BEYOND THE NUCLEAR FAMILY MODEL

Cross-Cultural Perspectives

Edited by
Luis Lenero-Otero

⑤ SAGE Studies in International Sociology 7
sponsored by the International Sociological Association/ISA

For information address

SAGE Publications Ltd.
44 Hatton Garden
London EC1N 8ER

SAGE Publications Inc.
275 South Beverly Drive
Beverly Hills, California 90212

International Standard Book Number
0 8039 9985 2 Cloth
0 8039 9986 0 Paper

Library of Congress Catalog Card Number
76–22901

First Printing

Printed and Bound
Biddles Ltd., Guildford, Surrey

CONTENTS

INTRODUCTION

Luis Lenero-Otero
Mexican Institute of Social Studies

The family is one of the most closely studied fields in contemporary Sociology. Researches on family structure are being conducted from widely differing approaches in every continent. There is a deep pre-occupation amongst sociologists to discover the direction followed by the structural change in the contemporary family institution.

It would seem that from within this perspective, the simplistic conception of universal family functions conceived in a static and uniform way is being overcome. Sociology is beginning to discover, analyse and put into perspective, a panorama of plural family typology, in which there appear, coexisting and interacting simultaneously and successively, diverse structural systems and different models on family life. It also seems increasingly evident that, in spite of the marked tendency towards uniformity in global life styles – owing mainly to the development of contemporary communication media and the implantation of a neo-colonialist system throughout the world – there exists a diverse situation regarding sociocultural patterns and local institutions. This brings about a social evolution that cannot be considered unilineal, and which presents us with dynamics, at times clearly dialectic in time and space or, in many other cases, highly ambiguous and ambivalent.

International aculturation processes are subject to variations of increasing complexity, provoked by the clash between the sociocultural neocolonialist forces, emanating from the technologically developed countries, and those of the local cultures.

The family, as an institution and system of human life, cannot withhold itself from the processes of equalization, diversification, imposition and liberation which operate in both the Third World countries and those more highly industrialized.

One of the first questions that comes to the mind of the family researcher, is that the broad generalizations frequently made concerning family life are basically ideological conceptions more than scientific knowledge of the family.

Nevertheless, many of the most important family sociologists, in their eagerness to grasp the universality of the interactions and processes of the family dynamics, have worked explicitly or implicitly, from the base of one of the family models, which moral, civil law and contemporary religions have presented as the prototype for the regulation of kin, living and sexual relationships: *the nuclear family model.*

Still further departing from this ideological conception of what ought to be the modern family life, methodological designs have been planned for the compilation of census data, vital statistics, the same as for housing, urbanization, social security, education and public welfare policies in the majority of countries, if not in all. Thousands of surveys have been conducted on the hypothesis that contemporary family living responds fundamentally to the net of husband – wife – children relationships, conceived as an integrated and unitary microcosm.

The nuclear family model has also been presented as the prospective key to the phenomenon of international uniformity in conjugal and kinship relations. William Goode, repeatedly cited in this book, is one of the most important sociologists who has worked from within this standpoint. Several scholars have depicted in turn, 'essential family characteristics and functions' in a society with a growing process of industrialization and urbanization, in a world highly populated, in a civilization of massive consumption and of a high density of impersonal relationships. They find in the nuclear family compensation for the mechanization of human relationships; in a society which exalts democracy and the equality — at least relative — between men and women, and which attempts to reconstruct the micro-nuclear family on the basis of community equality and individual development.

As a consequence of an urban family ideology which comprehends the nuclear model as an ideal type of family, when the reality is confronted with the model, society creates multiple mechanisms for the treatment of what is considered 'deviant behaviour'. From this view point, the deviations are seen rather as pathological, or at least 'not modern'. Therefore instead of accepting the existence of alternative family models, adjustments toward an ideal normality are sought. This is the reason that some social and cultural policies are not always adapted to reality, for example in the design of housing more or less appropriate for nuclear families but not suitable for extended or semi-extended families. This also happens when norms, rights and social responsibilities are established for the heads of households, who are always assumed to be male but not female.

However, this ideological perspective is being increasingly outdated not only by the new sociological research, but also, in many cases, by the planners as well as by the population itself.

[The insight that there prevails a plurality of family models which go 'beyond the nuclear family model', is born in the perception of a diverse reality, found in the plurality of cultures and subcultures all over the world.]

INTRODUCING THE PAPERS

On the basis of this new perspective a selective series of papers have been compiled. They were chosen from among nearly one hundred writing collaborations presented in the working sessions of the Family Research Committee of the International Sociological Association, in the VIII World Congress of Sociology, Toronto, August 1974.

The papers included reflect, in the first instance, a critique of the nuclear family model theory – without denying its relative importance; in the second place, they make up an analysis of the coexistence between both nuclear and non-nuclear family types; and finally, they offer several dimensions of individual and marital dynamics in the critical framework of contemporary conjugal family change principally relating, in the last group, to Western industrialized nations.

The authors, all social scientists with a high research and theoretical experience, outline their realistic perceptions of contemporary family behaviour, holding an extensive bibliography and using an illustrative set of data – from both official statistics and field researches – through the different cultures and subcultures of the countries they present: Japan, the Philippines, India and Iran, from Asia; Sweden and Poland, from Europe; the United States, from North America; Venezuela and Puerto Rico from Latin America; including multiple and varied illustrative and comparative references.

Special mention should be made to Blumberg's paper. The extension of its contribution – larger than the others – is justified by the importance and originality of the research made by her in a topic which becomes very substantial for this volume. In spite of the restrictions of space, we did not want to reduce the length of it, because we think it very illustrative of a cross-cultural analysis made in Venezuela, as well as in Negro families in the United States.

CRITIQUE OF THE NUCLEAR FAMILY MODEL THEORY

Professor Turowski, of the Catholic University of Lublin, and Liu, of the University of Notre Dame, begin with a critique of the nuclear family model application to urban society, in the respective countries they analyse, pointing out the inadequacy and the myth of the nuclear family model theory. Above all, they detail the presence of 'sui generis' types of the 'joint family' or quasi-nuclear family which appear in the contemporary life of those countries analysed, as a product of the coalescence and readjustment of family functions in a changing society

The same point is made by Yamane for Japan, by Trost for Sweden and the Scandinavian countries, and by Blumberg in her reference to Venezuela and to marginal population in the United States and other countries.

Therefore, there are made similar approaches to the problem through different references to variables dependently or independently analysed. This gives to this book a great variety and value.

For example, within the dependent or central variables we find references to the same phenomenon of the quantitative composition of the family as the key structural characterization.

Liu, Yamane, Trost and Blumberg all make special reference to the problem of structural characteristics in the family by means of the number and type of residents found in a single household. But their analyses about the family type go beyond mere census data, and try to extract the qualitative substance of the household composition. They all discover a new type of nuclear family which does not strictly correspond to the classical, atomistic, parent – children model, but instead pertains to a synthesis of extended family models (in its diverse form and tones) combined with the nuclear family model.

A study of the changing functions and meaning of kin, neighbourhood and sexual relationships appears in the paper presented here. Polygamy or contemporary neopolygamy, more or less evident or continual, is suggested by Blumberg in her study of mother – son families (which might be labelled semi-nuclear), as well as the 'syndiasmic cohabitation' of couples in consensual union, analysed by Trost.

Furthermore, an attempt is made to extract the meaning of kinship relations which make a semi-extended, neolocal family into a 'new nuclear family', which maintains or, at times even accentuates, the meaning of kinship as the real structural unit of its interacting dynamics.

In addition, questions of family demography were stated, mainly in the correlation of fertility with the type of family pattern. These matters being the preoccupation of Liu and Trost.

FAMILY LIFE CYCLES AND FAMILY TYPOLOGY

Special reference is made to one of the most important factors in the changing characterization of the family: that of the family cycle. It is evident from the work of many authors – mainly that of Reuben Hill, and here, in the analyses of Liu, Khatri, Yamane and Blumberg – that family structure and the meaning of relationships within the domestic nucleus change remarkably, depending on the stage of the life-cycle through which the family is passing. This leads us to affirm that a family cannot respond to a single family model, but that for evaluative normative and functional purposes, one has to adopt successive or alternative models, depending on their circumstances of development. Thus, we may speak of three-generation families becoming nuclear families, and vice versa, according to their stages in the life-cycle.

Divorce, consensual union and communal living amongst young people, or families in any given moment, tend almost always to establish changing situations in successive stages according to the structural model with which family relationships function in each life-cycle.

MACROSCOPIC VARIABLES RELATED TO FAMILY TYPE AND FUNCTIONS

On the other hand, in almost all the papers presented, there appear macrosocial variables as the characteristical frameworks which necessarily affect family typology. The *urban* or *rural* community, in all its levels of substructural or sectorial urbanization, refers to rural and urban families. Nevertheless, the generalization will not suffice to identify an extended or 'prenuclear' family type in what is understood to be rural environment. The results contained herein, as in the majority of current sociological researches, demonstrate the presence and varying dynamics of 'neoextended' families in an urban environment, as well as that of nuclear and 'neonuclear' families in a rural environment.

Industrialization is another independent variable with which nearly all the authors of the book interrelate the type of family and its functions. Yamane in particular refers to the industrialization process of Japan and Trost, Foss and Straus make the same point in connection with the countries studied by them; Blumberg, Turowski and Liu, in turn, include references to the phenomenon and its manifestations, treating it almost always as a general factor which influences family relationships.

It seems that the nuclear family system is not identified with industrial society, nor the extended family with preindustrial way of life; in fact, Liu and Turowski — among others — go some way towards demonstrating that the nuclear family exists and is conceived in a pre-industrial society, as the extended family is found within the industrial one.

On the other hand, it is of paramount importance to distinguish *social classes and strata* of the society to which the families under analysis belong, in order to characterize the sense of family life: behavioural patterns are affected by the social function and by the facilities or obstacles present in the different strata and classes of the social structure.

Trost refers to the qualitative difference that exists between couples who cohabit in consensual union belonging to the middle and upper classes of a given society – e.g. Sweden – and those from the lower and marginal classes of a country such as Mexico: in both cases, non-marital cohabitation have diverse meanings and dynamics.

In their turn, Liu, Khatri, and Blumberg make similar references to the importance of the social class variable in conjunction with the *means of production and employment.* Female employment is repeatedly singled out as a component affecting the shape and dynamics of the family. The traditional models of nuclear or extended families suffer a transformation when confronted by female employment or, para-doxically, revert to a model long since discarded.

FAMILY IDEOLOGY AND INDIVIDUAL DEVELOPMENT WITHIN THE FAMILY NETWORK

Another factor which, perhaps more than any other, stands out as a variable in the family model is that of *family ideology* related with the concept and way of *individual development.* Turowski emphasises the importance of the ideological model in family theory which is not reconciled to reality; Khatri, in an original analysis of family model literature, identifies English colonial ideology which introduced indivi-dualistic, egalitarian and democratic concepts in Indian family life, as the prime mover in family change.

Foss and Straus, in particular, develop and highly interesting experimental methodology of cross-cultural comparison, and an analysis of the individual development concept within parent – children family relationships. Their sophisticated appraisal of the interacting decision-taking process within the context of the semi-nuclear family, suggests patterns of behaviour based on cultures adopted by the individual and sifted by the interaction of the nuclear family.

Yamane writes about the change produced in new generations by the induction of education after the Second World War. Trost appears to find his working hypothesis in the suggestion of a non-stereotype Family Policy which concedes freedom to life-styles, options, and which analyses the functional convenience of a cohabitation model, within or without marriage, convenience understood as the point of view of those individuals which make up the couple.

Finally, Christensen, from a more general perspective involving marriage and the family, analyses the ideology behind a social movement such as women's liberation. His analytical proposition is that of the researcher who presents himself with a paradigm, in this case, of an interrelation: 'The equality and division of labor between the man and the woman'. Supposedly, his theoretical proposition may be applied to the conjugal relationship model and that of the nuclear family; nevertheless, he allows a revision or readjustment of the classic model of conjugal family in which the integration of wife – husband relationships implants an alternative typology on which to base differential applications. It follows that his essay, together with those of Foss, Straus, Trost and the majority of Blumberg's references, also reflect the initial statement: 'beyond the nuclear family model'. They are secured in a concept of individual development that goes some way to support itself by the research of its conditions and functions. As Blumberg and Trost emphasise, this leads us to a family policy grounded in reality and not in abstract preconceptions of what the family ought to be.

We have then, in this book, a representative sample of contemporary sociological research, with a wide international perspective, and at the same time an extraordinary thematic unity which justifies the title page.

The reader will, in the end, be aware that there is not only a 'beyond' in the methodology employed by the ten authors, but also a perspective of change and structural reality 'beyond' myopic empiricism; 'beyond' the constricting vision of a microsociology in which there appears the interrelation of macrosocial variables with the family life and models; and, above all, 'beyond' academic formalism without in any way depreciating scientific analysis which forms the central axis of a logic systematized by comprehensive research and complemented by empirical data. All these are placed in the context of a plural model of a family structure in the process of change throughout the modern world.

Luis Leñero-Otero
Mexico, August 1975

I FROM THE MYTH OF THE NUCLEAR FAMILY TO THE CONTEMPORARY PLURAL FAMILY STRUCTURE

1

INADEQUACY OF THE THEORY
OF THE NUCLEAR FAMILY
The Polish Experience

Jan Turowski
Catholic University of Lublin, Poland

The most known theory for understanding changes in the family in the contemporary world is the theory of the nuclear family. In particular, this theory describes and explains changes brought about by industrialization and urbanization.[1] The findings of Polish research in this field may hence be of interest since Polish society has been undergoing an accelerated process of industrialization and urbanization.[2] An American sociologist, L. Reissman, places Poland alongside France, Canada, Hungary and Italy in the third top group in the world according to the degree of urbanization, on the basis of four urbanization indicies applied to 45 countries.[3]

It is therefore in order to compare the findings of Polish research on the family with the statements of the theory of the nuclear family. The term 'nuclear family'[4] or, as preferred by W. Goode, 'conjugal family' is applied to the theory and propositions which elucidate trends and mechanisms of the change undergone by the contemporary family.

THE METHOD OF ANALYSIS

The basis of the statements of the theory of nuclear family is an abstract model of the family anticipated for pre-industrial, rural and peasant society and the same, constructed logically as its contradiction for understanding the pattern of family life in the urbanized and industrialized societies. So in the past the family fulfilled many functions. Today they are reduced, or the family has lost them; in the past the extended family existed, at present it disappears and changes into a small, conjugal, two-generation family. The family was in the past an institution, now it becomes a private companionship; and so on. This is not a simplification of that theory. The authors take into consideration the empirical data, but it is most often only the distinction of the family in different countries and cultures and the differentiation into urban and rural within the given countries. Meanwhile there are more types of families.

So, in a majority of Polish investigations the so-called concrete historical methods for scientific analysis of family changes are applied. Here are the following principles of this method:

(1) The traditional family life is observed or reconstructed very exactly on the basis of empirical sources for a given period in the past, or in the present.

(2) Many types of families are distinguished according to various factors which influence family life.

(3) Taken into consideration are not only similarities among many kinds of families of a given period but primarily diversities and specific features of each type.

(4) Family trends are established for each type of family on an individual basis according to the families' own features.

(5) The concept of linear changes in family life, which is the basic proposition used in the dychotomic analysis, is not accepted.

We will now present the results of Polish research in family changes and compare them with the statements of the theory of the nuclear family.

DIFFERENTIATION OF THE FAMILY
IN POLAND

The differentiation of the family is very complex. Thus, of the more than 9 million families in Poland 47.8 percent are rural and 52.2 percent are urban.[5] But the rural families are not uniform. They may be subdivided into the remnants of the traditional type of a peasant family representing traits characteristic of the oldest generation and seen in the most isolated regions. This type is principally reconstructed on the basis of historical and sociological sources. The most numerous type of rural families today is the modern rural-farm family which constitutes in Poland 27.2 percent of all families. Next come the part-time farmers' families, numbering 10.5–12.5 percent of the total. Then there is the distinct type of rural-worker families, about 8–10 percent, characterized by the employment of the head of the family in non-agricultural occupation but living in the village.

The urban family is also differentiated: 30–34 percent are families of workers, about 11 percent officials and petty bourgeois, and 7.2–8 percent intelligentsia. Both urban and rural populations are further differentiated by the type of local community. Rural families belonging to different social strata and residing in suburban villages in the direct zone of influence of a large city are characterized by a number of specific traits. Therefore the various strata of the urban population should be divided into large city families as compared to small town families. Also we must distinguish the urban family of rural origin which are undergoing the process of adaptation.

These types of differentiation are established by empirical research[6] and are confirmed by the respondents. This attests that the differences are also reflected in the social consciousness. Similar differentiation is to be noted in both economically advanced and developing countries.[7]

Our research on the Polish family indicates that the first factor of differentiation is the social and occupational affiliation of the heads of the families. The second is the type of local community (village, town) and its character (suburban, large city). The third factor is the pattern of family life propagated by various ideological institutions.

But families are also differentiated in another aspect: the number of children in the family] For example, in Poland in 1970 there were about 20 percent of families without children, 31 percent with one child, 27 percent with 2 children, 13 percent with 3 children, and 9 percent with 4 and more children. The number of children influences the economic status of the family, its internal organization, the division of duties in the family, and so on.]

The authors of the theory of the nuclear family do not take into consideration all these differences. The above typology cautions against an analysis of abstract types of families in the given countries or national cultures and against generalization of propositions based on similarities and not on diversities.

CHANGES IN THE FUNCTIONS OF THE FAMILY

An essential thesis of the theory of the nuclear family states that the functions of the family in industrial and urban society are being reduced. Ogburn maintains that only two out of seven functions of the pre-industrial family have remained in the modern family: the procreative and the emotional–associative.[8] Locke–Burgess in their famous work write about the reduced functions of the modern family and its transition from an institution to companionship.[9] According to Parsons, in industrial and urban societies the non-kinship units become of prime importance in a social structure. This means that the family has become a more specialized agency than before, probably more specialized than it has been in any previously known society.[10] He repeated this assertion at the World Congress of Sociology at Amsterdam.[11] More descriptions of the trends of change in the family's functions may be cited. But let us turn to the results of Polish research and explain what are real changes in families' functions.

The reconstruction of the traditional peasant family to be found in such works as *The Polish Peasant in Europe and America*,[12] in pre-war peasant autobiographies and diaries of the mid-war and post-war young generations, indicate that the traditional peasant family was not autonomous. In practice, both the three-generation and small traditional peasant family shared such functions as economical, educational and functions of insurance and social control with the local community, which as a whole or through its informal institutions, assisted the family. Thus the family functions in the so-called pre-industrial society were shared by the family with the local community and the circles of relatives and neighbours on which its organization rested. In the urban industrial society these tasks are taken over by public and government institutions when the traditional rural local community disintegrates. Hence the reduction of the family's functions primarily pertains to the fact that some of the functions formerly fulfilled by the local community have been taken over by institutions.]

An examination of the various types of families shows that the reduction of the so-called historical or universal (basic) functions takes place on a more or less limited scope. But all types of families continue to fulfil functions of insurance and protection while others are taken over on the basis of assistance. The economic function seems to be most sharply reduced. [Sociological research indicates without doubt that the productive function has been separated from the modern family, but it still persists in the families of farmers and in suburban villages.] However, one may ask if the productive function has disappeared completely in the urban-type family. Recent research on married couples and families among the intelligentsia and the free professions shows that work, or the preparation for it, has been partly shifted to the homes of many categories of white collar worker families. Is this a sign of the partial return of productive function of the urban family?[13]

The consumptive function, although partly limited, is still associated with the family. Apart from one meal taken outside the home–mainly in families of intelligentsia and officials–the morning and evening meals are still eaten at home. A strong tendency is reflected in respondents' declarations to limit consumption to the household. The more or less general return of the community of consumption in the family may be anticipated.

Discussions on the changes in the functions of the modern family have, however, failed to estimate adequately two very important processes indicated in Polish research. The first is the process of intensification of the partly reduced basic (universal) as well as historical functions.[14] An analysis of about 5,000 diaries submitted by rural youth during 1959–60 reveals an intensification in Polish families of the so-called integrative–expressive function[15] (also called after Parsons the emotional function of mutual adaptation). The declarations of the diarists are to the effect that members of the modern family, particularly of the young generation, should in their daily life and aspirations aim at creating opportunities for the family to shape its members' personalities, to share emotional response, spend their leisure time and relax together. This has become a central and dominant function which is intensified since it requires a greater expenditure of time and means as well as a conscious activity of family members.

Lobodzinska observed the same phenomenon among urban families. In the research conducted on a national sample of married couples of various urban social strata she established that while urban workers' families still stress the importance of the economical function, families of the intelligentsia stress primarily the integrative–expressive function.[16]

The intensification process pertains also to the function which has been most reduced, namely the family's educational function. Markowska in her research on changes in the last few generations of rural families in villages in the Cracow region, and later in villages of the industrialized Plock region and in the most isolated agricultural Podlasie region,[17] found that although the family's educational function has been partly taken over by public and government institutions, the remaining tasks still require more time and greater resources from the parents. This intensification process is associated with the phenomenon of the functions becoming independent of each other, i.e. the distribution and division of activities both in time and place.

⌈ The separation and distribution of functions appear very strongly in urban families where women take up outside employment. This does not enable the woman to combine her domestic role with employment outside which was possible in the traditional family. This separation of the roles and functions of the working woman causes tensions and collisions which are hard to reconcile.⌉

Moreover, the theory of linear changes in the family and of its transition from a multifunctional to a specialized group has not been confirmed. We can talk about the modification of family functions and a partial reduction of some functions and at the same time of their simultaneous intensification and separation. On the other hand, the integrative-expressive function is becoming a clearly dominant function in the modern family.[18]

INDIVIDUALIZATION OF THE SMALL FAMILY

The propositions of the disintegration of relations of kinship (including the three-generation family) and separation of the conjugal family from the maternal and kinship family, occupy an important place in the theory of the nuclear family. The concept 'individualization of the small family' is correctly distinguished from the concept of 'the family's social isolation'.[19] The findings of Polish research suggest the following determinations on this question.

(a) The theory of the nuclear family considers the traditional, i.e. the pre-industrial, family as the three-generational linked by a common economy and community of residence. This is a simplification. Research on the rural family shows that apart from the extended family there were also small families among the landless peasants, homeworkers, casual labourers, handicraftsmen where lack of farms created the need of newly formed families of young people seeking their own, independent means of subsistence. The same applies to the lower social strata of the pre-industrial small town. Consequently the former traditional family everywhere in Poland constituted a pluralistic system of various types, including the most widespread extended family.

(b) There is now a fairly large proportion of three-generation families in Poland, but they assume different forms. According to the research by Piotrowski, based on quota sampling of 3,000 old people at the age of 65 and more, in Poland old people live together with their children more often than in the West. In Poland as much as 67 percent of old people who have children (86 percent have children) live with them in one household. This is a very high index; for comparison the percentage in some of the Western countries is: UK 42 percent, US 28 percent, and Denmark 20 percent. This very high index in Poland is mainly due to the fact that 76 percent of the aged farmers live together with their children; but even outside agriculture this percentage is high, reaching 57 percent. Mutual habitation of older peasants with their children is connected with traditional family farming. In towns, the sharing of a household is motivated partly by the housing shortage and partly by the vitality of the modified extended family in Poland.[20] The data confirm the well-known adjustment made by Townsend, Willmott and others on the question of the character of the modern family.[21]

(c) In some population groups the existence of the three-generation family and even its rejuvenation is to be observed. This pertains especially to part-time farmers, rural workers, suburban villagers and even in some urban families. Part-time farmers are inclined to maintain the three-generation family. This enables both partners in a small family to work off the farm, share in the farm and make possible the participation of the grandparents in bringing up their grandchildren. A similar phenomenon, noted by one of the Polish investigators, is to be observed in villages inhabited by workers. The three-generation family is being revived in which the older generation works on the farm, helps to run the household while the young generation is engaged in outside employment, and raises the children.[22] The diffusion of this kind of family tie is conditioned by women's employment. This enables her to run a larger household under rural conditions. The possession of her own home in a common household and reduced differences in the way of life of the generations mean fewer conflicts than in the urban three-generation family. This phenomenon is also confirmed by research on the suburban family.

(d) A comparison of the modern extended family with the traditional three-generation family established its complete distinctness. As Markowska correctly pointed out in her sociological research in Poland, the modern three-generation agricultural, part-time farmer and suburban family is no longer the former patriarchal family in which the fate of the young people was subordinated to the farm and all their needs were satisfied by work and consumption in the common household. The present extended family is subordinated to the new young family and enables young couples to be employed. Grandparents run a farm or a household, look after the children or take part in some economic or other undertaking. This is why it should be called the modified extended family.)

(e) Besides various forms of the modified extended family there are of course numerous independent small families not linked by a common residence or common household with parents. The independent small family is more common in the cities among white-collar workers than among manual workers (especially families of steel workers and miners who mostly uphold former traditions) and is more frequent in cities than in small towns. But such families are as a rule linked by active kinship relationships and often by strong personal ties (or the so-called emotional). Sometimes they sustain a unity built up of common values and life patterns) Research in Warsaw, Poznań, Konin, Nowa Huta, Lublin and other Polish cities confirm the existence of various kinds of ties linking the small family with the maternal family.[23] There is even a certain revival of kinship relations as a counterweight to the anonymous relations of the large city community. Could it really be a new pattern of city life associated with the mass migration from the villages and small towns?

(f) There was also established a specific trend in the cycles of the conjugal family's life. (Lobodzinska in her investigation of married couples among engineers advanced the hypothesis that the younger family of white-collar workers comprises two phases: the phase of contracting marriage and immediately after the marriage when the young family shows a strong tendency to independence. The second phase comes when there are children to be brought up when the presence of parents enables the mother to look after the children while continuing her professional career.[24] Hence the parents' new roles at an older age favour the maintenance of the modified extended family, prompted not only by the family needs but also by the feeling of responsibility toward the old parents. This is why the proportion of three-generation families in new settlements and single family houses is higher than the average index for the urban family. This is confirmed by Goode.[25]

It is thus difficult to maintain that the modified extended family has been preserved on a larger scale in Poland than in the Western countries only because of hard housing conditions. The hypothesis may be advanced, after Lutynski, that '...under structural conditions, other than obtained in the West, factors appear which counteract the tendency towards shrinking of the family, factors which condition the persistence of elements of the multi-generational family...'.[26]

Let us conclude: the authors of the theory of the nuclear family over-estimate the importance of the community of residence or of the common household for the persistence of the family as a social group. Goode correctly considers that emotional ties were more important than the objective ones for the traditional extended family.[27] The thesis regarding the disintegration of kinship relations between the maternal family and the resulting small family requires correction. The separate and independent small and maternal families are both as a rule charac-terized by an intensified emotional community, expressed in wide personal relations (mutual visits and assistance) according to Rosen-mayer's known formula: intimacy but at a distance.[28] So, these state-ments do not confirm the thesis about the individualization of a conjugal family and the disappearing of the kinship relation outside a small family.

THE AUTONOMY OF THE INDIVIDUAL IN THE FAMILY

An essential proposition of the theory of the nuclear family is that the individual is becoming autonomous in the modern family and that egalitarian relations are becoming consolidated. This trend cannot be doubted. But Polish empirical studies point to the need for certain supplementation and more detailed determinations.

(a) Research on the internal structure of the rural family and on the urban worker's family puts to question the thesis regarding the genesis of the family partnership structure exclusively in the urban community. It was established that the structure should be sought in the family's socio-occupational structure. For decades the partnership patterns took shape (parallel with the urban family) in the rural community, in the group of day labourers, handicraftsmen, home workers and now among the working-class population. The latter possessed no land only their labour-power; often both partners earned the means of living with their labour and thus acquired their social status.[29] Rights and obligations in these families were shared equally between the man and the woman.

(b) The farmers and part-time farmers' families are undergoing a great change in relation to the traditional structure of the peasant family. There the woman had no independence but was consigned to the home and the farm and her activity did not go beyond that and the local community. The woman's social status in the farm family has now risen with the growth of her authority as a co-manager and representative of the family. There are in Poland about 3.5 million individual farms, most of which are operated only by women. Out of each ten individual farms six are run by women and four by men. Rural women are taking an active part in economic, social and cultural organizations. But this process is developing more in the realm of rights and authority than in the division of responsibility at home and on the farm, since the bulk of the new obligations and activities still devolve upon the woman and prevent her from a full development of her capacities and her intellectual and emotional life. Research on the social position of women in the Plock region — part-time farmers' families — reveals both the woman's growing position in the family and her limited possibilities of intellectual development and participation in culture.[30]

(c) The independence of women in the urban family is brought about by cultural advance, a wider range of activity outside the family, and by employment which improves her opportunity for co-partnership in the family and for a greater role in society. In Poland the occupational activization of women is particularly advanced. In 1960 married women constituted 55 percent of all working women while 42 percent of all married women were employed, as compared to about 55 percent in England, 30 percent in other European countries, and 33 percent in US.[31] However, because of the difficulties involved in bridging the gap between a woman's employment and her role in the family, an attempt is now under way to work out new patterns of a woman's independence by giving up outside occupation in favour of one's home and education of children, and raising her cultural status by participation in activities in the local or wider community.

(d) The phenomenon of the change in the individualization of the person in the family is manifested in the changed position of the child. [There has been a particularly great change in the position of children in the farm family where they traditionally constituted a source of manpower. The child is now assuming an independent role which is separated from the farm. This is expressed particularly in the sphere of education, in the choice of occupation, forms of leisure and participation in cultural life.] Citing the diaries *'The Young Rural Generation in the Polish People's Republic',* Chalasiński asserts that the desire for personal independence by acquiring new cultural patterns and an independent vocation is a characteristic trait of Poland's young rural generation.[32] However, this independence is not won without conflicts with the parents' generation.

This trend is even more marked in the part-time farmer's families. Also children and youth in the rural worker's family enjoy a high degree of independence. This is greatly facilitated in suburban villages where it is easy to obtain work in a town, to acquire an independent vocation, to study and to have access to city forms of spending leisure time and of entertainment. But this independence does not usually mean a complete break with local ties based not only on emotional disposition but also on common economic interests, home and various undertakings. But suburban villages are especially exposed to the phenomenon of cultural disharmony in the form of disjointed or dissonant values and patterns of behaviour. In this respect some families and even entire villages are undergoing a phase of social disorganization.[33]

[One of the features of the children's independence in urban workers' families is the fact that children as a whole no longer inherit their father's occupation. Therefore there is a growing influence of the young people in the choice of·school and occupation and later marriage and the decision to raise a family and a partner for marriage. Another feature is the very independent and even conflicting forms of leisure. In urban families, including those of the intelligentsia, there is growing isolation of young people from their parents, a tendency to live separately and an excessive orientation toward conspicuous consumption especially among groups of youth in the large cities.[34]

The claim has been made in relation to individual independence effecting the disintegration of the family, that the theory of the nuclear family has not established criteria for determining the kind and degree of independence which does not endanger the cohesion of the family, so indispensable to its functioning. On the contrary some authors regard all expressions of independence as necessary and determined by social development. It may therefore be in place to stress with Chalasinski upon studying the expressions of independence among Polish rural youth that a desire to attain the ideal of personal culture and an independent vocation constitute the scope and denote the limits of individual independence in the family.

CONCLUSION

The findings of Polish sociological research on the family correspond with the current of reasoning represented by Goode's *World Revolution and Family Patterns.* These findings suggest that both the traditional extended family and to some extent the conjugal family among Plebian strata existed in the pre-industrial society. It was therefore of a pluralistic character in the past and much more so in the present. The modified extended family are quite numerous in Poland, which seems to be connected with structural features. As hitherto established, family functions have been partly reduced or according to the better formulation of Thomas and Znaniecki, part of the tasks have been transferred to broader social groups or institutions. This process of transfer is accompanied by the seemingly contrary process of intensification of elementary (universal) functions which become dominant (rediscovering own functions, after McIver) and the process of separation of individual functions. This pertains particularly to the integrational–expressive and socialization functions. In Poland the family is one of the principal institutions which internalizes the values and patterns of life transmitted by political, ideological religious institutions. This is why the family has not lost its character as an 'institution' and has not become 'a private companionship'. However Locke and Burgess's thesis of the family's transition from institution to companionship is true as far as it signifies the preponderance of emotional, personal or spiritual ties in the modern family. The post-war Polish family is characterized by the increased role of these ties among family members which is also a result of the modified function of that social group as well as of the influence of ideological institutions.

The above also contradicts the proposition of McIver with regard to the family's passing over from the *Gemeinschaft* type group to that of the *Gesellschaft* type, according to the typology of Toennies. That thesis is also negated by the multiplicity and personal nature of the family functions and the character of its social ties which today mainly constitute the personal relations of friendship, love, kinship, etc. These kinds of relations is the differentia specifica of Toennies's Gemeinschaft type groups.

The egalitarian pattern of the family structure did not take shape exclusively in the urban community but also in the landless rural population. The process of the women and children gaining independence in the family is expressed in their choice of occupation and in the realization of personal culture. This process proceeds differently in various types of families. The theory of the nuclear family obliterates the differences between the independence of the individual in the family and expressions of its disorganization and the undesirable effects of the projected models. It thus creates a basis for formulating the ideology of the nuclear family in which all phenomena of disintegration are justified as developmental trends or are also regarded as normative ideals despite their previous destination as models for theoretical analysis.

NOTES

1. The present author identifies himself with the assertion of N. Bell and E. F. Vogel: 'We shall regard the family as an analytical concept, defined in terms

of the existence of relationships, recognized by the participants, between a man and woman, and between one or both of them and their children...' in: N. W. Bell and E. F. Vogel (eds), *The Family* (New York) 1968, 1. In Polish sociology the term 'large family', or 'multigenerational family' is used to designate the three-generation family running a common household and living together. The equivalent in English sociology is the extended family, grandparental family, joint family. In French – famille a nombreuses generations; in German – die erweiterte Familie, die Grossfamilie. The modern three-generation family geared to the realization of the aims of the small family, in which the relations between the nuclear family and the parents are based on a division of competence and decisions, is called here the modified extended family. When such families are not linked by a common farm and home and only by intensive personal, emotional or spiritual ties, they are called dispersed extended families.

The Polish terms 'small' or 'two-generation' family are synonymous with the 'nuclear family', 'conjugal family', 'famille elementaire', 'famille conjugale', 'Kernfamilie'. The terms 'task', 'duties' or 'activities' are used to define efforts on behalf of members of the family or the family as a whole and their sequences for the larger groups. The term 'function' is used in reference to the more general consequences of activities, after *The Family*, op. cit., 7.

2. M. Ciechocińska, 'Przeobrazenia w strukturze zawodowej Polski' ('Changes in Poland's Occupational Structure'), in: *Socjologia zawodow* (Warszawa), 1965, 91: *Rocznik Statystyczny*, 1971, 67 and others.

3. L. Reissman, *The Urban Process* (New York), 1964, 207.

4. The term 'nuclear family' is used (1) as an ideal type, after Max Weber, as the conceptual construction of a catalogue of a given phenomenon's traits, (2) as signifying the model desired by respondents or as the normative model regarded as obligatory in a given community, (3) as a conception and theory, hence as a set of judgements explaining changes the family undergoes, and (4) as signifying ideology, i.e. as a system of justifications of the nuclear family model as the most desirable and of determinations how to achieve it. W. J. Goode, *World Revolution and Family Patterns* (New York), 1968, 7 and others call attention to the need of distinguishing different meanings of the term.

5. The data on the number of families and the percentages of different types are estimated. The data on the proportions of the rural and urban populations maintaining themselves on non-agricultural occupations, on the number of households and housing premises, percentage of the working population, etc. are taken from *Rocznik Statystyczny* of 1971. The estimates should be regarded as orientating data.

6. Most data is contained in the work of I. Thomas and F. Znaniecki, *The Polish Peasant in Europe and America* (New York), 1958; *Pamietniki Chlopow* (Peasants' Diaries), (Warszawa), 1935; J. Chalasinski, *Mlode pokolenie chlopow* (The Young Peasant Generation), (Warszawa), 1933 as well as the following postwar works: M. Kwasniewska-Trawinska, '*Sytuacja spoleczna kobiety wiejskiej w*

ziemi krakowskiej w latach 1880-1914' ('The Social Situation of Rural Women in the Cracow Area, in 1880-1914'), *Prace i Materialy Etnograficzne,* 10 (2) 1967; K. Dobrowolski, 'Tradycyjna rodzina chlopska w Poludniowej Polsce na przelomie XIX i XX wieku' ('The Traditional Peasant Family in Southern Poland at the Turn of the 19 and 20 Centuries'), in: *Studia nad zyciem spolecznym i kultura (Studies in Social and Cultural Life)* (Wroclaw), 1966, 196-242; J. Turowski, 'Rodzina chlopska w okresie lat 1864-1918 w swietle zrodel pamietnikarskich' ('The Peasant Family in 1864-1918 in the Light of Diary Sources'), in: *Lodzkie Studia Etnograficzne,* IX, (1967); D. Markowska, 'Gospodarstwo i rodzina w tradycyjnej kulturze chlopskiej' ('The Farm and the Family in the Traditional Peasant Culture'), in: *Polskie Studia Slawistyczne,* series III (Warszawa), 1967 and by the same author: 'Rodzina wiejska na terenie dawnej Puszczy Zielonej' ('The Rural Family in the Former Puszcza Zielona'), in: *Kurpie, Puszcza Zielona* (Wroclaw), 1961, 95-161.

7. The part-time farmers' family is thus quite common. In the US this group constitutes about 20 percent of all farmers, in Yugoslavia and the GFR, about 51 percent. The distinction of the large city family is also quite general. The well known GFR rural sociologists Wurzbacher, Brepohl and Kotter call attention to the need to distinguish the specific traits of the suburban village and its family. Laszlo A. Vaskowicz points out the distinctness of the families of various social strata in: *Familie und Religiöse Socialisation* (Vienna), 1970.

8. W. F. Ogburn, 'The Changing Functions of the Family', in: *Selected Studies in Marriage and in the Family,* F. Winch (ed.) (New York), 1960, 158.

9. E. W. Burgess and H. J. Locke, *The Family* (New York), 1953, 24.

10. T. Parsons and R. F. Bales, *The Family, Socialization and Interaction Processes* (New York), 1955, 8-9.

11. *Transactions of the World Congress of Sociology,* VIII (London) 1956, 95.

12. W. I. Thomas and F. Znaniecki, op. cit., vol. I, 140.

13. For instance, in German sociology K. P. Bahrdt, *Humaner Städtebau* (Hamburg), 1968, 47-61.

14. D. Markowska, 'Kierunki przeobrazen wspolczesnej rodziny wiejskiej' ('Trends of Change in the Modern Rural Family'), in: *Roczniki Socjologii Wsi,* II, 1964.

15. F. Jakubczak, 'Ksztaltowanie sie integracyjno-ekspensyjnej funkcji rodziny wiejskiej' ('The Shaping of the Integrative-Expressive Function of the Rural Family'), in: *Roczniki Socjologii Wsi,* II, 82; J. Chalasinski, *Mlode pokolenie wsi Polski Ludowej* (The Young Rural *Generation in the Polish Peoples Republic),* Vol. I (Warszawa), 1964, and Vol. V (Warszawa), 1968.

16. B. Lobodzinska, *Malzenstwo w miescie (Marriage in the City)* (Warszawa), 1970, 212.

17. D. Markowska, *Rodzina w srodowisku wiejskim (The Family in the Rural Community)* (Wroclaw), 1964 and the same: 'Rodzina wiejska w rejonie

Plocka' ('The Rural Family in Plock Region'), in: *Zeszyty Badan Rehonow Uprzemyslowionych (Notebooks of Research on Industrialized Regions)*, 1963, No. 6; 'Family Patterns in a Polish Village', *The Polish Sociological Bulletin*, No. 2, 1963, as well as *Rodzina wiejska na Podlasiu (The Rural Family in Podlasie, 1864-1964)* (Wroclaw), 1979. See particularly the same author, 'Kierunki przeobrazen', op. cit.

18. A. Kloskowska, 'Rodzina w Polsce Ludowej' ('The Family in the Polish People's Republic'), in: A. Sarapata (ed.), *Przemiany spoleczne w Polsce Ludowej (Social Changes in the Polish People's Republic)* (Warszawa), 1965, 505-51.

19. The term 'individualization' is variously conceived and defined, more rarely as 'isolation' and more often as 'becoming independent'. Sometimes as independence within the broader systems of kinship and the local community and at other times as autonomy in the sphere of values, life pattern and family functions within the global society. In the last conception it approximates the meaning of individualization as the process of the family's transition from an institution to a companionship. One example may be the determination of A. Kocy, 'Urbanization and Nuclear Family Individualization. A Casual Connection', in: *The Sociology of the Family. Opatija Seminar, Current Sociology*, XII (1), 1963-64 (Oxford), 1964.

20. J. Piotrowski, *Ludzie starzy w Polsce i ich sprawnosc zyciowa (Poland's Older People and Their Fitness for Life)* (Warszawa), 1970, 22.

21. P. Townsend, *Family Life and Old People* (London), 1957; P. Willmott and M. Young, *Family and Class in a London Suburb* (London), 1960; *Social Structure and Family Generational Relations* (Englewood Cliffs), 1965; L. Rosenmayer and E. Kockeis, *Umwelt und Familie alter Menschen* (Neuwied-Berlin), 1965.

22. E. Pietraszek, *Wies robotnicza (A Workers' Village)* (Wroclaw), 1965.

23. J. Komorowska, 'Rodzina warszawska w swietle badan i statystyki' ('The Warsaw Family in the Light of Research and Statistics'), *Problemy Rodziny*, No. 5, 1969, and *Warszawa, Socjologiczne zagadnienia stolicy i aglomeracji (Warsaw. The Capital's Sociological Problems and Agglomeration)*, ed. S. Nowakowski (Warszawa), 1969; *Poznan. Spoleczno-przestrzenne skutki industrializacji (Poznan. The Social and Spatial Effects of Industrialization)*, ed. J. Ziolkowski (Warszawa), 1967; Z. Tyszka, *Przeobrazenia rodziny robotniczej w warunkach uprzemyslowienia i urbanizacji (Changes in the Worker's Family Effected by Industrialization and Urbanization)* (Warszawa), 1970; R. Siemienska, *Nowe Zycie w nowym miescie (The New Life in a New Town)* (Warszawa), 1969; J. Turowski, 'Rodzina w srodowisku wielkomiejskim' ('The Family in the Large City Community'), *Zeszyty Naukowe KUL*, No. 1, 1971. Two basic monographs are devoted to the urban workers' family in Silesia: W. Mrozek, *Rodzina Gornicza (The Miner's Family)* (Katowice) 1963-65; F. Adamski, *Hutnik i jego rodzina (The Steelworker and His Family)* (Katowice), 1966.

24. B. Lobodzinska, op. cit., 275.

25. W. J. Goode, 'Industrialization and the Family', in: B. E. Hoselitz and L. E. More (eds), *Industrialization and Society* (Paris), 1963.

26. J. Lutynski, 'Badania nad mlodymi malzenstwami' ('Research on Young Couples'), *Przeglad Socjologiczny,* 14 No. (1), 1960, 105–16.

27. W. J. Goode, 'The Process of Role Bargaining in the Impact of Urbanization and Industrialization. Family Systems', in: *The Sociology of the Family. Opatija Seminar, Current Sociology,* XII (1), 1963–64.

28. L. Rosenmayer and E. Kockeis, 'Housing Environment and Family Relations of the Aged', in: *Sociology in Austria* (Graz-Koln), 1960, 79–98.

29. E. Pietraszek, op. cit., 99–102; W. Kwasniewicz, *Wiejska spolecznosc rzemieslnicza w procesie przemian (The Rural Handicraftsmen Community in the Process of Change)* (Wroclaw), 1970, 179.

30. B. Tryfan, *Pozycja spoleczna kobiety wiejskiej (The Social Position of Rural Woman)* (Warszawa), 1968.

31. M. Sokolowska and W. Wrochno, 'Pozycja spoleczna kobiety w swietle statystyki' ('Woman's Social Position in the Light of Statistics'), in: *Kobieta Wspolczesna (The Modern Woman)* (Warszawa), 1966, 44–78.

32. *Awans pokolenia, t. I – Mlode pokolenie wsi Polski Ludowej (Advancement of a generation,* Vol. I, *The Young Rural Generation in the Polish People's Republic)* (Warszawa), 1964, 12.

33. Suburban villages were investigated by: D. Dobrowolska, *Przeobrazenia spoleczne wsi podmiejskiej (Social Change in Suburban Villages)* (Wroclaw), 1968; J. Sulimski, *Procesy urbanizacyjne w strefie podmiejskiej Krakowa (Urbanization Processes in the Cracow Suburban Zones)* (Wroclaw), 1967.

34. C. Czapow, *Rodzina a wychowanie (The Family and Upbringing)* (Warszawa), 1968.

2

THE MYTHS OF THE
NUCLEAR FAMILY AND
FERTILITY IN CENTRAL PHILIPPINES

William T. Liu
University of Notre Dame

Two questions are relevant to what this paper attempts to do. The first one concerns the impact of residential patterns on kin-relations. The second deals with Goode's assertion that there is a world-wide trend toward that change from the traditional extended family system to the nuclear family (Goode, 1963: 1-2; Taeuber, 1971:37). The first question is empirical and specific, with no attempt to generalize from a set of limited data collected in the mid-Visayas in the Philippines. The second question is general and the emphasis will be on the conceptual and analytical level and, when data can be drawn from varieties of sources, there will obviously be speculations as to what these data generally mean when applied to the question of the family in transition. At this point, one may take some risks by suggesting that some of the theoretical works on the family are undergoing processes of mutation. The answers may get to be less unclear until we have additional data to clarify them.

The two major questions raised here may be independent from each other, except for the fact that they both are raised when it comes to discussing family systems and variations of the levels of fertility (Burch, 1970; Burch and Gendell, 1971; Taeuber, 1971; Palmore et el., 1970, just to mention a few). This paper will attempt to relate these two questions and draw empirical data to bear on them.

FAMILY STRUCTURE, HOUSEHOLD
COMPOSITION AND FERTILITY

Studies dealing with the structure of the family and fertility almost invariably employ household statistics. While not accurate as a measure of family size, approximation of family size from household number has been generally satisfactory, at least for the Western nations, particularly in the United States (Ogburn and Nimkoff, 1955; Taeuber, 1971:41). There is the assumption that household composition is an indicator of the type of family system prevailing in that society; and residence pattern generally approximates the ideal rules of residence as well as the structure of jural authority inheritance and other relational norms of a family system. In countries where census data are available and reasonably accurate, household information is by far the most comprehensive and temporally useful information about the family system in that society. On the other hand, attempts in using household data as measures of family type in testing the hypothesis[1] that extended and/or corporate family systems generally favour higher marital fertility receive no convincing support from a variety of studies[2] (Nag, 1967; Pakrasi and Malaker, 1967: Liu, 1967; and Sennett, 1970).

Thus, the physical unit used for one purpose may not, in this case, be the best unit of observation for another purpose. There are, aside from disappointment from lack of empirical support of the Davis–Lorimer assumption (Cf. note 1), several inherent weaknesses of some of the commonly cited studies, almost all of which were associated with the conceptualization and the limitation of data. The first is the confusion between marital fertility and societal fertility. Burch and Gendell (1971:94), for example, raised the point that no attempt was made to compare a society dominated by extended family system with a society where the extended family is not the dominant type with respect to the level of fertility.

The second weakness is the lack of theoretically relevant (rather than the physically relevant) differentiation between the nuclear family and the extended family. For example, stem family is regarded as a non-extended type, but the structural requisite of the stem family gives priority to filial obligations over sibling solidarity. Even in industrialized countries kin helping patterns may be taken over the household structure as a form of modified extended family (Litwak, 1965; Hill et al., 1970). There is the confusion in terms of the criterion used in defining types of family structure. A third weakness is that residential patterns are obtained on a cross-sectional basis rather than on the longitudinal basis, for this reason relationships between any nuclear unit and kins may be functions of the family development cycle and are therefore quite independent from household composition (cf. Gore, 1961) especially in urban areas where housing patterns are not adaptive to population change (Freedman, 1957:30). A fourth weakness is that, even though historical data is available on the variations of family type along with socio-economic data of the head of the household (e.g. occupation), all but one (Palmore et al., 1970) had not taken into consideration the possible effect of the social class dimension of the household size. Finally, the fifth weakness is that household composition and residential patterns may be functions of economic factors, particularly that of capital investment in housing construction in that society at a given period. Other factors are migration (Gonzalez 1961; Taeuber, 1971: 70, 83), sex selective mortality rate (Anderson, 1971:55), or the mode of economic productivity (Gonzalez, 1969; Smith, 1956; Parish and Schwartz, 1972).

In anthropological writings, however, the application of rules of residence as a guide of defining family structure received empirical support (Murdock, 1949) as well as conceptual criticisms (Levy, 1969; Hsu, 1968). In Murdock's volume, an impressive amount of evidence was presented to illustrate that a society begins to change first through a modification of rules of residence, is then followed by the changes of the extended family with the eventual alteration of order of kins and terminology with which such relations are designated. Murdock, however, qualified the generalization by saying that rules of residence may be changed as a result of the change of economic and cultural conditions (Murdock, 1949:212, 221 et passim).

On the other hand, Hsu (1968:581) posited that it is important to view human relationships in their fundamental and dyadic forms, and that complex human relationships are multiplications and permutations of the basic dyadic form. These different patterns of dyadic interaction may be organized and called attributes.

> When more than one dyad is involved, their respective attributes affect each other through combination, co-ordination, modification or elimination so as to form an overall pattern which we term *content* (p.581, italics added).

Thus, Hsu differentiates structure from content; the former is the organization of the dyad, and the latter is the organization of attributes. The distinction between attributes and structure is significant. Even within one culture, the husband—wife relationship may be different in attributes but identical in structure. The fact that most of the research on family structure and fertility was arrived at without taking consideration of attributes, is understandable. Data on the structural aspects of human groups are more available than the data on corporate attributes. In measuring family systems in transition, however, structural changes often lag behind changes in attributes. This paper aims to contrast structural aspects of the Cebuano urban family with some of the attributional aspects of conjugal and kinship relationships.

HOUSEHOLD COMPOSITION DATA

First tabulation on household composition indicates that the extended family in the classical sense is not widespread in Cebu. Table 1 gives a descriptive profile of the residential pattern of families interviewed.

Household information from area probability samples indicate that about two-thirds of all classes of family dwellings contain nuclear families. Co-residence with relatives are rare, even for urban middle class sample. In interpreting the data, however, some considerations must be taken to include housing construction and neighbourhood composition. For the majority of the vast lower and lower-middle class dwellings, construction materials are not suitable for multiple units large enough to include more than one family. Houses are conjested, especially in the squatter areas throughout the city and in the urban fringe. Small structures are built behind a larger building; no zoning

TABLE 1

Composition of Households in Cebu, Philippines
(in percentages)

Social class	Type of household					
	Nuclear[a]	Nuclear[b] lateral	Joint[c]	Nuclear[d] lineal	Other[e]	Total
Urban (upper (N=101))	68.3	4.0	7.9	18.8	0.1	100.0
Urban (middle (N=720))	62.6	10.0	8.2	17.8	1.8	100.0
Urban (lower (N=700))	66.3	10.1	7.9	12.8	2.9	100.0
Rural (middle (N=179))	70.4	6.7	6.2	15.6	1.1	100.0
Rural (lower (N=403))	78.6	4.3	4.8	10.4	1.9	100.0

[a]Nuclear family is defined in the commonly accepted way as consisting of parents and their unmarried children.

[h]Nuclear lateral type is a nuclear household plus unmarried kin who are laterally and not lineally related to the head of the household.

[c]Joint families consist of two or more nuclear families that are either related laterally or lineally.

[d]Nuclear lineal type consists of the nuclear core plus lineal relations of the head of household whose parents are absent. Included in this category is the stem family.

[e]'Other' includes those in which our information of their family composition is incomplete, or those for which information is available but difficult to decipher and classify into the above family types.

laws effectively regulating the construction of structures may be the cause as well as the effect of widely scattered squatters throughout the city, including upper class residential neighbourhoods. Under these circumstances, the housing factor generally may be responsible for the overwhelming statistics on nuclear family types, which in turn changes the intensity of kin interaction in some cases. Although relatives may reside in detached dwellings with separate cooking facilities, their interactions may be sustained at a high level because of the sharing of a common yard, bath house, or a well from which water is fetched for all purposes of cooking, bathing and washing.

CO-RESIDENCE PATTERNS

In Table 2 a different arrangement of the residential pattern in shown. Here the data gives information on the living patterns for the most part after the marriage of the couple. The sample is divided into four parts:

(1) those who live in the same *sitio* (neighbourhood) as the parents of the husband or the wife;

(2) those that lived in the same house (hence, also in the same sitio with either the parents of the husband or the wife;

(3) those that do not live in the same sitio as the parents or parents-in-law; and

(4) if one or both parents or parents-in-law is (are) deceased at the time of marriage.

If 'living in the same sitio' and 'living in the same house' is combined, more than 60 percent of all of the respondents belong to this category for the urban population, and about 80 percent of the rural population belong to the same category. The corresponding percentage figures are smaller by about 10 to 20 points for co-residence with wife's parents.

In a region where intra-city residential mobility is low, where a substantial proportion of one's relatives live in the same sitio, and where streets and pathways are found between congested home sites, the accessibility of kinship relatives in spatial terms is high. Table 2 only includes the wife's and the husband's parents, married siblings, and siblings-in-law. Nephews and cousins are not included, nor are fictive relatives (compadrazgo or god-parents/god-siblings relations). The total number of related people who are likely to live near the respondent is probably much greater than emerges from the data shown in Table 2.

KINSHIP AND FRIENDSHIP RELATIONS

Table 3 indicates the proportion of those who claimed closest friends and are also related. The table indicates that husbands and wives are closely associated with their relatives in most cases, more than

TABLE 2

Residence of Relatives after Marriage
(in Percentage Figures) N = 2281

	Urban sample		Rural sample		
	Upper & Middle	Lower	Middle	Lower	Total
A. Husband's parents lived . . .					
(1) in the same house	31.2	30.2	28.4	41.3	31.2
(2) in the same sitio (but					
not in the same house)	24.4	21.5	27.0	35.9	25.8
(3) not in the same sitio	38.0	39.2	20.6	19.6	33.8
(4) deceased, either or both	7.4	10.9	11.1	7.6	9.2
B. Wife's parents lived . . .					
(1) in the same house	17.9	18.7	27.0	20.7	19.2
(2) in the same sitio (but					
not in the same house)	29.2	26.9	36.5	43.9	31.7
(3) not in the same sitio	46.9	45.9	28.6	29.3	41.9
(4) deceased, either or both	6.1	8.5	7.9	6.1	7.3
C. Husband's married siblings lived . . .					
(1) in the same house	6.4	5.9	1.6	3.4	5.3
(2) in the same sitio (but					
not in the same house)	43.7	40.7	37.3	55.6	43.7
(3) not in the same sitio	43.8	48.2	33.3	32.1	42.9
(4) deceased	9.2	8.6	9.5	5.5	8.1
D. Wife's married siblings lived . . .					
(1) in the same house	4.3	4.3	–	1.5	3.6
(2) in the same sitio (but					
not in the same house)	40.8	38.2	60.3	53.0	42.9
(3) not in the same sitio	46.7	48.3	33.3	37.1	44.9
(4) deceased	8.2	9.1	6.3	8.4	8.6

TABLE 3

Most of Closest Friends who are also Related to Respondents
(Wife Data Only)

Age groups		No.	% Related
24 or under	(N = 322)	127	39.4
25–34	(N = 924)	301	32.5
35–39	(N = 391)	133	34.0
40–44	(N = 269)	93	34.5
45 and over	(N = 61)	20	32.7

one-third of the sample, even when age is controlled. The way the question was addressed: 'are most of your closest friends or your husband's friends related to you?' indicates that perhaps the percentage figure is higher if *any* of the friends which the respondent claimed is a kin relative. The data can also be viewed in a different way, namely there is a conceptual or cognitive overlapping between *friend* and *relative.* Two related, but independently collected data in Cebu during the latter part of the sixties, when the present study took place, suggest that (1) relatives and neighbours do overlap a great deal (Duff, 1971); and (2) friends are frequently given kinship terms which, at least conceptually, tend to view one's close friends as a part of the 'family' (Jacobson, 1969). Thus, in organizational terms, the *social world* of the Cebuano is not divided into sets of mutually exclusive segments even in the urban areas.[3] On this point, Jacobsen (forthcoming, ms. p. 97) states that:

> While the boundaries between kin the family, and kin and non-kin may be clearly demarcated, they are not absolute in the sense that they do not always cover the same range in the former case and that kinship models may be used for friendship relationships in the latter. For example, close relatives can be defined to include or exclude different ranges of cousins, some people drawing the line at the first cousin range and others at second cousins. In the context of friendship ties, some friends are like 'brothers and sisters'. What this means in operation is that there is a considerable amount of flexibility in the mode of recognition of both kinship and friendship ties.

Long-time friendship ties do undergo changes as one's life-cycle changes. There is, furthermore, a difference between the sexes. Men ordinarily keep there pre-marital friends, especially friends made during the teen years, known in the Cebuano dialect as 'barkada'. Women, on the other hand, tend to incorporate pre-marital friends into fictive kin circles, so that they form the matrix of sponsors on birth, baptisms, confirmations of their children, and become a part of the consanguineal kin network (Liu et al., 1969:399).

CO-RESIDENCE AND FERTILITY

One logical question to be raised at this point is the relationship between *co-residence and fertility* in contrast to *relational extensions* of the conjugal family and fertility. The former is based on the traditional definition of sharing the household with kin-relatives; the latter is to be viewed as the constellation of relatives and friends which differentiates itself in *content* from the nuclear family.

With respect to the co-residence pattern, the complete data is difficult to present since co-living with relatives is a function of the life-cycle dependence of the married offspring on their parents or parents-in-law. Most of the couples who claimed to have lived with their parents, parents-in-law, or married siblings lived with them at the time of marriage and averaged less than three years shortly after the second child is born (Liu et al., 1969:398). Thus, taking into consideration the temporal and durational dimension of such co-living arrangement with relatives, Table 4 shows the length of time elapsed between marriage and the birth of the first child *for normally fecund couples only.*

The total sample means, in terms of months, between marriage and the first birth is fifteen months. Those who lived with the husband's parents at the time had a mean of 15.1 months. For those who lived with the wife's parents, the mean is 14.8 months. For those who lived with the husband's siblings and with the wife's siblings, the mean months are 17.0 and 16.9, respectively. For those who did not live with any relatives, the mean month is 14.5. Thus, the entire range is only about 2.5 months which can hardly be considered significant.

TABLE 4

Length of Time Elapsed Between Marriage and First Birth by Types of Residential Arrangements

	Living with Husband's Parents	Living with Wife's Parents	Husband's Married Siblings	Wife's Married Siblings	Nuclear Household only	Total
Mean months	15.0	14.9	16.8	17.1	14.8	15.0
P M P through 6 months (%)	28.6	17.6	4.9	3.3	45.6	100

CONJUGAL ROLE STRUCTURE

Table 1 gave the household data, the classification of family types, and also suggested that the nuclear family and its variants dominate the Cebuano communities, both urban and rural. Table 5 shows that conjugal role structure is markedly segregated Cebu, characteristic of sex-determined activities.

Role segregation within the nuclear family, however, was not accompanied by an autistic pattern of unrelated activities. It is, as indicated by Bott (1957), marked by the respective network of interpersonal relations, with little overlapping of obligations and relations beyond the nuclear unit. Thus, the emotional expressions between the husband and wife are less intense, and less exclusive. To illustrate this consider Figure 1 which displays three hypothetical cases (Liu's previous works have come close to the approximation of the ideal pattern).

The two dimensions of conjugal relations, power differentials and affectivity, are represented in the figure. An assumption implicit here is that intenseness of emotional involvement, as measured by affectivity (positive or negative), and power differentials are inherently related. The nuclear family is characterized by a high degree of affective bond between the conjugal pair and a minimum degree of authority or power differentials. On the other hand, the traditional extended family would be characterized by a high degree of power differentials and a low

TABLE 5

Conjugal Role Constellation, Cebu Urban Families, by Social Class, in Percentage Figures, $N = 1,521$

Item	Ha Hd	Ha Bd	Ha Wd	Ba Hd	Ba Bd	Ba Wd	Wa Hd	Wa Bd	Wa Wd	Social class
Food	—	—	—	—	*	*	*	5.7	88.6	Upper
	*	—	*	—	*	*	*	*	83.8	Middle
	—	—	—	*	—	*	*	*	85.8	Lower
Health	*	*	12.0	*	9.0	25.0	*	—	46.0	Upper
	—	*	12.8	—	*	22.2	—	*	53.2	Middle
	—	—	—	*	*	—	12.7	24.7	53.8	Lower
Spending money	*	*	6.2	5.2	17.5	14.4	*	10.3	37.1	Upper
	*	*	5.9	*	10.0	7.7	7.2	19.4	37.0	Middle
	5.6	*	6.5	*	8.3	14.5	8.6	6.8	43.9	Lower
Child	18.4	—	*	7.1	33.7	12.2	*	*	23.5	Upper
	11.4	*	*	*	18.0	5.4	12.0	6.8	38.7	Middle
	12.6	*	10.5	*	17.0	5.1	*	5.1	14.2	Lower
Economic planning	20.6	*	8.2	15.5	20.6	15.5	6.2	*	7.2	Upper
	9.3	*	*	7.9	16.7	23.1	6.4	6.7	20.9	Middle
	8.0	5.1	7.6	*	15.4	6.9	*	25.6	25.0	Lower
School	*	—	6.5	6.6	31.5	35.9	—	—	17.4	Upper
	7.5	*	13.6	*	17.4	35.3	—	*	14.2	Middle
	7.2	7.6	*	*	18.1	*	11.0	32.2	18.7	Lower
Leisure	11.5	*	9.4	*	32.3	26.0	*	*	11.5	Upper
	8.6	17.5	11.6	5.1	30.7	17.4	*	*	14.1	Middle
	8.3	6.3	*	6.1	29.5	*	11.3	17.7	16.9	Lower

Key: * denotes less than five percent;   -- denotes less than one percent.
Ha = activity by Husband alone   Hd = decision by Husband   Wa = activity by Wife alone
Wd = decision by Wife   Ba = joint activity   Bd = joint decision

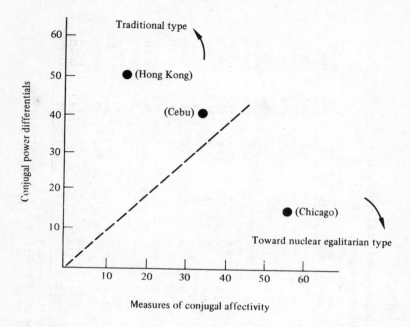

Figure I. Relationships between Affective Exchange and Power Differentials as measured by the Revealed Difference Method for Hong Kong couples, Philipino couples, and American middle class couples in Chicago. Plotted positions are approximations for illustrative purposes.

degree of affective involvement. The positions of Hong Kong families and of Philippino families were collected at different times (Liu, 1970; Hutchison, 1970) by using the same procedure and instruments. The position represented by the Chicago data was collected by Strodtbeck (1964) among middle class families. Individual families in each sample are given separate scores along these dimensions, but are not represented here in the illustrative figure. The figure, which is a visual presentation of data collected during the last decade in Chicago, Hong Kong and the Philippines (as a part of the Cebu Family Health Project data) suggest that the direction of change (i.e. nuclearization) of the family system can be assessed in terms of conjugal relations. This does not mean that such relational analysis is a substitute of the household analysis. These

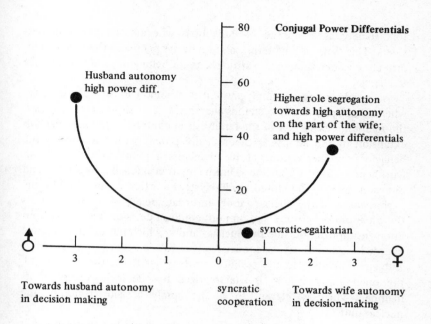

Figure II. Relationships between Conjugal Role Structure and Power Differentials. Plotting based on judges ratings, for illustrative purposes only.

are conceptualized on two different planes.

One perspective based on which the nuclear family can be conceptually clarified is to look at the *relational dimension of the family structure* (Liu et al., 1970a). A nuclear family can be either 'open' or 'closed'. In the open system, obligations and interactions among family members are *extended* beyond the membership of the basic nuclear unit. In the closed system, such relations are not as extended beyond the basic unit. The distinction between an open family system and a closed family system provides a useful differentiation in one's attempt to describe variations and change in family relations. The concept itself is a classic one, going back to Weber who spoke about a closed social group as being one in which outsiders were excluded, limited or subjected to particular conditions of participation (Weber, 1947:

folk society as composed of individuals who are isolated from outsiders. This type of long-term isolation brings people in the folk society
into close association, with a strong sense of belonging, and a reluctance
to change.

As a rule, a closed family system is common in an open society,
whereas an open family system is characteristic of closed society. Thus,
the *relational* extension of the family, as in contrast to the *membership*
extension of the family, is theoretically potent with reference to the
behavioral predispositions of its members, a point so ably made in
Durkheim's study of suicide (Durkheim, translated by Spaulding and
Simpson, 1951). The closed family system — often exemplified by the
exclusiveness of the nuclear family in urban society of the West — puts
the premium on privacy and on joint conjugal decision-making without
intervention from outside the nuclear family; which places all non-home
oriented activities as 'secondary'. The role of kinship relatives is
ambiguous relative to the conjugal process itself. On the other hand,
the open-family system is characterized by the inclusiveness of its
members which is relevant to all the family decision regarding the
nuclear unit.

The *intensiveness* of the nuclear family is neither uniformly felt
throughout the social status spectrum nor the same for every member
in the family. The significance of treating interpersonal relationships
both within and outside the nuclear family to include kinship members
is particularly crucial in conjugal relations. Nuclear units may link
with other nuclear units of the kinship corporate group in various
forms if the family is open. There are at least five areas where such
concern may be conceptually relevant. First, there is the obvious
property inheritance rule which provides the economic basis of the
power for either the male or the female heir. Under the rule of
primogeniture, the power of the first-born male is legitimized by his
right to inherit, who then has the complete discretion in what
provisions are made for his younger siblings, although in actual practice
he may not exercise his full rights. The exact relationship between the
male in the household of a patrilineal system contra his wife is not
clear. Secondly, in the sphere of child—parent relations, the unilineal
system allows the grandparents to exercise direct influence of

child-bearing, thus making it possible for members of the affinal group to dilute the power of the mother and, indirectly, her bargaining power vis-à-vis her husband. Thirdly, in case of the matrilineal system, since the mother's power is largely transferred to her brother's domain, the actual power of the natural father would have to be greatly lessened even if the segregation of role performance in the nuclear household gives the male head de facto power. Fourthly, lineal groupings give an unequal probability for members of the nuclear family to associate with relatives of one side over the other. Finally, the lineage system has a differential impact on the mobility of its members, both in terms of the occupational and the residential choices. In contrast to the unilineal system, the bilateral system allows a greater freedom and autonomy on the part of the nuclear unit, thus lessening the influence and control of the larger kinship network.

In addition to the power differentials of the conjugal pair in the nuclear family, patterns of intranuclear family communications may differ considerably between the open and the closed family system. Spontaneous communication between the married couple is, in a sense, a function of the power differentials between them and the relative participation, joint or segregated, of household chores. Thus the 'social context' of communication styles, as indicated in a recent paper by Liu (1972), becomes relevant in the consideration of the family system and spousal interaction. Regrettably, little systematic study has been done on the decision-making process of an open family system. Moreover historical material is unfortunately mote on conjugal interaction. Thus, to search in the period during which traditional family commenced to change in these regards would not be possible. Rather than to assert that shrinkage of family size is associated with the nuclear family system, one may well entertain the notion that the *intenseness* of the nuclear family life as well as its emotional *exclusiveness* may in fact require an increased affective and effective communication between the husband and wife, which had begun during and even before the shrinking size of the family in the city took place.

RELATIONAL PERSPECTIVE
ON THE CEBU DATA

To view the data from the relational perspective, the procedure is a bit complex. Two tables are presented here. Table 6 indicates the way husbands and wives relate either conjointly or separately to their relatives and friends and how such network of relationships may be related to the level of marital fertility. To do this a simple typology of the family is constructed; each type of family relationship is then related to the fertility ratio. Table 7, however, is an attempt to juxtapose friendship pattern, kinship involvement and co-residence pattern.

In Table 6, in order to compress the massive amount of data dealing with family relations and friendship network, the first step is to separate out families typified by a 'loosely-knit' network, in which the individual spouse knows and has friendship ties with people who are not related to each other and has only a weak tie among them. This type of family relation is characterized by the closed and more intense conjugal relations. The second type then is the open system where relations are extended out and networks outside the family are strongly knit by either kinship or close friendship relations. The tendency, in the latter case, is for such strong outside network relations to draw husband and wife closer together even though the conjugal relations are not intense or exclusive.

There is, however, a third group in which the strong and tightly-knit friends and kinship networks are mutually segregated along sex-determined associations. In this case, one may assume that the network relations outside the conjugal bond tend to dilute the emotional affectivitiy of the couple rather than bringing them together, as there exists the competition of exclusiveness between one's peers and friends, and one's spouse. Thus, the three types of family relations are as follows:

Type I. Tightly-knit friendship and kin-network involving both husband and wife.

Type II. Tightly-knit friendship and kin-network, respectively, separating husband and wife.

Type III. Loosely knit friendship network, respectively separating husband and wife, but bringing couple closer together.

TABLE 6

Friendship Network and Desired Family Size, and Fertility Ratio, by Age Cohorts, Total Sample, $N = 1,931$

Age Cohort and types of friendship	Number of children/ woman	Desired size	Number of cases
24 or under			
Type I	2.1	3.9	69
Type II	2.3	3.4	28
Type III	2.2	3.5	195
25–34 Type I	3.9	5.1	211
Type II	3.8	3.8	90
Type III	3.7	3.8	623
35–39 Type I	5.8	6.2	102
Type II	6.2	4.3	31
Type III	5.6	4.2	258
40–44 Type I	5.9	5.2	68
Type II	5.8	3.8	25
Type III	5.2	4.2	176
45 or over			
Type I	8.5	6.9	14
Type II	7.0	5.5	6
Type III	5.2	4.2	41

The data here suggest that Type I families (i.e. tightly-knit friendship and kin-network relations involving both husbands and wives) have higher completed fertility ratio (8.5 per couple). The total number of Type I families is not large ($N=464$). The total number in the Type II group is 1,293, confirming the sex-segregated association pattern. On the other hand, Type III, involving families with weak-linkage outside the conjugal bond, has the lowest completed fertility ratio. In looking at other age cohorts, fertility ratios are less differentiated by type of the family association. However, the desired family size does show a clear distinction between Types I, II and III families. The difference is is about one child for women 25 years old or over, and above half a child for those under 25 years old. Since friendship pattern and kin-network relations are based on self-reported data from the wife, errors may be introduced here. More rigorous design with possible interactive sampling may give the hypothesis on the nuclear-extended family relations and fertility a better and more definitive test.

Table 7 is based on two sets of information. The first pertains to how many of the wife's own friends are also related to each other. Those who stated that more than half of their best friends are also related, are used in the analysis. (N=840). This may be a crude measure of the extensiveness of kin-involvement and the strength of the kin-network relations. The second information pertains to the co-residence pattern of the conjugal unit with either the wife's parents or the husband's parents any time after their marriage. Only urban samples are used.

In either case, the exploratory computer run indicates that living patterns for those couples who are closely related to their relatives (defined here as extended families by relational inclusion) do not differ

TABLE 7

Fertility Ratio and Co-residence Pattern

	Number of cases	Children ever born	Fertility ratio	S. D.
A. Co-living with wife's parents				
(1) for at least some time	294	1384	4.7	2.8
(2) never	479	2280	4.8	2.7
(3) non-classified	67	338	5.0	3.1
Total	840	4002	4.8	2.7
B. Co-living with husband's parents				
(1) for at least some time	359	1715	4.8	2.9
(2) never	412	1944	4.7	2.8
(3) non-classified	69	343	5.0	2.9
Total	840	4002	4.8	2.7

significantly in their respective fertility ratio. Two weaknesses are apparent in this table: the lack of control of age groups and the high standard deviations from all comparing groups.

Answers to these and other questions do not stop at the statistical level. Because of the cultural tradition, the economic levels and employment opportunities, lack of Western medical facilities in parts of the urban neighbourhoods and the majority of the rural *barrios,* and patterns of social stratification in the society, much of the fertility behaviour of Cebuano women are deeply rooted with these interlocking socio-economic factors for which statistical data do not always clearly reflect. Some carefully written fieldnotes and open-ended interviews on kinship data have considerably strengthened the argument that fertility behaviour and family and kinship dynamics are deeply interwoven beyond what some of the household data can indicate.

Without going deeply into these materials, however, some examples can be given here to illustrate this point. The first is that there is a wide range of kinship behaviour from one social class to another. Whereas lower class kinship reciprocity may be considerably weaker due to sheer economic difficulties, the middle class dweller is under pressure to render a helping hand to kinship relatives with rather meager resources. In contrast, the upper class relies upon internuclear households to solidify its financial and political alliances (Hollesteiner, 1963; Liu et al., 1969). Secondly, a repeated theme in the Philippine scene is the belief that social positions and employment opportunities can be achieved through the manipulation of 'connections' or contacts. In order to sustain and to operate in the system, kinship solidarity is maintained in a selective manner, and non-kin can be included as fictive kin-relatives, to broaden one's circles of contacts. In the same vein, investments in the educational needs of one's relatives where possible may be considered as an investment in future opportunities through 'human resources' from which one expects reciprocity. It is through these human network mechanisms that kinship solidarity is interwoven in a complex manner with politics, religious rituals, education and business.

FAMILY TRANSITION,
THE MYTH OF NUCLEARIZATION

Goode (1963:25) suggests that all societies are changing toward the nuclear family system, and rejected technology as the prime moving factor while maintaining that factors underlying the change are yet to be identified. Supporting Goode, Taeuber (1971:37, italics added) states:

> Ideal families [in premodern period] were multigenerational kin groups. Marriage occurred at early ages and fertility was limited only marginally by traditional taboos or practices; growth potential was high when and if mortality declined. The premodern family was thus incompatible with modernization. *With industrialization and urbanization, there was transition to a nuclear or conjugal family.*

Urban economy as an environment which calls for ramifying readjustment of the family dynamics has been the thesis of Parsons (1955). A more recent volume (Sennett, 1970) on the change of the family system in Chicago between 1872 and 1890 suggests that economic impact forced middle class husbands to withdraw from community life. Hence, the nuclear family came about in the urban scene because of the collapse of multiple primary groups, thereby making the family the only medium for interpersonal expression. In Sennett's words (p.50):

> Fathers were no longer leaders but rather the supporters of direoting mothers; the home had, in some way, become the focus for a new kind of intense family life, a life that was private and isolated. While the older families were home-oriented in their values, they were anything but isolated from others of the same set in Union Park.

The history of this section of Chicago community shed considerable light on the theory of family transition. Documents secured and interpreted by Sennett provide answers to such specific questions as how the authority pattern changed during the 1870s and the 1880s, which reversed the moral power of the father, and how family life has become intense and eclusive and the structure closed. Thus, aside from the household composition, Parsons, the American sociologist, and Aries, the French historian, both spoke of the urban nuclear family in terms of the weak allegiance to kin relatives. They both attempted to describe a cluster of conditions which shape a private and exclusive family system but they gave different reasons (Parsons, 1955; Aries, 1965).

In any event, there is little evidence that pre-modern families are characterized by the dominant type of joint family system in practice. Many factors intervened as can be inferred from the works of other scholars on the family. Among such factors are: (1) the achievement of nuclear family by default vis-à-vis the conception of nuclear family as an ideal only (Levy, 1955); and (2) regional variation of the particular family ideal, as evidenced by the works of Ho (1965), Hau (1943), Taeuber (1971), and Freedman (1957; 1966).

If only historical data on when family change first took place were available, it would be extremely helpful in showing how relations among kin changed from inclusiveness to exclusiveness. But such data are not available aside from illustrative materials. Sennett's data on the Chicago families during the 1880s, however, are useful in permitting the following propositions to be formulated:

Proposition I: Nuclear family system, as in contrast to the extended family system, is a response to the demand of urban living and wage system, shaped by industrialization, and hence is characterized by intenseness of conjugal relations, with marked decline of the importance of kinship contacts (Sennett, 1970).

Corollary A: Nuclear family system, as in contrast to the extended family system, is characterized by syncratic co-operations rather than segregation of task roles in the family (Herbst, 1952; Liu, 1970).

Corollary B: Nuclear family system, as in contrast to extended family system, is characterized by expressive affective interchange between husband and wife (Liu, 1970).

Proposition II: Nuclear family system, as in contrast to the extended family system, is characterized by the egalitarian role relations, rather than clearly marked male over female authority patterns (Ogburn and Nimkoff, 1955; Burgess et al., 1963; Goode, 1963).

Proposition III: Bilateral system, because of the structural requisites for a more balanced interchange between the nuclear unit and its

duo-lineal kins, is more adaptive to the urban economy and is, therefore, less resistant to the transition from the extended to the nuclear
family system (Fortes, 1953:17–41).

These propositions, mainly derived explicitly or implicitly from
previous writings, may be combined with other empirical works or
assumptions. For example, if the Davis–Lorimer proposition on the
higher fertility among extended and/or corporate system is true, a
derivative from Proposition III above suggests that unilineal system
presents more a structural obstacle, as compared with the bilateral
system, for the family to adapt to the industrial-wage economy, and
would therefore be more apt to have a higher marital fertility. At
present, however, not enough is known about specific conditions under
which the derived postulate can be validly tested across cultures. Data
on the non-lineal type of family, however, suggests that this is true
(Fortes, 1953).

Furthermore, from Propositions I, II and III it is possible to obtain
the derivative assumption that the bilateral system tends to be more
conductive to egalitarian conjugal relations, greater affective interchange
between husband and wife, and thus exhibits within the nuclear unit a
greater degree of syncratic co-operation between husband and wife,
and a syndrome of social psychological factors which typifies the
nuclear family ideal in the European–American sense. These assumptions have yet to be systematically tested with a wider range of
comparable cross-national data.

Family structure, because it is regarded as a focal point of the
recent discussions on demographic processes, is consequently regarded
as a spatial arrangement of co-residence pattern. Generally, three
factors may be identified as being responsible for such conceptual
approach and research procedures. The first is that available data,
historical and cross-national, have been largely if not exclusively
extracted from enumerative censuses, parish records, and household
data. Secondly, family type variations, such as rules of residence, jural
authority, marriage customs and inheritance rules, have generally been
regarded as legitimate and important topics for ethnological investigations, embodied in the formal elicitation of social organizations. As
such, formal rules of practice are usually more important in explaining

the lines and processes of a society; deviations from such rules have ordinarily been neglected. Finally, relational data about a large number of families are not generally available. Thus, the analysis of family types have largely been *quasi-structural*, rather than structural. The former is the analysis of the social unit by using proportions of one category of role and/or status in relation to all others. Significant examples are the works of Coale (1965), Burch (1970), and more recently, the excellent paper by Parish and Schwartz (1972). The latter (structural) approach is the analysis of the relations and norms of relations of members of the group. Examples of the latter may be the works of Parsons and Bales (1955), Aries (1962) and Freedman (1966). One significant exception which combined both of these approaches is exemplified by Taeuber's study of the Japanese family (Taeuber, 1958, chapter on the family).

None the less, household composition has been identified as the way in which people shape their living pattern in order to adjust to their economic environment most efficiently. The works of LePlay (1870), Bloch (1931), Parish and Schwartz (1972), Habakkuk (1955), Nimkoff and Middleton (1960); as well as more recently the work by Winch and Blumberg (1968) also pointed to the importance of economic factors in shaping the family co-residence pattern, principally in such activities as management of agricultural works and the control of family estates. Important as the economic forces may be, other social forces, which have not been rigorously researched, may also play a part.

For example, as Nelson (1969) pointed out, a great deal of the lower class urban residents in all LDC are recent migrants from rural areas. In Latin America, as much as 40 percent of the lower class residents are thus classified. Poverty and housing shortages may constitute the major reason of single household, characterized by incomplete nuclear unit. The situation is reported by Mitchaell in Hong Kong (Mitchaell, 1971). The disruption of family life is not entirely explained by economic variables, but it has major economic as well a political consequences. Family life may be a reflection of, and adjustment, to such disruptions. It seems that residential patterns are good indices to measure certain organizational characteristics only if they are used in conjunction with socio-cultural data about a population or a sub-population.

NOTES

1. The hypotheses on family type and fertility were set forth by Lorimer (1954), Davis (1955), and Davis and Black (1956) after careful and thorough discussions on various historical and cross-cultural materials. These hypotheses, though stated in somewhat different details and forms, were essentially supportive of the extended and corporate systems favour higher marital and societal fertility and that nuclear and independent family system tends to have lower societal fertility.

2. For a good summary, see Burch and Gendell (1971), also Hawthorn (1970:18–33). Burch and Gendell dealt only with family type, whereas Hawthorn dealt with associated factors, including marriage age, coitus frequency, etc. all of which, however, dealt with data which may not be comparable because of definition of household and the periods for which data was available. Sennett (1970), however, dealt only with Chicago data during the period of urban transition in the late nineteenth century.

3. This may be an over simplification, since at least one author (Lynch, 1964) observed that his informants do make such distinctions and priorities are assigned. But in personal terms, the labelling of good friends as kin indicate that inclusion is used.

REFERENCES

Adams, Bert (1967), *The Second Sowing*. San Francisco: Chandler.

Anderson, Michael (1971), *Family Structure in Nineteenth Century Lancashire*. Cambridge: Cambridge University Press.

Aries, Philippe (1965), *Centuries of Childhood*. New York: Vintage Books.

Bloch, Marc (1931), *Les Caracteres Originaux de l'histoire Rurale Francaise*. Paris: Armand Colin, 1952.

Bott, Elizabeth (1957), *Family and Social Network*. London: Tavistock Publications, Ltd.

Burch, T.K. (1970), 'Some Demographic Determinants of Average Household

Size: An Analytic Approach', *Demography* 7 (February): 61-69.

Burch, T.K. and Murray Gendell (1971), 'Extended Family Structure and Fertility: Some Conceptual and Methodological Issues', in Steve Polgar (ed.), *Culture and Population: A Collection of Current Studies.* Chapel Hill: Carolina Population Center, Monograph 9, pp. 87-104.

Burgess, Ernest W., Harvey J. Locke and M. M. Thomas (1963), *The Family: From Institution to Companionship.* New York: American Books, Inc.

Coale, A. J. (1965), 'Estimates of Average Size of Household', in A. J. Coale et al. (eds.), *Aspects of the Analysis of Family Structure.* Princeton: Princeton University Press.

Davis, Kingsley (1955), 'Institutional Patterns Favouring High Fertility in Under-developed Areas', *Eugencis Quarterly* 2 (March): 33-39.

Davis, Kingsley and Judith Blake (1956), 'Social Structure and Fertility: An Analytic Framework', *Economic Development and Cultural Change* 4 (April): 211-235.

Demo, Nieva (1972), 'The Midwives: A Functional Analysis of Social Changes', Unpublished M.A. Thesis. Cebu, Philippines: San Carlos University.

Duff, Robert W. (1971), 'Neighbourhood of Residence and Knowledge, Attitudes and Practices with Regard to Conception Control in a Philippine City', Ph.D. Thesis, University of Notre Dame.

Durkheim, Emile (1951), *Suicide.* Transalted by John A. Spaulding and George Simpson. Glencoe: The Free Press.

Fortes. M. (1953), 'The Structure of Nonlineal Descent Groups', *American Anthropologist* 55 (January): 17-41.

Freedman, Maurice (1957), *Chinese Family and Marriage in Singapore.* London: HMSO.

— — (1966), *Chinese Lineage and Society: Fukien and Kwangtung.* London: Athlone Press.

Gonzalez, N. L. S. (1961), 'Family Organization in Five Types of Migratory Wage Labor', *American Anthropologist* 63: 1264-80.

— — (1969), *Black Carib Household Structure: A Study of Migration and Modernization.* Seattle: University of Washington Press.

Goode, William J. (1963), *World Revolution of Family Patterns.* New York: The Free Press of Glencoe.

Habakkuk, H. Jr (1955), 'Family Structure and Economic Change in Nineteenth Century Europe', *Journal of Economic History* 15: 1-12.

Hawthorn, Geoffrey (1970), *The Sociology of Fertility.* London: Collier—Macmillan, Ltd.

Herbst, P. G. (1952), 'The Measurement of Family Relationships', *Human Relations* 5 (February): 3-35.

Ho, Ping-ti (1965), 'An Historian's View of the Chinese Family System', in Seymour M. Farber et al. (eds), *Man and Civilization, The Family's Search for Survival.* New York: McGraw-Hill.

Hollesteiner, Mary (1963), *The Dynamics of Power in a Philippine Community.*
      Quezon City: University of the Philippines Press.
Hsu. Francis L. K. (1943), 'The Myth of Chinese Family Size', *American Journal
      of Sociology*, 48:555-562.
— — (1965), 'The Effect on Dominant Kinship Relationships on Kin and Non-Kin
      Behavior: A Hypothesis', *American Anthropologist* 67:638-61.
— — (1968), 'Chinese Kinship and Chinese Behavior', in Ho and Tsou, *China in
      Crisis*, Vol. 1; Book 2. Chicago: University of Chicago Press.
Hutchison, Ira W. (1970). 'Husband–Wife Interaction and Fertility Patterns in the
      Philippines', Ph.D. Thesis, University of Notre Dame.
Jacobson, Helga, E. (1970), 'Urbanization and Family Ties: A Problem in the
      Analysis of Change', *Journal of Asian and African Studies* 4 (October):
      302-307.
— — (forthcoming), 'Tradition and Change in Cebu City' (unpublished manuscript,
      forthcoming in Developing Nation's Monograph Series. Winston-Salem: Wake
      Forest University).
Kosa, John, Leo Rachiele and Cyril Schommer (1960), 'Sharing the Home with
      Relatives'. *Marriage and Family Living* 22 (May): 129-131.
LePlay, F. (1870), *L'Organisation de la Famille.* Paris: Dentu.
Levy, Marion J. (1955), 'Some Aspects of Individualism and the Problem of
      Modernization in China and Japan', *Economic Development and Cultural
      Change* 10 (1962):225-240.
— — (1969), 'Aspects of the Analysis of Social Structure' in Ansley I. Coale et al.
      (eds), *Aspects of the Analysis of Social Structure.* Princeton: Princeton
      University Press.
Lieban, Richard (1967), *Cebuano Sorcery: Maligu Magic in the Philippines.*
      Berkeley: University of California Press.
Litwak, Eugene (1965), 'Extended Kin Relations and Industrial Democratic
      Society', in E. Shanas and G. Streib (eds), *Social Structure and The Family:
      Generational Relations.* Englewood Cliffs, N.J.: Prentice-Hall.
Liu, P. K. C. (1967), *The Use of Household Registration Records in Measuring
      the Fertility Level in Taiwan.* Taipei: Institute of Economics. Academia Sinica.
Liu, William T. (1970) 'On the Use of the Revealed Difference Method in Family
      Study and Its Cross-Cultural Significance', *Transactions of the Sixth World
      Congress of Sociology,* Evian, 1966.
— — (1972), 'Conjugal Interaction and Fertility Behavior: Some Conceptual
      Problems in Research', Paper given at the Comparative Sociology Institute
      Conference on *Family and Fertility,* Ohio State University.
Liu, William T., Arthur J. Rubel and Elena Yu (1969), 'The Urban Family of
      Cebu: A Profile Analysis', *Journal of Marriage and the Family* 31 (May):
      393-402.
Liu, William T., Ira W. Hutchison and Lawrence Hong (1970a), 'Conjugal Power
      and Decision-Making: A Methodological Note on the Cross-Cultural Study of

the Family', Paper given at the Seventh World Congress of the International Sociological Association, Varna, Bulgaria.

Liu, William T., Arthur J. Rubel and Virginia Pato (1970b), *The Cebu Family Health Project.* Notre Dame: Centre for the Study of Man in Contemporary Society, University of Notre Dame.

Lorimer, F. (1954), *Culture and Human Fertility.* Paris: UNESCO.

Lynch, Frank (1964), 'Social Acceptance' in *Four Readings on Philippines Values.* Frank Lynch (ed), Ateneo de Manila University Press (Quezon City, Philippines) 1-21.

Mitchaell, Robert E. (1969), 'Family Life in Urban Hong Kong', *Urban Family Life Survey* (mimeo).

— — (1971), 'Residential Patterns and Family Networks', Part I and Part II. Unpublished working papers (mimeo) based on The Urban Family Life Survey of Hong Kong.

Murdock, George (1949), *Social Structure.* New York: The Macmillan Co.

Nag, Moni (1967), 'Family Type and Fertility', in *World Population Conference Proceedings,* 1965, Vol. II. New York: United Nations, pp. 160-163.

Nelson, Joan (2969), *Migrants, Urban Poverty, and Instability in Developing Nations.* Harvard University Centre for International Affairs, Occasional Papers..

Nimkoff, M. F. and R. Middleton (1960), 'Types of Family and Types of Economy', *American Journal of Sociology* 66:215-25.

Ogburn, W. F. and M. F. Nimkoff (1955), *Technology and the Family.* Boston: Houghton Mifflin Co.

Pakrasi, K. and C. Malaker (1967), 'The Relationship Between Family Type and Fertility', *Milbank Memorial Fund Quarterly* 45 (October): 461-60.

Palmore, James A. Robert E. Klein and Ariffin Bin Marzuki (1970), 'Class and Family in a Modernizing Society', *American Journal of Sociology* 76 (November): 375-98.

Parish, William L. and Moshe Schwartz (1972), 'Household Complexity in Nineteenth Century France', *American Sociological Review,* 37 (April 1972): 154-172.

Parsons, Talcott and R. F. Bales (1955), *The Family: Socialization and Interaction Process.* Glencoe: The Free Press.

Redfield, Robert (1947), 'The Folk Society'. *American Journal of Sociology* 52: 293-308.

Safilios-Rothschild, Constantina (1971), 'The Study of Family Power Structure: A Review 1960-1969', *Journal of Marriage and The Family* 32: 539-52.

Sennett, Richard (1970), *Families Against the City: Middle Class Homes of Industrial Chicago, 1872-1890.* Cambridge: Harvard University Press.

Smith, R. T. (1956), *The Negro Family in British Guiana.* London: Routledge & Kegan Paul.

Strodtbeck, F. L. (1964), 'A Summary of Current Works on Family Interaction Studies Using Revealed Differences', Working paper 31, Social Psychology

Laboratory, University of Chicago (mimeo).

Taeuber, Irene (1958), *The Population of Japan*. Princeton: Princeton University Press.

── (1971) 'Change and Transition in Family Structure', in *Fogarty International Center Proceedings*, No. 3, Washington, D.C.: U. S. Government Printing Office.

Weber, Max (1947), *The Theory of Social and Economic Organization*. New York: Oxford University Press.

Winch, Robert F. and R. L. Blumberg (1968), 'Societal Complexity and Familial Organization', in R. F. Winch et al. (eds), *Selected Studies in Marriage and The Family*. New York: Holt, Rinehart & Winston.

Young, Michael and Peter Willmott (1957), *Family and Kinship in East London*. London: Routledge & Kegan Paul.

II COEXISTENCE AND CHANGE IN THE EXTENDED AND NUCLEAR FAMILIES

3

UNDERSTANDING CHANGES IN THE FAMILY IN CONTEMPORARY INDIA
A Few Hypotheses

A. A. Khatri
University of Alabama, USA

In this paper, an attempt has been made first to offer a rationale for the use of imaginative literature as sociologically relevant data, secondly to illustrate this use for study of family changes by quantitative and qualitative analysis of 45 Gujarati social novels from three periods (pre-1912, 1931–37, and 1956–62) by the means of a category system of 143 items and 699 sub-items (with intra-coder reliability of 85.7 percent and an intra-coder reliability of 68.6 percent), and thirdly to consider Goode's hypothesis about the role of exposure to ideology and Kirkpatrick's hypotheses about urban residence, youth and upper social class specifically intelligence and higher education and examine their applicability as change agents to the Indian family. Mention is also made of specific hypotheses about changes in the Indian family developed by the present author and the case study technique employed by him. The paper ends with global evaluation of changes in the Indian family as derived from analysis of data of imaginative literature.

This paper was presented and formally discussed in the session, 'Theories for Understanding Changes in Conjugal Family in the Contemporary World' of the Committee on Family Research of International Sociological Association during VIII World Congress of Sociology held in August, 1974 at Toronto, Canada. It is a revised and abbreviated version of sections of a chapter, 'Social Change in Marriage and Family Relationships' of the thesis entitled 'Marriage and Family Relationship in Gujarati Fiction' accepted in fulfilment of requirements of PhD Degree by the University of London, London, England.

A number of hypotheses and investigative techniques to test them can be derived from the writings of sociologists for sharpening our understanding of changes in the family organization in different parts of the world. One difficulty experienced by research investigators interested in understanding changes is that data concerning the diverse variables of the family in the past are not now available and most of which are irretrievable.

With data base of the past family being so tenuous, ways and means have to be explored for partial rejuvenation of the past, understanding of which becomes necessary for shedding light on the contemporary family. It is submitted here that imaginative literature of the past in general and of social novels avowedly devoted to description of the then extant society in particular brings back to some extent relatively unexplored fields otherwise lost to sociologists concerned with family change.

In this paper it is proposed (1) to offer rationale for the use of imaginative literature for the study of aspects of social reality and social change; (2) to illustrate the use of a method of quantitative and qualitative analysis of social novels by consideration of a few hypotheses about family change and examine their applicability to the Indian family; and (3) to present global evaluation of changes in the Indian family as revealed by fictional analysis.

RATIONALE FOR THE USE OF
IMAGINATIVE LITERATURE AS
SOCIOLOGICALLY RELEVANT DOCUMENTS

If one is not looking for equivalence of fictional incidents in reality of the social world, but if one is interested in understanding basic values, assumptions, roles, expectations, attitudes and modes of inter-personal orientation, a study of social novels is likely to shed a flood of light on intra-personal processes and intimate inter-personal relations not easily investigated by questionnaires, interviews, observation and other methods, which predominantly rely upon verbal imparting of information on the part of respondents.

Here we are prompted to make a special mention of emphasis on the use of fiction by Lowenthal (1961:143) as 'genuinely primary source for a study of the penetration of the most private and intimate spheres of individual life by the social climate'. Equating fictional study with laboratory experimentation, he says (p. 158),

Nevertheless an extremely inexpensive social laboratory might be suggested when no living beings need to be interviewed with all the paraphernalia of money-and-time outlay . . . it might be worthwhile reviving . . . the figures of his imagination with artificial respiration and subjecting them to questions and psychological experiments on the most advanced level.

In words of Coser (1972, pp. xv-xvi),

Sociologists have but rarely utilized works of literature in their investigations and yet it would appear obvious that the trained sensibilities of a novelist or a poet may provide a richer source of social insight than, say, the impressions of untrained informants on which so much sociological research currently rests.

The usefulness of literary accounts for gaining insights into concreteness of social processes is attested to by Tavuchis and Goode (1975). They state (p. xii), 'Even if the sociologist does not fully trust such literary accounts, they may furnish interesting interpretative ideas or hypotheses that deserve testing'. 'As models, the societies described in science fiction can generate serious inquiry into the nature of contemporary social reality' (Milstead et al., 1974, p. xiii).

Allport, a strong proponent of the use of personal documents including literary productions states: 'Raw documents have served as the sea upon which authentic scientific voyages of discovery have been launched' (1951:176). Cantril and Bumstead (1960:4) also stress the significance of non-scientific documents for scientists thus: ' . . . vivid descriptions of human experience by non-scientists may . . . supply protocol data with which the scientist may begin his task of cross-examining nature . . .'.

Warner et al (1949) suggest reading of imaginative literature for understanding social stratification. Coleman (1956) does likewise for getting insight into abnormal behaviour. Kenkel's (1969) Presidential address before the 1968 meeting of National Council of Family Relations deals with 'Marriage and the Family in modern science fiction'. Somerville

(1963; 1964; 1966), Clear (1966) and Smardan (1966) have limelighted importance of imaginative literature for the study of family and family life education. Dealing with 'Social problems in fiction', Mukerji (1958: 297) states, 'Problems are the very texture of some fine modern novels, their very bone of bones, their flesh, their very own'. Veena Das (1973) has studied a sample of Urdu novels 'in order to understand the structure of marriage preferences in West Pakistani society' (p. 32). In her view 'The fictionalized accounts of the politics of marriage can yield rich insights into our understanding of marriage strategies' (p. 31).

Further illustrations for the use of literature for sharpening our understanding of various concepts, social processes and institutions are provided by Dabaghian (1970), Ofshe (1970), Coser (1972), Fernandez (1972), Milstead et al. (1974), and Tavuchis and Goode (1975). This rationale for the use of imaginative literature is followed by a brief description of the procedure employed by the present author in his study.

Procedure

A sample of 45 social novels fulfilling certain specified criteria was selected from three periods: pre-1912 (beginning with the first novel in 1866), 1931–37, and 1956–62. For the latter two periods, rural novels were also included. After a series of revisions, a category system consisting of 143 items and 699 sub-items was developed for quantitative and qualitative content analysis. The category system had an intra-coder reliability of 85.7 percent and an inter-coder reliability of 68.6 percent. Advantages and disadvantages of using novels as social documents as well as usefulness and limitations of content analysis as a research technique have received extended discussion elsewhere (Berelson, 1952; Khatri, 1970b, 1975). However, it may be mentioned here that no assumption of quantitatively factual representation of social reality in imaginative literature has been made. As the sample consists of Gujarati social novels of different periods, it cannot also be assumed that similar findings about changes in the Indian family are bound to emerge as a result of analysis of social novels written in other regional languages of India. These limitations to the generalization of findings should be kept in mind while interpreting the results of the present study.

CERTAIN HYPOTHESES
ABOUT CHANGES IN THE FAMILY

First of all, we will state Goode's proposition concerning the role of ideology as a determinant of family change. According to Goode (1963:2), 'Ideological and value changes, partially independent of industrialization also have some effect on family action'. In relation to 'Changing family patterns in India', he says (p. 207) . . . India exhibits more change in family relations than would be expected if industrialization were the sole moving variable'.

It is hypothesized here that the nature and direction of social change in the Hindu family during the last hundred years or so have been influenced considerably by contact with the British culture, specifically exposure to British education, their family organization, their ideology of democracy, liberty and equality. We will deal with the relevant evidence from fiction as it bears upon this hypothesis.

Many novels, particularly pre-1912, contain references to British education, British mate selection process, British ideas about man—woman relations in general and husband—wife in particular. Usually these modes and models are presented in highly eulogistic terms. Sometimes, however, they are portrayed negatively with concomitant idealization of ancient Aryan culture. In 1931—37 and 1956—62 novels, explicit references to British culture have been scanty; however, their modes and models continue to be depicted as values to be cherished and ideals to be followed. Thus, contact with the British culture through various media has significantly influenced treatment of attitudes, values, aspirations, intra-personal and inter-personal conflicts and intra-familial relations in general.

The very first novel (Nandshanker, 1866) refers to the British model of self-selection in marriage in highly positive terms and the prevalent Hindu custom of arranged marriage in negative terms. Another novel written in the same year (Nilakanth, 1866) devotes itself to describe ills of the 'rotten' Hindu society and advocates reforms. Thus, social change appears to be salient in the consciousness of these authors of the first two novels. This consciousness becomes sharpened later and characters with reformist ideology are introduced in novels that follow. It is also interesting to note that almost in the same breath the terms 'English education' and 'reformed' are used. The term English education as used by novelists means here formal education imparted in schools and colleges in India and the United Kingdom as distinguished from education imparted at home in Sanskrit, scriptures, etc. It is presumed that those who have been exposed to English education are also reformed and are interested in social change.

Either the persons who have had English education put forth ideas which seek to bring about social change or whenever any of these ideas are put they are considered to have originated from persons who have been so educated. Some of the ideas attributed to English education are as follows: late marriage as opposed to child marriage, autonomy in mate selection as opposed to familial arrangement, extra-mural gainful work for women as opposed to intra-mural work as housewives, establishment of an independent household by the groom after marriage as opposed to living with his parents, permissiveness regarding meeting of boys and girls, man—woman equality, respect for women, and desirability for divorce in certain situations.

Characters exposed under the influence of British ideology criticize the traditional ideas, attitudes and modes of behaviour and advocate change towards acceptance of British ideas, attitudes and behaviour. We can discern the conflict of ideology (British and Hindu) as characters argue with each other, oppose each other, criticize each other for their ideological commitment and activities. This conflict has been the salient focus of consciousness of many authors of the pre-1912 period (Beginning from 1866). As industrialization was relatively insignificant in the pre-1912 period, we can safely assume that one of major operative change agents was exposure to British ideology.

Goode (1963) has also hypothesized that the family organizations all over the world are gravitating gradually but inevitably towards the ideal typical Western model of the conjugal family. Khatri (1970b:155) formulated one index of the above broad hypothesis as follows: 'There is increasing tendency on the part of newly married couples to establish an independent household of their own'. He (Khatri, 1974) has discussed this hypothesis in somewhat more detail and presented evidence to the effect that trends of the Indian family toward the ideal type of the conjugal family are myths rather than verified aspects of reality. Kirkpatrick (1963) has formulated five other trans-cultural hypotheses concerning patterns in family change. Three of these will be quoted and the extent of their applicability to fiction data will be examined briefly.

(1) 'The modifications in family structure tend to come first in urban rather than rural areas. A background rural area tends to reveal a picture of family life such as existed at an earlier historical period'.

Quantitative and qualitative analysis repeatedly reveals at various points that modes of mate selection, of marriage and family relations in rural novels of 1931–37 and 1956–62 were more or less the same as pre-1912 novels on dimensions of the traditional form of marriage and hierarchically oriented family relations, namely arrangement of betrothal-marriage by families without consultation of mates involved, often during the latter's childhood with considerations of family status ('Kule') and bride or groom price, and disregard of characteristics of the mates and their happiness, expectations of submissiveness from a married woman to her husband and mother-in-law, wife-beating, observance of the Rule of Avoidance and restrictions on personal mobility for married women in the family of in-laws. It appears as if passage of time has almost no impact on these and related dimensions for individuals and families populating rural novels.

(2) 'Younger generation spearheads family change'.

In the mate selection area where the maximum amount of social change has been found, the above hypothesis has received confirmation. In each of the three periods, inter-generational conflicts regarding choice of mate have been reported with the younger generation seeking approval for their chosen mate or disapproving family arrangement. There are some youths who silently suffer or give in to parents. More often than not, parents have to give in. An almost equal number of males and females have been involved in these inter-generational conflicts. In a few cases brothers of females waging this fight against family elders lend support to them. There are, however, some parents in 1931–37 and 1956–62 novels who have accepted and even encouraged autonomy in mate selection. In other spheres of social change also like widow-remarriage, adoption of non-traditional mode of marriage ceremony, refusal to accept domination of parent—son relation over the latter's conjugal relations, it is the younger generation that has taken initiative and has been involved.

In sum, wherever social change in the sphere of marriage and family relations has taken place, it is the younger generation that has spear-headed it.

(3) 'Changes in regard to the family may be spearheaded at the upper levels of the social structure and involve the more intelligent and highly educated people'.

The hypothesis also gets considerable confirmation from the fiction data. Available evidence is succinctly summarized below.

Most of the males involved in family change are college-educated. Many of them belong to middle or upper class, with their families being involved in business or holding important government positions. Females in the pre-1912 period are not college-educated but most of them belong to upper class or royalty. In 1931—37 and 1956—62 novels, many of the females involved are both college-educated and also belong to middle or upper class.

On the basis of evidence of studies on the Indian family then available (Agarwala, 1955; Desai, 1955; 1956; Ghurye, 1952, 1954, 1955; Kapadia, 1954—59; Karve, 1953; Kuppuswami, 1957; Mehta, 1934; and others) and out of his own observations, Khatri (1962) formulated trends in family change from the traditional Hindu family to its emergent forms in contemporary India.

These hypotheses include the following themes: involvement of boys and girls in the mate selection process, role of romantic love, caste endogamy, dowry, education, earning capability, physical appearance and personality characteristics of potential mates in the mate selection process, increase in age at marriage, extent of neolocal residence, trends towards formation of lineal joint families and nuclear families, and increase of widow-remarriage. Evidence from fictional analysis and other empirical investigations concerning these hypotheses and other indices of family changes have been discussed elsewhere (Khatri, 1964; 1966;

1970a; 1970b; 1972; 1974). Space considerations prevent treatment of any of these hypotheses here. However, global evaluation of social change as depicted in Gujarati fiction can be presented succinctly as follows.

Most 'evils' described in pre-1912 novels, namely bride or groom price, bigamy, childhood marriages, wide disparity in spousal age, girls being uneducated, negatively perceived and equated with a bundle of serpents, mother-in-law's extreme dominance and torture of daughter-in-law, marriage debt, obscene songs at marriage, sex segregation and restrictions on personal mobility — all are rarely referred to in urban novels of 1931—37 and 1956—62. In urban novels of 1956—62 the predominant picture is depicted as follows.

More and more girls are being educated to matriculate, graduate and beyond that. Boys and girls move about unchaperoned and relatively freely and also meet each other. Girls are also found being involved in extra-mural gainful work. Rarely one finds reference to prenatal marriage negotiations and cradle betrothals. The role of 'Kule' (family status), bride or groom price has dwindled into insignificance. Although inter-caste marriages raise a controversy and conflict of generations sometimes takes place, inter-caste marriages do take place, without even parental opposition. There is hardly any reference to obscene songs sung at the marriage ceremony. Divorce is not ruled out as a possibility; it becomes a subject of controversy and sometimes takes place without raising a hornet's nest. Caste dinners and chest-beating after death are rarely reported by authors of these urban novels. It appears as if most of the reforms advocated in pre-1912 novels have been achieved to a considerable extent for many urban characters, particularly of 1956—62.

However, social change in other dimensions like widow-remarriage, companionship of husband—wife, equalitarian intra-family relations; these in terms of frequency, their salience in consciousness of novelists, their implementation by actual incidence is least reflected. We can say that in the broad field of marriage and family relations, just a few pebbles have been thrown in the ocean of tradition, causing some ripples and no more.

To foster a further understanding of the changes in the family and to gain insight into the internal dynamic processes and relationships within the family and other related social institutions, a case study technique was adopted by the present author in his analysis of fiction. From each of the three periods (pre-1912, 1931—37, 1956—62) under investigation, case studies were developed in the areas of mate selection, marriage, spousal relations, father—son, mother—daughter and other significant family relationships. Juxtaposition of case studies from each of the three periods deepened understanding of changes in variables not readily accessible to the usual investigative techniques, namely basic value-orientations, culturally prescribed assumptions, roles, intra-family attitudes and modes of inter-personal relations, motives, frustrations and intra-psychic and inter-personal conflicts, idiosyncratic personality manifestations of familial goals and values, intra-individual and inter-individual variabilities in approximations to the ideal typical family models, etc.

SUMMARY AND CONCLUDING REMARKS

In this paper, an attempt has been made first to offer a rationale for the use of imaginative literature as sociologically relevant data; secondly to illustrate its use for study of family change by the procedure of quantitative and qualitative analysis of 45 social novels from three periods (pre-1912, 1931—37 and 1956—62); thirdly to consider a few hypotheses about family changes as derived from Goode and Kirkpatrick and offer evidence from analysis of social novels written in Gujarati — a regional Indian language; and finally to refer to the case study method and specific hypotheses developed by the present investigator about the changes in the Indian family and offer global evaluation thereof.

It is submitted here that for cross-cultural analysis of certain family variables — specifically attitudinal and value dimensions — systematic comparative analysis of imaginative literature by means of pretested and rigorously developed category system can be a fruitful research technique for sharpening our understanding of inter-cultural variabilities and also cultural changes.

REFERENCES

Agarwala, B. R. (1955), 'In a Mobile Commercial Community'. 'In Symposium: Caste and Joint Family', *Sociological Bulletin,* 4 (September): 138-46.

Allport, C. W. (1951), *The Use of Personal Documents in Psychological Science.* New York: Social Science Research Council.

Berelson, B. (1952), *Content Analysis in Communication Research.* University of Chicago, Glencoe: The Free Press.

Cantril, H. and Bumstead, C. (1960), 'Reflections on the Human Venture', in Norman Kiell, *The Universal Experience of Adolescence.* New York: International Universities Press, 1964.

Clear, J. (1966), 'Marriage Education Through Novels and Biography', *Journal of Marriage and the Family,* 28 (May): 217-19.

Coleman, J. C. (1956), *Abnormal Psychology and Modern Life.* Chicago: Scott Foresman.

Coser, L. A. (1972), *Sociology through Literature,* 2nd edn. Englewood Cliffs, New Jersey: Prentice-Hall.

Desai, I. P. (1955), 'An Analysis'. 'In Symposium: Caste and Joint Family', *Sociological Bulletin,* 4 (September): 97-117.

Dabaghian, J. (1970), *Mirror of Man: Readings in Sociology and Literature.* Boston: Little, Brown and Company.

Fernandez, R. (1972), *Social Psychology through Literature.* New York: Wiley & Sons.

Ghurye, G. S. (1952) and (1954), 'Social Change in Maharastra', *Sociological Bulletin,* 1 (March); 3 (March): 41-60.

—— (1955), *Family and Kin in Indo-European Culture.* Bombay: Oxford University Press.

Goode, William J. (1963), *World Revolution and Family Patterns.* New York: The Free Press of Glencoe.

Kapadia, K. M. (1954-55), 'Changing Patterns of Hindu Marriage and Family', Sociological Bulletin, 3 (March): 61-67; 3 (September); 4 (September 1955): 161-92.

—— (1956), 'Rural Family Patterns', *Sociological Bulletin,* 5 (September): 111-26.

—— (1957), A Perspective Necessary For the Study of Social Change in India', *Sociological Bulletin,* 6 (March): 43-60.

—— (1958), *Marriage and Family in India.* 2nd edn. Bombay: Oxford University Press.

—— (1959), 'The Family in Transition', *Sociological Bulletin,* 8 (September): 68-99.

Karve, I. (1953), *Kinship Organization in India*. Poona: Deccan College Monograph Series 11.

Kenkel, W. F. (1969), 'Marriage and the Family in modern Science Fiction', *Journal of Marriage and the Family*, 31 (February): 6-14.

Khatri, A. A. (1962), 'Social Change in the Hindu Family and Its Possible Impact on Personality and Mental Health', *Sociological Bulletin*, 11 (March and September): 146-65.

— — (1964), 'Hetero-sexual Friendships and Involvement in The Mate Selection Process of Secondary and Primary Teacher Trainees in Ahmedabad', to be published as a chapter in *The Family in India: A Modern Regional View*, edited by George Kurian. The Hague: Mouton.

— — (1966), 'Marriage and Family in India — An Overview of Researches', in *Researches in Child Development, Marriage and Family Relations Done in Indian Institutions of Teaching and Research*, Baroda: Department of Child Development, Faculty of Home Science, University of Baroda.

— — (1970a), 'Personality and Mental Health of Indians (Hindus)-in The Context of Their Changing Family Organization', in E. J. Anthony and C. Koupernik (eds), *The Child in His Family*. New York: John Wiley.

— — (1970b), 'Marriage and Family Relationships in Gujarati Fiction', Ph.D. thesis, University of London, London, England.

— — (1972), 'The Indian Family: An Empirically Derived Analysis of Shifts in Size and Types', *Journal of Marriage and The Family*, 34 (November): 725-34.

— — (1974), 'The Joint Family in India Today', a paper presented before the Family Section of The American Sociological Association Meeting at Montreal, during August, 1974. To be published in the *Journal of Marriage and The Family*, August, 1975.

— — (1975), 'Analysis of Fiction for Comparative Study of Family Systems', a paper to be presented during the annual meeting of The Society for the Study of Social Problems, August, 1975 at San Francisco.

Kirkpatrick, C. (1963), *The Family: As Process and Institution*. New York: Ronald Press.

Kuppuswami, B. (1957), *A Study of Opinion Regarding Marriage and Divorce*. Bombay: Asia Publishing House.

Lowenthal, L. (1961), *Literature — Popular Culture and Society*. Englewood Cliffs, New Jersey: Prentice-Hall.

Mehta, S. (1934), *Gujarati Lagna Vyavastha and Kutumb Sanstha (Marriage System and Family Institution of Gujarat)*. Ahmedabad: Gujarati Vernacular Society (in Gujarati).

Milstead, J. W. et al. (1974), *Sociology through Science Fiction*. New York: St Martin Press.

Mukerji, D. P. (1958), *Diversities — Essays in Economics, Sociology and Other Social Problems*, New Delhi: People's Publishing House.

Nandshanker, T. (1866), (The First Gujarati Novel) *Karanghelo,* 5th edn, 1899. Bombay: Gujarati Printing Press.

Nilakanth, M. R. (1866), *Sasu Vahuni Ladai (Mother-in-law – Daughter-in-law Conflict),* Nilakanth second edition 1893. Ahmedabad: Mahipatram Rupram (in Gujarati).

Ofshe, R. (1970), *The Sociology of the Possible.* Englewood Cliffs, New Jersey: Prentice-Hall.

Smardan, L. E. (1966), 'The Use of Drama in Teaching Family Relationships', *Journal of Marriage and the Family,* 28 (May): 219-22.

Somerville, R. M. (1963), 'Imaginative Literature in Family Life Education', *Journal of Home Economics,* 55 (June): 409-12.

— — (1964), *Family Insights through the Short Story.* New York: Teachers College Press.

— — (1966), 'Creative Literature for Study of the Family', *Journal of Marriage and the Family,* 28 (May): 213-14.

Warner, E. L. et al. (1949), *Social Class in America.* Chicago: Science Research Association.

Tavuchis, N. and Goode, W. S. (1975), *The Family Through Literature,* New York: McGraw-Hill.

Veena Das (1973), 'The Structure of Marriage Preferences: An Account from Pakistani Fiction', Man, 8 (1) (March): 30-45.

4

THE NUCLEAR FAMILY WITHIN THE THREE-GENERATIONAL HOUSEHOLD IN MODERN JAPAN

Tsuneo Yamane
Osaka City University, Japan

⌊An **outstanding feature** of the traditional Japanese family system was the stress it placed upon family continuity. Ideally the family name, property, occupation, mores and so on were to be transmitted through the male line for generation after generation. To this end, in pre-war law codes the status of family head was given strong support while the status of wife was weakened and was subject to discrimination of one sort or another.⌋

To ensure family continuity one son, ordinarily the eldest, would be designated as heir and receive preferential treatment over his siblings. In return he would become responsible for the household when he was made head. He would take a wife and bring her to live in the same dwelling with his parents. By contrast his brothers, when they grew up, would leave to form their own families of procreation; his sisters, when they grew up, would marry into other families.

⌈ The heir's spouse was regarded primarily as the daughter of his

This article is based on the paper prepared for and read at the Eighth World Congress of Sociology held in Toronto in August, 1974. The investigation data were collected under the author's guidance by Mrs. Sachiko Hayashi who is currently teacher of home economics at a high school in Kyoto Prefecture. The author wishes to acknowledge a favour given by Professor David W. Plath of the University of Illinois, who read the manuscript and corrected English sentence.

parents and only secondarily as his wife. Consequently her position depended more upon whether she was dutiful to her parents-in-law than upon whether she was a good wife to her husband. Often enough even a 'good wife' was divorced because she was not adequately caring for her parents-in-law. To the extent that her position was precarious within the household the position of the aged parents was secure.

[Seen as a kinship system, this traditional Japanese family pattern was predominantly partilineal, patrilocal and patriarchal.]

[The ideal which people sought to achieve in pre-war times was that of three generations living together harmoniously under the same roof.]

Recent writers, however, stress what they call the 'nucleation' of the Japanese family. By this they usually mean that independent two-generation nuclear families (consisting of husband, wife and offspring) have become the dominant type, and that three-generation families are declining in number. We must bear in mind, though, that even in the past nuclear families were present along with lineally-extended families. These nuclear families were the ones formed by the non-heir sons who, when they grew up, were obliged to marry outside the line of their family of orientation. Cross-sectional statistics from earlier periods thus show a considerable proportion of nuclear families at any one point in time, even though the lineally-extended family was the ideal.

There is a resemblance here to conditions in a polygynous society. Murdock (1949:28) considers a society polygynous when it meets two criteria: (1) that polygyny is strongly favoured, and (2) that polygynous unions occur in more than 20 percent of all marriages — although he selected this percentage arbitrarily. In any event, because of the sex ration all marriages in a society could not be polygynous no matter how much it is preferred. Likewise all families in Japan cannot be lineally-extended because only one child is allowed to remain in the parental home. So it is no wonder that in 1920, when the traditional family system in Japan was being enforced legally and when the lineally-extended household was preferred culturally, 55 percent of the families were nuclear.

However, we must take care when comparing the nuclear family of 1920 with that of today. Under the traditional system, parents in a nuclear family fully expected that one son would continue to live with them, bring in a wife, and in time transform the household into a lineally-extended one. In this sense the nuclear family of that era was not strictly an 'independent' one as Murdock has defined it (1949:32). The time factor must be considered. As was stated in an earlier essay, what existed under the traditional Japanese family system was a 'temporary nuclear family' or a 'potential lineal family' (Yamane and Nonoyama 1967:785).

This no longer is necessarily true for nuclear families being formed today. In terms of value orientations at least, a man and a woman unite today to form their own family of procreation. No longer is there a legal sanction in favour of patrilineality and patrilocality. In the present-day situation we can indeed speak of an independent nuclear family in Japan. Although surnames continue to descend patrilineally, behaviour patterns are approaching bilaterality in that kin ties through each parent are coming more and more to be given equal weight. And though residence still tends to be patrilocal, young couples show a strong preference for neolocality.

Thus the modern or present-day nuclear family does not transform into a lineally-extended one. Formed at marriage, it grows larger with the birth of children, becomes smaller as children marry out, and ceases to exist at the death of the last remaining spouse. It is not linked to an ideal of family continuity; it is, in Parson's terms, a self-liquidating group (1954).

These trends toward 'nucleation' might be summarized as follows: from patrilineal to bilateral descent, from patrilocal to neolocal residence, from patriarchal to equalitarian relationships, and from continuity to self-liquidation.

Looked at statistically the trend has been thus: in 1920, 55.3 percent of all households in Japan were nuclear, and by 1970 the figure has risen to 63.4 percent. An 8 percent increase over half a century might lead one to conclude that 'nucleation' has not been very dramatic in the Japanese case. Certainly the rate of change seems slow when contrasted with rates of such phenomena as economic growth, lengthening life expectancy, or declining rates of births and deaths.

But we must not be deceived by simple census figures. First, a recent increase in the percentage of one-person households partially masks the increase in the percentage of nuclear households. Subtract one-person households from the total, and the proportion of nuclear households will rise considerably. Secondly, a quite different picture emerges when we directly compare the numbers of nuclear and extended households. In 1920 the ratio of nuclear to extended households was 1.4:1, but by 1970 it was 2.5:1. The increase in this ratio was particularly marked in the decade 1960—70 when the number of nuclear households continued to rise but the number of extended households remained almost unchanged. Thirdly, what is particularly noteworthy is that recently there has been a rapid decrease in the number of extended households containing both grandparents, whereas there has been no change in the number containing only a single grandparent.

On the other hand there is evidence that preference for a lineally-extended family still exist and are by no means negligible. A 1973 Japanese government opinion survey on the problems of old age found that among persons 65 and older 57.4 percent were living with their married children. The figure rises to 75.3 percent if we include those living with unmarried children. Only 18.9 percent live apart from a child. The survey also asked people about residence preferences, and found that of persons 50 and older 76 percent hope to live with a married child while only 14 percent definitely wish to live apart. A similar study in 1969 also asked whether people preferred to live with a married son or a married daughter; 'son' was the overwhelming choice. Figures such as these have led some analysts to argue that the traditional family system remains strongly rooted in Japanese consciousness and that it will continue to regulate much Japanese behaviour.

I am doubtful about this argument. First, note that these 'traditional' preferences are held mainly by people 50 and older — the pre-war generation who were born and raised under the old system. Generation differences always need to be scrutinized carefully when one is analysing changes in family systems. This is particularly important in Japan's case because of the striking differences between pre- and post-war patterns.

Secondly, in this connection we must remember that forms of the family at any point in time are to some degree reflections of earlier conditions — in the sense that families now being formed are the unions of persons born a quarter century ago. In recent decades, mean age at marriage has been fairly stable in Japan; for males at age 27 and for females at age 24. Thus family patterns as they appear in the 1970 census largely reflect the value orientations of people born before the end of the Pacific War.

We also must allow for generational factors when we try to forecast further changes in family patterns. As I suggested earlier, the proportion of nuclear families in the population is related to the average number of children born per household and to cultural values regarding descent and residence and the like. If a preference for patrilocality prevails, we can hypothesize that the more children born per family the higher will be the proportion of nuclear families. And conversely, the fewer children per family, the higher the proportion of lineally-extended families.

Trends in Japanese vital statistics show a rapid decrease since 1960 in the mean number of members per household; in 1970 the number stood at 3.69. If this trend continues, then we might predict that after 1985, when those born after 1960 begin to marry, the percentage of lineally-extended families will begin to climb. This, however, is contingent upon the preference for patrilocal resident remaining strong. If a preference for neolocality comes to prevail, then after 1985 the percentage of nuclear families would rise.

The problem then reduces to one of determining future preferences with regard to residence. A 1971 Japanese government opinion study reveals that preference for neolocal residence becomes stronger with each succeeding younger generation. I have already mentioned that in the past ten years the number of neolocal marriages has been increasing. Putting these two kinds of evidence together, we can assume that neolocality will probably continue to grow more and more manifest.

Nevertheless, the 1971 survey also shows that even among people in their twenties about half still prefer patrilocality. This seems to be due mainly to th marginal character of this group: they were born just before and after the end of the war, and they have internalized some of their parents' attitudes toward the family system even though they have been more or less liberated from the pre-war values taught in the school system. This marginal group is now beginning to marry, and presumably about 1990 their offspring in turn will marry. It can be expected therefore that second post-way generation will be even more free from traditional orientations to the family than are their parents.

Thus two countervailing forces may intersect after 1990. One is a demographic vector tending to decrease the number of children per family; the other is a values vector, the preference for neolocality. It is likely that preferences for neolocality will be much influenced by government policies with regard to support for education and for old-age welfare.

The 1970 census reported 3,661,524 three-generation households in Japan. This is about 14 percent of all households in the nation. What conditions prevail within these households? [Under the traditional system a nuclear family had some functional boundaries within an extended households, at least for sexual and reproductive activities. But aside from these — for example in economic and political activites — the functional unit was the extended household itself as a whole. All property and income was at the disposal of the head, and it was the head who took the initiative in family activities and who represented the family to outside institutions. The lineally-extended household was also an emotional unit, in the sense that all members were required to integrate with the head as the central figure. And lastly it was the unit of socialization, in the sense that not only parents but all members participated in child care and discipline.]

Today, however, a young couple lives with parents by mutal consent rather than by institutional sanction. In keeping with this, we can assume that role relationships between parents and married children are changing, and that the nuclear family is ceasing to be submerged within the extended household unity.

METHOD OF STUDY

On the basis of these assumptions about changes in family relationships, I have been carrying out empirical studies concerning the living arrangements that the Japanese anticipate in old age and concerning functional relations that now exist between married adults and their parents.

The data were collected in 1973 at two locations in Kyoto prefecture. One is Nishijin district in Kyoto city, long famous for the brocades it produces; the other is Nagaokakyo, an emerging suburb. Questionnaires were distributed by several primary schools in each location, and were given to pupils who have at least one grandparent living in their home. The questionnaire was to be filled out by the pupil's parents and returned within one week. Most of the respondents are presumed to be middle class economically. Most are in their thirties or forties, with the aged parents in their sixties or seventies. In Nishijin 165 questionnaires were returned completed; for Nagaokakyo the figure is 148. This is about 60 percent of the number distributed.

The questionnaire had two parts, one asking for certain kinds of factual information and the other asking opinions. The opinion section consisted of five questions to be answered by each parent. They were asked

(1) whether or not they wanted to live with a married child when they became old;

(2) whether they preferred to live with a married son or a married daugher;

(3) if they wanted to live with a married child, whether the two families would integrate or segregate their activities;

(4) if they want to live apart from married children, whether they wanted to live nearby a married child; and

(5) whether they would want to continue living alone after their spouse had died.

The factural section was to be completed by the pupil's mother. It attempted to elucidate relations between parents and grandparents in 15 daily activity areas: room arrangements, food, meal preparation, seating at meals, dishwashing, washing clothes, shopping, mending clothes, room cleaning, income, spending, child care, child discipline, leisure, and decision on major issues.

FINDINGS

I want to underline the fact that these respondents are from a marginal generation. All were born before the end of the Pacific War and were brought up by parents who had firmly internalized the values of the traditional family system, yet in their adult years they have lived through drastic changes pertaining both to the family and to value orientations. Thus they have internalized portions of the traditional outlook but are likely to be ambivalent about it. Indeed they probably are more ambivalent in this regard than are people in the first postwar generation.

Table 1 shows that there is rather little difference, particularly in Nishijin, between the proportion of persons who say that when they are old they want to live with, and those who want to live apart from, a married child. This contrasts with the findings of the government surveys mentioned earlier, probably because the respondents in my study are younger. What is most important to note, however, is that the most frequent response is 'either will do'. This seems to indicate that traditional preferences for patrilocality have weakened.

An unexpected result is that people in Nishijin seem to favour living apart from a married child more strongly than do those in Nagaokakyo. Nishijin is predominantly popoulated by families that engage in cottage industry, in which aged parents would continue to have a role as labourers: Nagaokakyo on the other hand is mostly a residential area for salarymen. Speculatively, it may be that this Nishijin preference for living apart is a projection of discontent with current living arrangements.

Of those who wish to live with a married child, more than seven out of ten want it to be with a son. In a bilateral kinship system one might expect that closer relations would develop with the wife's kin rather than the husband's, since she is more likely to be in the home and to be in frequent contact with her parents than he is. In this regard the preference for living with a married son seems to indicate that traditional values on continuity through the male line remain strong.

Those who said they prefer to live with a married child were further asked if they wanted to merge family activities or to keep them separated. A clear majority said that they want to integrate family functions. People in Nagaokakyo seem to favour separation-within-

TABLE 1

Expectations about Life in Old Age (percent)

	Nishijin		Nagaokakyo	
	Husband	Wife	Husband	Wife
Want to live together	25	29	39	33
Want to live separately	24	29	18	28
Either will do	47	39	40	34
N.A.	4	3	3	5
Total	100	100	100	100
Live with married son	85	73	74	71
Live with married daughter	15	23	24	27
N.A.	0	4	2	2
Total	100	100	100	100
Live together integratedly	80	77	62	71
Live together but independently	20	19	28	25
N.A.	0	4	10	4
Total	100	100	100	100
Live near married child	74	81	85	78
Don't live near married child	16	19	15	18
N.A.	10	0	0	4
Total	100	100	100	100
Want to live apart even when bereaved	74	60	65	71
Want to live together when bereaved	16	36	31	27
N.A.	10	4	4	2
Total	100	100	100	100

coresidence more than do those in Nishijin, and this may relate to differences between white collar and cottage industry life-styles.

Those who said, on the other hand, that they wish to live apart from a married child were asked two further questions: 'Which do you prefer, living near your child or not?' and 'Do you want to live apart from a married child even when you have lost your spouse, or would you move in with the children then?' The most favoured pattern is to live near a married child but not in the same household. This fits the 'intimacy at a distance' hypothesis proposed by Rosenmayr and Kockeis (1963: 418-419). What I find curious is that the majority say they would rather continue to live apart even in widowhood or widowerhood. They would prefer to be alone. Perhaps this too reflects disatisfaction with present living arrangements.

Now let us turn to look at actual behaviour patterns within these households. As Table 2 shows, in these families the majority of aged parents have a separate room of their own, and thus some measure of privacy. Where they do not have a separate room, the reason seems mainly to be that the house simply is too small.

TABLE 2

Do the Aged Parents Have Their Own Room or Not?

	Yes	No	Unknown	Total
Nishijin	66	33	1	100%
Nagaokakyo	78	20	2	100%

With regard to finances (Table 3), fewer than one-fifth of these old couples have no income of their own and are entirely dependent economically on the younger generation. Slightly more of these families regard the incomes of older and younger generations as separate than regard them as indistinguishable, but where expenditures are concerned the vast majority pool their purchasing operations. By 'completely separated' here we mean that the aged parents are fully autonomous economically: they pay for their upkeep and buy personal belongings with their own funds. 'Partially separated' indicates those who are supported by the

TABLE 3

Differentiation in Dealing With Incomes and Expenses
Between Married Couples and their Aged Parents
Within Three-Generational Households

	Completely Separated	Completely Integrated	Aged Parents no Income	Partially Separated	Unknown	Total
Income						
Nishijin	38	31	20		11	100%
Nagaokakyo	45	34	14		7	100%
Expenses						
Nishijin	16	70		7	7	100%
Nagaokakyo	13	76		5	6	100%

younger generation but who have some money of their own for small personal expenses. The different patterns of integration of income and expenditures remain puzzling and cannot be explained with our present data. These patterns of money management will need investigation with more elaborate instruments.

What about the divison of labour? We examined six household tasks that ordinarily are regarded as 'woman's work' (Table 4). As the table shows, the broad pattern is roughly the same both in Nishijin and in Nagaokakyo: and from this one can anticipate that a similar pattern of task differentiation will be found throughout the urban middle class in modern Japan.

First, in almost no instances does the grandmother manage all household tasks. This would be likely to occur only if the junior wife is employed full-time outside the home. In more than half of these families the junior wife prepares the meals and looks after the daily shopping.

Secondly, tasks are most often divided when they involve washing, cleaning or mending. 'Segregation' in this context means that each generation looks after its own needs, not helping the other. Perhaps the chief reason why mending is done separately by each generation is that clothing styles differ markedly for each. Also, many old women regard sedentary tasks such as mending as a kind of hobby.

TABLE 4

Division of Functions Within Three-Generational Households Pertaining to Six Activities

	Segregated		Housewife does		Grandmother does		Co-operate		Unknown		Total	
	Ni	Na	Ni	Na	Ni	Na	Ni	Na	Ni	Na	Ni	Na
Preparing the meal	5	5	63	62	8	8	21	24	3	1	100%	100%
Doing the dishes	7	5	50	50	5	2	34	40	4	3	100%	100%
Washing clothes	29	22	36	39	4	1	28	35	3	3	100%	100%
Shopping	4	4	66	70	7	2	21	22	2	2	100%	100%
Mending clothes	41	40	27	19	3	5	27	34	2	2	100%	100%
Cleaning the room	27	31	27	23	2	2	40	42	4	2	100%	100%

Ni = Nishijin; Na = Nagaokakyo.

TABLE 5

Do You Consult the Old Folks When Deciding Important Matters Such as a Major Purchase or Moving to Another House?

	No, never	Yes	Unknown	Total
Nishijin	20	75	5	100%
Nagaokakyo	23	68	9	100%

Thirdly, although a grandmother rarely manages all the household work, she also rarely limits her efforts to tasks that only concern the senior generation. Indeed in all of these six task areas from one-fifth to two-fifths of the grandmothers will be found helping the junior wife. This is particularly true for washing dishes and cleaning the rooms.

As regards decision-making, Table 5 shows that seven out of ten of the younger parents report that they consult with the old folks on important family issues. From this question alone one cannot determine who took the initiative in the consultation, or how differences were resolved, and so on. Complex processes such as those of decision-making will have to be investigated by more refined methods.

Questions about patterns of eating, seating, and leisure activities were an attempt to uncover the expressive side of family interaction in these three-generation households (see Table 6). There is a kind of daily breathing pattern to family activities. Ordinarily in the daytime the members are absorbed each in their own tasks, whether they are in the home or not; but in the evenings they return and reunite. The physical separation is obvious enough, but as Zelditch (1965) has pointed out, the behavioural and attitudinal spacing is even more crucial. One of the major functions of the family as a group is to provide satisfactions, of a kind that may not be available elsewhere, for individual emotional needs, and thus to enable members to revitalize themselves psycho-physically and make ready for the instrumental chores of the day ahead.

Eating has a central place in this provision of emotional gratification and solidarity. Everywhere, through the ages, the heart of family life has been the act of communal dining. As Table 6 indicates, in fewer than one out of ten of these Kyoto households do the aged parents eat apart from the rest of the family. (There are, of course, obvious economies of labour, time, and money when the whole family eats together).

The old folks are much less likely, however, to share in the leisure activities of others in the family. About half of them join in 'sometimes', but one-fifth of them 'never'. Perhaps this unavoidable, given the usual disparities in tastes and interests among the generations.

In the family in traditional Japan, child-rearing, including both physical care and discipline, was the business of every adult member. Table 7 shows that today more than half of the families expect grandparents in the home to help with child-rearing, but another quarter do not expect or encourage the grandparents to help at all, particularly with discipline. This would seem to be a new trend, indicative of generation differences in attitudes toward family responsibility. At the other extreme, in only a few instances is child training left entirely to the grandparents — usually because the mother is working full time away from home.

TABLE 6

Behavioural Patterns in Food, Seating at Table, Leisure Between Aged Parents and Other Members Within Three-Generational Households

	Separated	Always together	Sometimes together	Unknown	Total
Food					
Nishijin	8	84	7	1	100%
Nagaokakyo	9	86	4	1	100%
Seating at Table					
Nishijin	7	86	3	4	100%
Nagaokakyo	8	80	8	4	100%
Leisure					
Nishijin	23	12	60	5	100%
Nagaokakyo	21	19	57	3	100%

TABLE 7

Role Differentiation in Child-Rearing Practices Within Three-Generational Households

	Leave to grandparents	Get grandparents to help	Don't make grandparents do	Unknown	Total
Physical Care					
Nishijin	1	64	16	19	100%
Nagaokakyo	3	65	26	6	100%
Discipline					
Nishijin	1	64	27	8	100%
Nagaokakyo	1	63	27	9	100%

CONCLUDING REMARKS

Despite the progressive 'nucleation' of the family, about 14 percent of the household in Japan still contain three generations of members. What is more a patrilocal bias — that aged parents should live with a married son — remains among the older generation and to some extent among the younger ones as well. However, the content of family relationships in these three-generation units today differs in important respects from what obtained in three-generation households under the traditional Japanese family system. My aim here has been to elucidate this difference.

The investigation reported here was a preliminary one, without elaborate sampling or a lengthy questionnaire. Given the small sample size and the arbitrary nature of the sample, no significant relationships were found with usual survey variables such as age, sex, education, occupation, etc. The most dramatically evident variable is that of whether or not the wife is working outside the house. However, it seems probable that with larger samples and more refined methods significant relationships will be found between factors such as age or occupation and the patterning of interaction in these three-generation households.

The data show clearly (despite their shortcomings) that three-generation household patterns are much the same in Japan whether in a new white-collar suburb or in an old inner-city craftsman's quarter. Activities of many kinds are shared by all members of the household, and this is particularly true of expressive behaviour. However, there also is a tendency to segregate the seniormost generation with respect to the handling of income and child-rearing.

From this one may infer a long-term trend toward the segregation of nuclear families within the lineally-extended household; functional boundaries between them are becoming more distinct. In this sense then we can say that 'nucleation' is taking place in Japan today even within three-generation households. To put this another way: under the traditional family system the main boundary enclosed the lineally-extended household, and there were sub-boundaries around its constituent nuclear families. Today the main boundary tends to enclose each nuclear family, with a sort of super-boundary secondarily encircling the extended household.

In keeping with this, role structures are thought to be undergoing marked change.[As nuclear family units become more independent, the status of the elderly becomes less secure. No longer are they the central figures they were under the traditional family system; they are more dependent upon their offspring and must take on more of the burden of co-operation with them. The young wife, once seen as a sort of pseudo-daughter to her husband's parents, comes more and more to be an ordinary in-law.]

How should we interpret this phenomenon of nucleation? One view would be that it signals the decay of the lineally-extended family in Japan; but it might also be seen as the emergence of a new three-generation pattern of family relationships. Perhaps the key is in the feelings of the aged parents themselves. If they feel genuinely isolated or alienated, then decay may have set in. If on the other hand they feel emotionally secure in their growing autonomy and separateness within the household, then perhaps a new pattern is taking shape. We cannot answer this just now; we must carry it over as unfinished sociological business.

REFERENCES

Murdock, George P. (1949), *Social Structure*, New York: Macmillan.

Parsons, Talcott (1954), 'The Incest Taboo in Relation to Social Structure', *The British Journal of Sociology*, 5:101-17.

Rosenmayr, Leopold and Kockeis, Eva (1963), 'Propositions for a Sociological Theory of Ageing and the Family', *International Social Science Journal*, 15 (3):418-19.

Yamane, Tsuneo and Nonoyama, Hisaya (1967), 'Isolation of the Nuclear Family and Kinship Organization in Japan: A Hypothetical Approach to the Relationships Between the Family and Society', *Journal of Marriage and the Family*, 29 (4):783-96.

Zelditch, Morris, Jr (1956), 'Role Differentiation in the Nuclear Family: A Comparative Study', in Talcott Parsons and Robert F. Bales (eds), *Family, Socialization and Interaction Process*. London: Routledge & Kegan Paul, p. 311.

III THE NUCLEAR OR QUASI-NUCLEAR FAMILY SEEN THROUGH THE INDIVIDUAL DEVELOPMENT PERSPECTIVE

5

THE POLITICAL ECONOMY OF THE MOTHER-CHILD FAMILY
A Cross-Societal View

Rae Lesser Blumberg
University of California, San Diego, USA
with Maria Pilar Garcia
University of Chicago, USA

INTRODUCTION

In this paper we shall consider two forms of the mother–child household that are characterized by the absence of a resident male head: first and foremost, we shall treat the mother-*headed* family common among marginal lower classes in diverse wage labour societies; and then consider the mother–child *residential arrangement* found among certain polygynous largely horticultural tribes. We juxtapose these two apparently so different forms because we believe that they share certain economic variables that account for their emergence despite the widely differing circumstances. For each, we shall review extant conceptualizations, formulate our own structural hypotheses, and then present data to explore the propositions. The data concerning female-headed families come from the US Census and a sample of lower class shacktown residents in Caracas, Venezuela. The hypotheses concerning the mother–child dwelling unit are tested with data from the 1,170 preindustrial societies of Murdock's Ethnographic Atlas (1967). In both cases, our hypotheses look to the relationship of the woman to her society's mode of production to account for the emergence of a male-absent household, and to her society's political economy to account for its persistence. In contrast, much of the literature makes it appear that both these cases occur primarily among people of black African origins. Consequently, a major thrust of this paper will be to assert and demonstrate that it is economic conditions — and not race — that is relevant in the occurrence of both types of mother–child household.

THE MOTHER-HEADED FAMILY

DEFINITIONS AND
REVIEW OF LITERATURE

(1) The *mother-headed family* is linked to the *mother–child dwelling unit* on the grounds of race: until recently, the majority of studies of mother-*headed* families involved US and Caribbean blacks; and mother–child *residential* arrangements are described almost exclusively among black African tribes (see Murdock and Wilson, 1972). In fact, a main reason for considering the mother–child housing unit in this paper is precisely to reinterpret the findings of Murdock and Wilson, which seemingly lend new support to the racial–historical interpretation of mother-centred familism among New World blacks that finally had been dying in the literature. We shall argue that the relation with race is spurious, both on racial–historical and racial–biological grounds.

(2) The *mother-headed family* is linked to two other forms usually described as mother-centred: the *consanguineal* and the *matrifocal* — on the grounds that all three tend to occur among the economically marginal lower classes in a wide variety of wage labour societies. Neither of these other two forms, however, are defined as requiring the absence of a resident male head. Solien de Gonzalez (1959) provides definitions best distinguishing these types. To her, the *consanguineal* household is a 'co-residential kinship group which includes no regularly present male

in the role of husband—father. Rather the effective and enduring-relationships within the group are those existing between consanguineal kin'. This does not mean that the *head* of the house is a female: mother's brothers or other male uterine kin may run the show (as among the traditional Nayar — see Gough, 1952). In contrast, she means by *matrifocality:* 'a general tendency to emphasize the mother as *the* stable figure and decision-maker within the family as well as an emphasis upon her kinsmen over those of the father and his kinsmen' (1970b). The lower class East Londoners described by Young and Wilmott (1957) are matrifocal by this definition, even though marriages are stable and the males present. In short, some consanguineal households may be matrifocal, and vice versa, and some of each type may be *headed* by the mother, but all three dimensions are analytically distinct.

Unfortunately, these three dimensions are generally jumbled together in the voluminous literature on mother-centred families. A more serious problem in this literature arises from the fact that early studies of this type of familism are confined to US and Caribbean blacks, and until recently the dominant interpretation stresses either or both racial—historical or social pathology factors.

The *racial—historical* approach divides into two schools. The first emphasizes *African origins,* citing the mother—child dwelling unit found in many polygynous African societies and the relative economic autonomy of the women (see Herskovits, 1937, 1941, 1943; Herskovits et al., 1947; Bascom, 1941; and Murdock and Wilson, 1972). The second school harks back to the effects of *plantation slavery* on New World blacks (see Frazier, 1939, for the most influential statement; see also Campbell, 1943; Henriques, 1953; King, 1945; Myrdal, 1944; Powdermaker, 1939; Simey, 1946; and Woofter, 1930). Under slavery, it is held, strong structural bars to stable nuclear families emerged (e.g. absence of legal marriage among slaves). Later, continuing economic and other effects of racial discrimination militated against the lower class black male becoming the dominant figure in a stable family, the argument of this school asserts.

The slavery-based approach shades off into the *social pathology* interpretation. Frazier himself (1950) views families deviating from the stable nuclear model as disorganized. He notes: 'the widespread family disorganization among Negroes has resulted from the failure of the father to play the role in family life required by American society'. 'Family disorganization', in turn, 'has been partially responsible for a large amount of juvenile delinquency and adult crime among Negroes'.

Probably the epitome of the approach linking social pathology and the black family was reached in the controversial Moynihan Report (1965). It is clear that Moynihan considers the increasing incidence of female-headed households among poor urban blacks as a growing social cancer in the ghetto. In his words: 'at the centre of the tangle of pathology is the weakness of the family structure. Once or twice removed, it will be found to be the principal source of most of the aberrant, inadequate, or anti-social behaviour that did not establish, *but now serves to perpetuate* the cycle of poverty and deprivation' (p. 30, emphasis added).

The orientations that link the female-headed family with blacks, social pathology, or more subtly, a self-perpetuating 'culture of poverty'[1] have been in decline in the literature of late. First, a long list of studies of both mother-*headed* and mother-*centred* familism in non-black populations has emerged, swamping an exclusively racial view (see Adams, 1960, for statistics on female-headed families in a variety of Central and South American countries); in addition to Latin America, matrifocality has been observed in diverse Pacific groups (Calley, 1956 − Australian aboriginal 'mixed bloods'; Geertz, 1959 − Java; Kay, 1963 − Tahiti), Native American tribes (Aginsky and Aginsky, 1947, 1949 − Pomo of California; Boyer, 1964 − Mescalero Apache), European populations (Lopreato, 1965 − South Italian peasants; Smith, 1956 − Scotland; Young and Wilmott, 1957 − East London) and other far-flung sites. Secondly, the social pathology focus also has come under criticism from those stressing structural approaches. These structural views involve one or both of two main tenets: (1) the mother-headed family is not 'abnormal' in and of itself; and/or (2) it is linked with structurally-caused poverty in wage labour societies, especially the economic marginality of the *male*.

With respect to the first tenet, Adams (1960) has been influential in justifying the non-deviant nature of the mother−child family. It is not surprising that previous social scientists had considered the female-headed unit an aberration, for this was a group that tended to view the nuclear family as universal (see, e.g., Murdock, 1949; Parsons, 1955; Bell and Vogel, 1960) and the male as the rightful head of the house (e.g. Parsons and Bales, 1955). Adams rejects the view that the nuclear family is universal and universally fulfils a list of well-agreed upon functions. Instead he proposes a structural conceptualization of the family, based on the *dyad* (of which the mother–child dyad is perhaps the basic biological unit) as the primary building block of family structure. This removes the mother–child family from the 'social disorganization' category while rendering irrelevant arguments as to just what universal functions the nuclear family is best filling, and/or whether it is indeed universal.

The second tenet, linking the mother-headed family to poverty and the larger class system of a wage labour society, was first argued influentially by Smith (1956), but in a curiously non-structural way. In his empirical study of three poor black villages in Guyana (then British Guiana), he found over a third female-headed families in two of them. He explains this in a roundabout way as resulting mainly from the low *social status* in the larger colour-class system of the 'undifferentiated' occupations available to the men in the village economy. These confer insufficient prestige (or steady income) to be important to household functioning 'at certain stages of its development'. Consequently, males feel — and act — marginal in their husband–father roles. The end result is matrifocality and a high proportion of female-headed households. But the data Smith presents seem to suggest a less psychological explanation: he shows how marginal village economic opportunities are for both sexes, and the extent to which the males act as a migratory reserve labour force in the larger capitalist economy (cutting cane on the sugar plantations for several months a year during 'crop', migrating for long periods to work in the bauxite mines, etc.). Moreover, even though Smith emphasizes that the sex ratio was evenly balanced only in the village that had fewest (17 percent) mother-headed families, he provides information suggesting another non-demographic reason for that village's low proportion of female-headed households: 'there are also *fewer opportunities for women to find work* in that area, so that their dependence on the earning power of men is greater' (p. 65, emphasis added). Still, Smith's study provides a non-racial, non-social–pathological interpretation of matrifocality, and some valuable empirical information. (Particularly suggestive are his observations showing that economic opportunities available to women are even more marginal than those available to men – and that half the female-headed units are 'grandmother families' headed by a woman over 60. In contrast, the median age of male heads is in the early 40s. Female heads supplement any income they earn with whatever contributions they can get from adult sons, the lovers of adult resident daughters, and sometimes these daughters' earnings.)

Smith has been criticized by Greenfield (1966), who argues that his explanation ignores the historical process whereby women-centred families arose; and by Solien de Gonzalez (1970a), who feels he gives too much weight to the psychological effects of the male's inability to provide cash income to the household.

Greenfield's own study is of Barbados, and he agrees thoroughly with Smith on the immediate causes of female-headed familism among the poor (i.e. that low occupational prestige and low, unreliable income in the male create a psychological situation conducive to his departure). Furthermore, Greenfield's well-presented data show a similar familism picture, even though he regards the village he studied as somewhat more 'middle class' occupationally than Smith's groups: in fact, a full 44 percent of its households are based on the mother-child dyad (p. 143). (Also, similar to Smith, Greenfield found that female heads are older than their male counterparts; that average age of family head is high for both sexes; that without property marriage is rare; and that older women outnumber older men.) Economically, the Barbados revealed in Greenfield's data seems even more distorted than Guyana; the island is a classic example of a one-crop (sugar) capitalist economy – there is not even any important subsistence agriculture. Furthermore, Barbados is greatly overpopulated (despite emigration) and its people apparently act primarily as a reserve labour force for the capitalist, technologically-saturated, sugar plantations.[2] Only a quarter of the labour force is directly employed by the sugar plantations, and many of these only for the 20 weeks per year of labour-intensive 'crop' activities. During the remaining 32 weeks, 'hard times', people are pushed to alternative, even more marginal, economic pursuits. In sum, Greenfield provides a detailed

portrait of mother-centred familism on Barbados and excellent docu-
mentation of the structural factors that would seem to cause both the
economic marginality and the low incidence of stable male-headed
families among these people.

Amazingly, though, the explanation proposed by Greenfield for the
origin of both the island's nuclear and mother-headed family forms
involves not the structural conditions long characterizing Barbados's
plantation economy, but rather historical diffusion from seventeenth-
century England. Capitalism, wage labour, and the small nuclear or
mother-headed family arrived together, as part of a larger Anglo-Saxon
culture stream 'into which the emancipated slaves were drawn two
centuries later', he asserts. In medieval English villages, he documents,
legal marriage was contracted only if property were involved ('husband'
meant a propertied villager; 'wed' is the gift the groom gave the bride to
signify her being vested in inheritance rights to his property). In
addition, records imply not only that the propertyless in rural villages
lived in common-law unions, but also that many poor families had no
resident males (p. 165). Yet rather than considering the structural
parallels as causal (i.e. the common position of the English and
Barbadian poor villagers vis-a-vis the means of production), Greenfield
implies that cultural diffusion is reason enough: 'the Barbadian Negro
is an English rustic in black skin', he quotes (citing Cruickshank, 1916,
p. 172). This further means that Greenfield is deliberately silent on how
matrifocality emerged in neighbouring Caribbean islands lacking an
Anglo-Saxon heritage. Contrarywise, he asserts that the essentially
similar market-exchange capitalism and family forms of Barbados and
the US may be due to *common origin.* Thus, the correlation between
economy and family might be the result of diffusion[3] rather than a
functional relationship (p. 168). Greenfield's explanation might be more
convincing if we did not have such a wide variety of studies showing
functional relationships between economic factors and family form.
These studies extend beyond the mother-centred familism literature
(where all the studies mentioned to this point show the covariation of
economic marginality in a wage labour economy and matrifocality).
Let us cite just three diverse examples: Handwerker (1973) on how
economic factors affect family structure among Bassa migrants to

Monrovia, Liberia; Opler's (1943) overview of the economic concomitants of polyandry; and Blumberg and Winch's (1973) study of family organization in 289 preindustrial societies which showed that two economic variables — inheritance and mode of subsistence — accounted for three-quarters of explained variance in familial structure.[4]

Gonzalez's (1970a) criticisms of Smith are similar to ours. However, despite her clarification of definitional issues in mother-centred familism, greater awareness of structural factors affecting poverty and underdevelopment[5] and well-done research on 'consanguineal' families (1959, 1969, 1970b), her suggested theories have drawbacks as explanatory devices. She posits matrifocality as adaptive to bilateral decent groups in a marginal position with respect to a larger political economic system (we agree). Then she suggests a *differentiation theory* to account for matrifocality: as societies industrialize, there is increasing separation of what she terms the 'domestic, supradomestic and jural' domains. Moreover, 'it is precisely in those where the domestic and jural[6] domains *tend to be separated the farthest* that we might expect to find the complex of phenomena that we are calling matrifocality' — especially among those lower class groups where control over the 'jural' domain 'has been taken almost completely out of the particular sub-society itself' (p. 241, emphasis added). Yet the strongest cases of matrifocality, consanguineality and female-headed familism do not come from the lower classes of the most industrialized societies — those with the most differentiated 'domestic' and 'jural' domains. Rather they are encountered among lower class groups in those Third World societies (she terms them 'neoteric' — 1970b) where both sexes participate in the 'jural' domain under conditions of great marginality. Greenfield, for one, seems to imply that matrifocality in Barbados was even higher in the immediate post-slavery period — when both sexes remained bound to the plantation estates, and *women did the same work at the same pay* as the men (p. 58, emphasis ours).

That mother-head families would be more frequent where women have economic options comparable to those of the males of their class is proposed in Winch and Blumberg (1968: 90-91) and Blumberg (1970: 207-11). The greater participation of lower class women in the labour force is also cited, and its correlation with domestic power discussed.

Poverty and wage labour, the two old stand-bys of the matrifocal literature, are also invoked in these two studies. In addition, another factor is posited in the 1968 article and further explicated in the 1970 work: the absence of the family as the unit of labour, and the relationship of this factor to the mode of production. Thus, Blumberg contrasts the different sorts of occupations in which blacks and East Indians are found in Guyana. The blacks, about whose mother-headed familism Smith has written, tend to work as individuals for wages in settings such as factories or public bureaucracies (where members of a family would not normally even be employed together). The East Indians never are discussed as having matrifocal familism. And, as both Blumberg (1970) and Despres (1970) note, they tend to be found in economic pursuits which are *family*-based (e.g. family farms and family-run shops). More generally, Blumberg observes, cross-cultural evidence suggests that family organization contracts and becomes more flexible under circumstances of unreliable or inadequate subsistence (Nimkoff and Middleton, 1960). The specific nature of the mode of production of the society will affect the sexual division of labour (see also Brown, 1970; Murdock and Provost, 1973; Blumberg, 1974a, 1974b). Jointly, Blumberg (1970) implies, these factors tell us whether the 'minimum family structure' expected to emerge under conditions of unreliable or marginal subsistence would be dyadic or require a male. Thus, where women contribute little to subsistence, she suggests, the minimum family unit that can survive is that headed by a male (p. 211).[7] Despite these suggestions concerning the unit of labour and the economic role of women, the Winch–Blumberg (1968) and Blumberg (1970) studies did not present an integrated theory accounting for the emergence, prevalence and persistence of female-headed families.

In order to do so, we suggest, we would have to go beyond the extant structural interpretations of mother-headed units in two ways. First, we must systematically treat the relation of the *mother* to the economic sector and the impact of this relation on her child-care responsibilities at different stages of the family cycle. This may give us some of the 'missing links' to account for the origin of mother-headed families in certain groups. But in order to account for their *persistence*, a second new element is necessary: a thorough analysis of the role of the larger political economy in *maintaining* the structural concomitants of mother-headed familism in a given group — regardless of state rhetoric that may condemn such families as 'disorganized', or a threat to the polity.

At this point, let us outline in preliminary form the conditions under which we believe the mother-headed family emerges and persists.

SOME CONDITIONS FOR THE EMERGENCE, PREVALENCE AND PERSISTENCE OF MOTHER-HEADED FAMILIES

In general, although such units are most prevalent among the economically marginal lower class in a variety of wage labour societies, not all economically marginal lower class groups in such societies have mother-centred familism. Conversely, female-headed units may be found in wage labour societies among groups which are not economically marginal (although, we suggest, not in very high proportion).

Accordingly, we distinguish four conditions for the emergence and prevalence of female-headed familism, in general, and an additional one for its persistence when encountered among the economically marginal lower class in wage labour societies. Actually, Conditions I, II and III tell us among which groups (and when in their family cycle) mother-headed families can emerge; Condition IV adds a specification affecting how prevalent mother-headed families might become in a group. The word 'poverty' is never mentioned in these four conditions. Yet, we suggest they are fulfilled most frequently among groups which are not only poor, but also constitute a *surplus labour population* in the context of a *larger political economy*. Condition V ties together surplus labour and political economy to predict the circumstances where female-headed families *persist* in this class over time. All five conditions are ultimately related to the mode of production, we suggest.[8]

Condition I: that the unit of labour, the unit of compensation, and the unit of property accumulation be the *individual,* independent of sex. (In societies where families are the unit of labour, and/or compensation is paid to the male head, and/or family property is corporately held, females rarely emerge as heads of families.)[9]

Condition II: that the females have *independent access to subsistence* opportunities. This condition is a function of (1) there being *viable* economic opportunities open to females[10] via: (a) their own work; (b) those of economically productive children whose labour or compensation they have access to; (c) inheritance; and/or (d) state-provided welfare; and (2) females being permitted, and in fact able, to head a separate residence and control property.

Condition III: that those subsistence opportunities open to females can somehow be reconciled with *child-care responsibilities.* First we must determine whether the female's own subsistence pursuits can be carried on simultaneously with child-care responsibilities (e.g. cottage industry, gathering).[11] If so, Condition III is satisfied. If not, satisfaction of Condition II might involve postponing formation of a mother-headed unit until young children can be cared for by a sibling old enough to do so, and/or some other child care agent; or until no young children are left; and/or until the woman can arrange sufficient remuneration from a working child, property, inheritance, and/or state welfare to permit her to stay home.

Condition IV: that the woman's subsistence opportunities from all sources in the absence of a male head not be drastically less than those of the men of her class.

As noted, all these conditions most frequently obtain among the economically marginal in wage labour societies, accounting for the concentration of female-centred and female-headed families among such groups. In other words, mother-headed families are most prevalent among groups characterized as *surplus labour.* For mother-headed families to persist in a society over time, we argue, so too must the class of surplus labour. Accordingly, to account for the *persistence* of mother-headed families, we invoke:

Condition V: that the political economy of the society produces and profits from a surplus labour population, and that the female-headed family unit successfully *reproduces* the surplus labour population to the benefit of those who control the political economy.)(To the extent that a society's political economy is controlled by outside, e.g. extranational, factors, the size of any surplus population and the extent to which it is internally beneficial to the society's elite becomes independent of their wishes.) Where Condition V is fulfilled, we predict that state rhetoric to the contrary, programmes that successfully reduce poor female-headed families will not be undertaken in the absence of a change in the structural conditions.

DISCUSSION OF THE CONDITIONS

We shall first discuss some interesting general implications of the Conditions before deriving the specific hypotheses we shall test in this paper.

Is bilateral kinship a necessary condition for mother-headed familism, or just a correlate?

Gonzalez (1970a) is unique in suggesting that although the two always seem to occur together, they both might be determined by another factor. We propose that Condition II — that females have viable independent subsistence opportunities — is almost never fulfilled in the absence of Condition I — that rights to the means of subsistence be individuated. And Condition I, is, we suggest, what most often breaks down existing unilineal systems. Therefore, we do not consider it necessary for a fully bilateral descent system to be present before mother-headed units can begin to emerge. The writings on contemporary Africa almost invariably show a link between the individuation of subsistence opportunities or property and the modification of traditional unilineal family patterns. Handwerker, for example, shows a wide variety of flexible household structures among the patrilineal Bassa migrants in Monrovia, Liberia — including 13.6 percent female-headed households containing only *maternal* kin. The strongest immediate determinants of household composition in his sample seem to be economic marginality and ownership of property.

When might a patrilineal system *not* move in the direction of matrifocality if brought into a commodity-production economy under conditions of poverty?

Despres' (1970) description of the East Indians who came to the Guyana sugar estates as indentured workers is quote suggestive. Both the East Indians and the African slaves who preceded them had patrilineal systems but slavery forcibly had destroyed the African system. In contrast, the conditions of the East Indians' contracts guaranteed job security, (minimal but steady) subsistence, and permitted a strategy of family employment. Men, women, and young boys worked in separate labour gangs (presumably, young girls did child care). By contract, a certain proportion of their labour time was for pay, rather than for the estate. With the pooled income, they could rent more land to add to the family wet rice plot the owner assigned them, and work that collectively in their 'free time' as well. They could grow rice as a *cash* crop because their own food was guaranteed. The family thus was able to act as the capital formation unit, and many families had accumulated enough at the end of the contract to trade their return passage rights for the right to buy government-subsidized irrigated land suitable for wet rice cultivation on a family basis. With family property, patrilineal inheritance patterns could be retained, and further family business ventures (such as urban trade) financed by kin group venture capital. Thus, in answer to our question: how might a patrilineally-oriented family system persist when brought into a commodity-production economy at poverty level, it seems that: (1) the early opportunities for a family employment and capital accumulation strategy permitted continuation of the patrilineal pattern; and (2) the 'minimum guaranteed subsistence' of the contract obviated the patterns of ad hoc reshuffling of household arrangements and resources that, we suggest, accompany 'feast and famine' economic *uncertainty* among other subsistence level groups.

In general, then, what effect does a 'feast and famine' pattern of unreliable subsistence have on the adaptation strategy of a group, especially its familism patterns?

Proposition A: environmental *uncertainty* leads to *flexibility*. Whether among certain US corporations (see, e.g., Perrow, 1967; Harvey, 1968), hunting and gathering bands (e.g., Lee, 1968, 1969, on the !Kung bushmen), or economic marginals in wage labour societies (e.g., Stack, 1970; Calley, 1956), groups that have to cope with environmental uncertainty are characterized by flexibility of organization. Their adaptive strategies are dynamic and loosely structured in response to fluctuating conditions.

Proposition B: unpredictable *fluctuations of scarce resources* lead to *sharing and exchange*. This kind of redistribution has been documented for both hunting and gathering groups (Lombardi, 1973; and Sahlins, 1965, give numerous references), and wage labour society marginals (see Valentine, 1970; Stack, 1970, 1974 for exchange networks among certain US urban blacks; and Calley, 1956 for same among Australian Aboriginal 'mixed bloods'). Conversely, adding the scarce resources criterion effectively excludes Perrow's and Harvey's formal organizations. Generalizing, it appears that groups facing *inconsistent surplus* tend to adopt a strategy of *sharing and exchange* of resources. Moreover, it seems to work: Lombardi (1973) shows mathematically how such redistribution serves to smooth out fluctuations in net available resources, and then demonstrates empirically how for one US welfare household, 'without exchange, the net available wealth would have dropped below zero for three successive days, while with exchange it never falls to zero'. Incidentally, the study by Calley bridges hunting—gathering and wage labour society marginal groups: the Australian Aboriginal 'mixed bloods' had practised generalized redistribution in their traditional economy, and now practised various kinds of 'borrowing and counter-borrowing' on their reserves in Northern New South Wales where they eked out a precarious existence, functioning as the sporadically employed and underpaid local reserve labour force (government relief prevented outright starvation). To generalize, it appears that in the hunting—gathering situation, the fluctuating and generally low levels of resources are caused by a combination of technology and habitat; whereas in the wage labour marginality situation they are caused by the relation of the group to the larger political economy.

Proposition C: the flexibility, and sharing and exchange characterizing groups facing inconsistent surplus extend even to household members; with the composition of co-residential groups changing flexibly and dynamically with changing circumstances — within the general bounds of the kinship pattern. This is best illustrated by Stack (1970) in her study of the 'kindred of Viola Jackson', a US black woman. (Lee, 1968, 1969 also describes shifting band composition among the !Kung Bushmen.) Indeed, many of the studies we have cited concerning the matrifocal family in wage labour societies show instances of flexible family composition as adaptive strategy. Under the impact of economic and interpersonal changes in the situations of their members, household units form and reform, and often children are shifted around or informally 'adopted'. Yet, what is striking in this literature is that despite adversity, these children do get cared for. Redistributing family members seems as adaptive a strategy for these people facing inconsistent surplus as redistributing food, money and other resources. Two further points should be noted concerning this flexible family composition. First, Stack shows that the pool of eligibles for this sort of exchange includes a loose *bilateral* group, rather than just maternal consanguineals, as indicated by Gonzalez (1969, 1970a). Secondly, Calley too found family composition frequently in flux — but, throughout it all, he found that the *proportion* of mother-headed families (about one-third) in one group he studied remained 'fairly constant'.

The answer then, to our question of how a subsistence pattern involving fluctuation of scarce resources affects familism, seems to involve: (1) organizational flexibility; (2) sharing and exchange; and (3) adaptive recomposition of households. All three characterize the households of wage labour society marginals whose general levels of mother-headed families we propose to be determined by Conditions I through V.

Under what conditions will the proportion of female-headed units increase in wage labour societies among groups which are *not* economically marginal?

Here, we look to Condition IV concerning the sex gap in resources. Does this mean that mother-headed families should multiply among middle class women in industrial societies around the world as they enter the labour force in increasing numbers? Not necessarily Presently, in a number of Western industrial societies, the higher the social class, the lower the rate of marital instability (see Winch and Blumberg, 1968; Goode, 1963). We suggest that this is related to the fact that the size of the sex gap in resources also *increases* with higher social class: the income, education, and prospects of the wife of a lawyer working as a secretary (or even a teacher) are much worse compared to her husband's than is the case with the woman at the next typewriter married to a bus driver. Thus, it makes sense for the lawyer's wife to protect her own and her children's upper-middle-class lifestyle and status by staying married. After all, numerous studies have revealed how infrequent is court-awarded alimony and how very prevalent is male non- or under-compliance with court-ordered child support. In one example, Bart studied all whites receiving divorces in Chicago's Cook County three years previously and found that only half of the women reported receiving what child support the court had decreed (Bart, personal communication, 1974 – based on 50 percent rate of questionnaire return).[12]

Nor does the evidence show that the increasing participation of middle class women in the labour force is accompanied by a shrinking in the male–female gap in earnings or even education. Quite to the contrary, Knudsen (1969) demonstrates the gap in these areas has *increased* during the recent years of economic expansion that pulled so many US married women into the labour force (see Oppenheimer, 1973). None the less, as more women achieve the possibility – via work or welfare – of a *viable* (if lower) income by their own efforts, they may increasingly choose to set up a 'home of one's own', to paraphrase Woolf (1929). Recent statistics seem to bear this out.

In the US, the last decades may not have seen a general shrinking of the earnings gap between males and females, but one group – black females – did increase its real income faster than whites of either sex, or black males. The income of non-white women rose 260 percent from 1950 to 1968, versus for example, only 160 percent among non-white males (see Farley, 1970). Also, especially since the mid-1960s, transfer payments (Social Security, welfare, etc.) have risen. Consequently, it is not surprising that the US Department of Labour (1973) shows a concomitant rise in the proportion of households headed by females of all races, and especially, black ones. The explanation of the general rise in female-headed units since roughly 1960 seems to lie in the greater ability of certain groups of women to maintain an independent household rather than living with relatives. Among white women, the largest percentage gains were registered among those over 65, who tended to live alone (US Department of Labour, 1973). However, among black women, Farley (1970) shows that it was among younger females 15—34 and especially 35—44 that rates of family headship increased. Contrary to Moynihan's empirically misleading pronouncements of a breakdown in the ghetto black family, this was not achieved by a reduction in the proportion of non-white married males heading families (this figure in fact, increased somewhat). Rather, Farley suggests, these additional female-headed units came from women who previously had been living with relatives — and now were able to make it on their own. (See also Billingsley, 1973; Hill, 1971; and Staples, 1972).

In conclusion, even within rising general levels of absolute affluence and female-headed households, we would predict a higher proportion of mother-headed units among groups where the *relative* sex gap in resources is narrow, a situation still most frequent among the lower classes.

Before turning to the hypotheses we shall test empirically in this paper, we address — much too superficially here — the implications of Condition V: (1) under what conditions does a society's political economy produce and profit from a surplus labour population; and (2) how does the female-headed family articulate with the surplus labour population?

With respect to the first question, critics of capitalism argue that the existence of a marginal lower class is a *'necessary and inevitable consequence* of a mature industrial capitalist system'(Sackrey, 1973, discussing the assumptions of Baran and Sweezy's (1966) *Monopoly Capital*, emphasis in original). However, a strong case can be made for the 'necessity and inevitability' of such a class in two other types of society as well: (a) traditional agrarian ones, and (b) contemporary Third World nations. In all three types of society, we suggest the mechanism that makes inevitable such a class consists of the *conjunction* of two factors. (1) On the one hand, those who control the political economy seem to benefit in two ways from the existence of adults who are normally marginal to the labour force: these adults reduce the bargaining power of the mainstream labour force (e.g. peasants in agrarian societies) by serving as potential replacements; and moreover, they are conveniently available to be pulled into the mainstream labour force only when and if the need arises. (2) On the other hand, many of the poor in those societies may find children to represent a benefit, not a cost – a possible solution to the problem of their poverty rather than its cause (see Mamdani, 1972).

Let us now consider the three types of societies where a surplus labour force tends to emerge.

(1) Traditional agrarian societies. Here, Lenski (1966) argues that 5–15 percent of the urban population in such societies consisted of a class he calls the 'expendables' – coolies, beggars, prostitutes, street-vendors, thieves, etc. – whose life conditions were so miserable they did not reproduce themselves. But, suggests Lenski, they were replaced in each generation because they represented the peasant population in excess of what the governing elite was willing to let survive, even at minimum subsistence level. Just because these sons and daughters of the peasantry were barely even a surplus labour force as adults does not mean they were not useful to their parents as children: often the only one of the three factors of production (land, labour, capital) the peasant producer can control is labour costs – by growing his own labour force (see, e.g. Polgar, 1972). For peasants, children typically represent a net benefit in labour over the small costs of maintaining them; and thus a large family is a 'rational' investment under a mode of production where surplus is usually skimmed off the top by the governing elite before peasants can attempt to look after their own needs (see Wolf, 1966).

(2) Third World nations. Similarly, it has been argued that for large segments of the marginal urban poor in capitalist wage labour societies – especially underdeveloped ones – children represent to their parents a potential net benefit rather than a cost (e.g. Schnaiberg and Reed, 1974; Blumberg, 1973), even if they ultimately swell the size of the surplus

labour population. And it is precisely in the size of this reserve labour force that Third World societies are distinguished from both historical agrarian ones and advanced industrial—capitalist nations. The truth of the matter is that these countries have tended to lose control of the size of their surplus populations.

Many of these Third World countries were previously traditional agrarian systems (and producers of a surplus population) before they were drawn into the world commodity-exchange system. Today, they tend to be experiencing capitalist development in their cities and key resource sectors while in the countryside cash crops are replacing subsistence agriculture without major reforms in the land tenure arrangements that had led to surplus population under the traditional system.[13] Add malaria control, smallpox vaccination campaigns and other infant-mortality-reducing measures, and the level of population pressure in the countryside should encourage either or both fragmentation of holdings or migration to the cities. Given the vagaries of the commodity cycle in the world market and the small size of these countries' 'modern industrial' (and frequently capitalist, export-oriented) sector, it follows that the growth of urban jobs falls increasingly short of the supply of hopeful job-seekers. (This phenomenon is often known as 'overurbanization' — see Hauser, 1963; Browning, 1967). Moreover, most of these countries are too poor to have adequate welfare programmes.

In general, where viable subsistence opportunities exist for *females* in such societies, the probabilities are high for flexible bilateral kinship, and various manifestations of 'matrifocal' families — including female-headed units. But the absence of welfare and the fact that the size of the surplus population may easily get out of hand may have especially disastrous consequences for such family units in this type of society.[14]

(3) Western industrial nations. The situation in many of these countries is complicated by their exchange of marginal populations (when the economy is expanding the northwestern European countries import as temporary workers some of the reserve labour force of countries to the south; the influx of illegal Latin and Caribbean immigrants is the US analogue. Here, we shall confine our attention to the US. Here, we find both a comprehensive welfare system, and relatively high proportions of female-headed families among the urban poor.

Moreover, scholars have argued that the welfare system — especially the Aid to Families with Dependent Children (AFDC) programme — actually *promotes* female-headed families by making it difficult for a family to get assistance while an able-bodied male head lives in the house (see, e.g. Safa, 1964).

A stronger criticism of US public assistance charges that in this affluent country the primary effect — and perhaps purpose — of welfare has been *to guarantee a marginal work force at the bottom of the economic order'* (Sackrey, 1973, p. 111, emphasis in original). Piven and Cloward (1971) make a forceful and detailed argument that the chief function of relief is to regulate labour, by (1) expanding relief to restore order when social conditions such as 'mass unemployment' threaten turbulence (figures on post-Watts-riot welfare expenditures tend to support this view);[15] and (2) treating welfare recipients in times of full employment in such a degrading and punitive manner as to convince the labouring masses that this is a fate to be avoided if even the 'meanest labour at the meanest rates' can be obtained (p. 4). In other words, welfare and unemployment compensation are pitched sufficiently below the prevailing wage rates as to make them a subsistence—maintenance programme into which surplus labour (especially male surplus) safely can be pushed in and easily pulled out as political—economic conditions warrant.[16] To Piven and Cloward, 'relief arrangements are ancillary to economic arrangements' (p. 3).

But why should relief arrangements favour the formation of female-headed units when government rhetoric (e.g. the Moynihan Report) condemns that type of family as disorganized, crime-producing and poverty-perpetuating? Faced with this paradox, should we give greater credence to the 'relief arrangements' or the rhetoric? Levin (1973) writing about why US schools are financed to invest so much more money in wealthy than in poor pupils, invokes what he terms the 'principle of correspondence' to argue that we should give greater weight to the *activities* and *outcomes* of a long-established institutional sector than to its official liturgy.[17]

By this criterion, then, we find that despite conflicting and often cross-cutting interests among different sectors of industry, southern versus northern states, and a patchwork of welfare and unemployment compensation laws, one outcome is clear:[18] policies that consistently favour the long-term sustenance of only women and children (among the able-bodied) have been with us for a long time. Not only are the existing number of marginal women and their families sustained, but we have never heard of a woman's welfare cheque being *cut* for having an extra child. So it seems reasonable to take the long-established built-in mechanisms that encourage and maintain female-headed families (albeit below the poverty line)[19] as an indication that this type of family arrangement is *successfully* reproducing the next generation of the 'marginal work force at the bottom of the economic order'.

In answer to our second question, concerning the articulation of female-headed families and the surplus labour population in these different types of societies, we may conclude: in agrarian and Third World societies, the absence of welfare seems to mean that the crucial determinant will be the extent to which the woman can achieve a viable subsistence by her own and/or her children's efforts. Since the jobs open to such women might safely be characterized as marginal, and since welfare is not generally available, a woman might well have to have both independent access to employment *and* the contribution of some of her children before making a go of a female-headed unit. This points to using children as possible solutions to the problem of her poverty (although it may not mean that mother-headed families have more offspring than nuclear ones of the same class). The individuation of property and the unit of labour make the mother-headed family much more likely in the Third World than the agrarian situation. In the US by contrast, the economically marginal woman heading her own family has access to a welfare system that guarantees against starvation. If she stays on it, she may not be penalized for having additional children, and if she goes off welfare, she is unlikely to get beyond the status of 'working poor', i.e. become a member of a volatile, ill-paid secondary labour force[20] — where once again a larger family may ultimately turn out to be a bonus if she can smooth out fluctuations in resources by her access to a flexible kin-based exchange network. Because of the nature of the welfare system, we must conclude that the articulation of the female-headed family with the larger political economy seems most direct in the US case — where such a family unit is encouraged to form and grow by long-standing laws.

HYPOTHESES ABOUT MOTHER-HEADED
FAMILIES TESTABLE WITH AVAILABLE DATA

Despite the rather broad discussion of the implications of our five structural Conditions presented in the preceding pages, what we actually are able to test at this point is limited by the available data. On the one hand we shall propose that in the US structure and not race is involved in producing high proportions of mother-headed units among certain sectors of the population — specifically, poor, urban residents. This we shall test with published data from the US Census. On the other hand, we shall attempt to use data on a sample of lower income, predominantly shacktown residents in Caracas, Venezuela — where there is no comprehensive welfare system — to explore a series of relatively low-level hypotheses concerning labour force participation and stage of family cycle of women who head their own households.

Let us start with the US. As we have pointed out above, much of the discussion of female-headed families in the US is framed in terms of the phenomenon being one of social pathology among poor urban blacks. And a first (but misleading) glance at the figures tends to confirm that impression. Looking at a 1970 report (US Bureau of the Census, 1970), we find that 23.0 percent of all urban households are female-headed. By race, however, this figure breaks down as follows: Blacks — 35.0 percent female-headed units; Spanish heritage — 18.4 percent; Whites (figure includes a tiny percentage of Orientals and Native Americans as well) — 21.8 percent (see Table 1, Part 1). Given that both the blacks and the Spanish-surnamed tend to be poorer than the whites, yet the black rate is nearly double the Spanish heritage group, the notion that this is a specifically racial problem seems initially plausible. However, to test the structural hypothesis, we shall break down the total urban population by income categories. In 1969, the year of these income data, the poverty line stood at $3,700 for a family of four (Stein, 1970:3). The US Census table we shall use gives income in $1,000 intervals for

TABLE 1

Numbers of US Urban Households by Selected Levels of Income in 1969 and by Sex and Race of Head, 1970*

Race and Sex of Head of Household	Number	Per cent	Median Income	Households with Income under $2,000		Households with Income under $4,000	
				Number	%	Number	%
Total	47,672,276	100.0	$8920	4,998,230	100.0	10,152,905	100.0
Male	36,670,772	76.9	10431	1,773,922	35.5	4,534,666	44.7
Female	11,001,504	23.1	3892	3,224,308	64.5	5,618,239	55.3
Black	5,259,391	100.0	5740	1,004,485	100.0	1,909,805	100.0
Male	3,417,324	65.0	7363	349,111	34.8	779,653	40.8
Female	1,842,067	35.0	3038	655,374	65.2	1,130,152	59.2
Spanish heritage	2,057,818	100.0	7282	227,802	100.0	507,066	100.0
Male	1,679,156	81.6	8144	108,794	47.8	284,213	56.1
Female	378,662	18.4	3317	119,008	52.2	222,853	43.9
Other[a]	40,355,067	100.0	b	3,765,943	100.0	7,736,034	100.0
Male	31,574,292	78.2	b	1,316,017	34.9	3,470,800	44.9
Female	8,780,775	21.8	b	2,449,926	65.1	4,265,234	55.1

* *Source*: US Bureau of the Census. *Census of Population: 1970.* Vol. 1. *Characteristics of Population.* Part 1, US Summary — Section 2, Table 258, pp. 960-961.

a The 'other' category is derived by subtraction of black and Spanish heritage from the total. Since the proportion of Orientals and Native Americans is very small, it is virtually equivalent to white.

b Since values for the 'other' category were derived by subtraction, no values for median income were available for this category.

low-income groups. As a rough approximation of the really poor — those earning well below the poverty line — we examine all urban households earning under $2,000 for 1969. Even remembering that the data refer to households, not just families, and thus can include people living alone such as elderly widows, it is sobering to find that fully 64.5 percent of households earning under $2,000 are female-headed. Broken down by race, the figure is even more startling: Blacks — 65.2 percent female-headed households; Spanish heritage — 52.2 percent; Whites (including those Orientals and Native Americans again, because this is the residual category) — 65.1 percent. Thus, the figures for black versus white Americans are within 0.1 percent of being identical. And although we do not have data, some of the reason for the low figure among Spanish-surname may be explained by the problem of illegal immigration: people who are in the US illegally are less likely to risk the female-headed-family-facilitating welfare rolls; moreover, if an accurate count of Spanish heritage people were possible, it might show a male-skewed sex ratio of the sort found among other immigrant streams that would give the females of the group more opportunity to remain in male-headed households.

Now let us examine all urban households earning under $4,000 in 1969, which, given average household size, should give us mostly people at or below the poverty line. Here, female-headed households are still a majority: 55.3 percent. The figures by race show: Blacks — 59.2 percent female-headed; Spanish heritage — 44.0 percent; Whites (i.e. the remainder) — 55.1 percent. Clearly, the 4 percent difference between white and black Americans is nothing on which to base a theory of racial pathology.*

The reason, of course, why the total figures are so misleading is that median incomes are sharply different for each racial and sex group, as Part 1 of Table 1 shows. Blacks of both sexes earn considerably less than their Spanish heritage counterparts, and far less than whites. (The table also gives data to calculate the extent of the sex gap in earnings, with

---

*We find similar results when we examine poor *non-urban* households: for both rural farm and rural nonfarm categories, there is no difference in the proportions of blacks and whites having female-headed families at incomes under $2,000 or $4,000 per year.

the average family headed by an urban *white female* earning 37.3 percent of that earned by a white *male,* and 52.3 percent of that earned by
the average *black* male; meanwhile, the black males average 70.6 percent
of their white counterparts.)

Reflecting once again on the Conditions, it is perhaps not so surprising
that a majority of the poorest households of even urban *whites* should
be female-headed in the US. Two factors particularly seem important:
(1) the US's high rates of female labour force participation (1970 Census
data show that 50 of every 100 women aged 18–64 were in the labour
force, and the figure has risen since); and (2) its fail-safe welfare system,
Aid to Families with Dependent Children, which underwrites their
survival.

At this point, we turn to mother-headed familism in Venezuela, a
country without so many opportunities for female employment – only
19.5 percent of females over age 10 are in the labour force (Encuesta
del Hogar, 1970) – and lacking the cushion of a widespread welfare
system. What sort of mother-headed familism might we expect under
such conditions? Most of our expectations (the low-level hypotheses
that follow) are derived from the above circumstances plus Condition
III – concerning the mutual accommodation of the female's economic
activities and her child-care responsibilities. The way in which this
potential conflict is accommodated depends on the nature of the subsistence activities open to the woman – specifically, whether they are of
a sort which can be combined with care of her young children. Activities
that meet that description are those that: can be easily interrupted and
resumed; are not dangerous; do not require fast and long spatial mobility;
and do not involve a workplace from which children are excluded.

Surprisingly, many of the marginal economic activities engaged in
by lower class women in even today's wage labour societies fit that
description. Especially prevalent in a number of underdeveloped societies
are cottage industry, taking in washing or ironing, street vending, market
or kiosk selling, as well as many farm pursuits – all of which can usually
be done without having to make child-care arrangements for preschool
children. Accordingly, if these opportunities are available to a woman,
there need be no restriction on the stage of the family cycle at which
the mother-headed family is likely to form.

Unfortunately, all the activities listed tend to be so marginal and low-income that it is unlikely that they would be sufficient in themselves to provide a woman viable subsistence for herself and her children. Such a woman may not be able to head a separate unit until she has access to the earnings of some of her children as well. This would tend to delay formation of a mother-headed family to the later childbearing years.

Conversely, many of the better-paid jobs are not only 'modern sector' but automatically require a workplace to which young children cannot be brought. A mother without a resident spouse in such a predicament would have to make alternative child-care arrangements in order to work. Sometimes she could manage to have the young children looked after by a cooperative relative, or could afford to arrange for another child-care agent (including taking in a relative's child for this purpose). At other times, she herself would have to enter another household where these services could be provided — rather than maintaining her own unit. Alternatively, she might succeed in forming her own household only when one of her children became old enough to watch the younger, or when no very young child remained in the home (this might mean waiting for the child to grow, or farming out the baby to an appropriate relative). Ultimately, income from working children or other sources (e.g. welfare, pension) might permit her to stay home.

It is clear that all of the above situations (and these are just examples of a wide list of possibilities) have implications for (a) increasing the probability of the mother being in the labour force if she is head of her family; and (b) delaying the stage of the family cycle at which mother-headed families become most prevalent.

From these two general statements, seven commonsense hypotheses follow immediately. The first three concern the labour force participation rates of females heading families, and the last four predict that such families emerge at a later stage in the family cycle than do male-headed units.

H_1: Women heading their own families are more likely to work than their counterparts living in male-headed families.

H_2: Moreover, for each category based on (a) age of eldest child; and also (b) age of youngest child, women family heads have a higher labour force participation rate than their sisters in conjugal unions.

Because of the material we have presented showing that grown children so frequently contribute to the maintenance of mother-headed units on the one hand, and the difficulties involved in a woman's working when her eldest child is still very young, we expect the age of the eldest child to be related to females' labour force participation. Accordingly, we propose:

H_3: *Within* groups of women family heads (as well as wives), age of eldest child is curvilinearly related to labour force participation, so that those with the youngest (preschool) and oldest (adult) eldest children are less likely to work than women with an eldest child in the school-age range.

The four hypotheses predicting that female-headed households tend to involve a later stage of the family cycle are:

H_4: Within cohorts based on age of eldest child, the older the youngster, the higher the proportion of female-headed families in the group.

H_5: More generally, women who are family heads have older children than wives living in male-headed families.

H_6: Moreover, it follows that women who are family heads are themselves older than their sisters in male-headed conjugal units.

H_7: In addition, women family heads tend to be somewhat older than male family heads.

In keeping with the situation in most countries, we also predict that women have less education than men, lower income, and lower occupational attainment. (This is based primarily on the society's opportunity structure, which generally offers women less access to education, restricted job opportunities, and lower pay − even in the case of 'equal work'. Accordingly, we predict that female family heads will have lower SES characteristics than their male counterparts.

THE VENEZUELAN SAMPLE
AND RELEVANT FINDINGS

Given the findings of other studies of mother-headed families in the literature, and the commonsense nature of these hypotheses, it should come as no surprise to the reader that all were supported by the data. Nevertheless, because of problems with the nature of the sample, these findings must be interpreted with considerable caution.

The data for the study were collected by CEVEPOF, the Centro Venezolano de Estudios de Poblacion y Familia, a government/private-sponsored research organization studying population and family matters. The study was conducted in 1971 in Caracas, the Venezuelan capital, a city of roughly 2.3 million, of which a growing proportion – now estimated at well over one-third[21] – live in shacktowns, or *barrios*. The aim of the CEVEPOF study (see CEVEPOF and CISOR, 1971 and 1972) was to compare barrio households headed by (a) an employed person; (b) an *under*employed person; (c) an *un*employed person; and (d) a person not in the labour force. Accordingly, although the shacktowns were selected by a stratified random process from a typology encompassing 237 of the city's close to 400 barrios, the households were not. Instead, the four employment categories were sampled by quota within the randomly chosen shacktowns. This produced 468 interviews; we have data on 400 of them, encompassing 36 percent employed, 30 percent underemployed, 24 percent unemployed, and 10 percent out of the labour force. These were supplemented by a control group of 100 randomly selected cases from two randomly selected low-to-moderate income *urbanizaciones* (neighbourhoods, more or less; one was actually a public housing development). Of the 500 households for which we have sex of head data, 114 (22.8 percent) are female-headed: 25 percent of the non-shacktown cases, and 22.2 percent in the *barrios*.

The female-headed percentage is in line with previous data showing between a fifth and a quarter of Venezuelan households female-headed (see, e.g. IX Venezuelan Census, 1961), and with a study of Venezuelan housing (Banco Nacional, 1971) which found 25 percent women heads among lower income Caracas units. In the US as of March 1972, women constituted 22 percent of household heads, but only 12 percent of family heads (US Department of Labour, 1973). The discrepancy between household and family in the US figures is caused by the large numbers of older women living alone. In the Venezuelan CEVEPOF sample, by contrast, only 4.4 percent of the female heads lived without family members in the house, i.e. they were much more likely to be family, rather than mere household, heads.

Hypothesis 1: Our figures here must be considered with caution, because four-fifths of the CEVEPOF sample cases were chosen by quota according to the labour force status of the head of the house. And even though that selection was made without regard to sex of head of household (in fact, the two urbanizaciones, which were not chosen by quota, show a slightly higher rate of female-headed households than the shacktowns), it confounds in an unknown, although probably conservative way, the labour force participation rates of our female heads.[22] None the less, we note that 39 percent of the women heading households are presently working, versus 17 percent of their sisters living as spouses (legal or common law) of male household heads (Table 2).

TABLE 2

(H_1): Percent of Women Currently Working, by Household Status

Household status of Woman	Not working		Working	Total
	Does not want to work	Wants to work		
Spouse = head		83.4%* (292)	16.6% (58)	100.0% (350)
Woman = head	39.8% (45)	21.2%* (24)	38.9% (44)	99.9% (113)
Total − women working			22.0%	(463)

* Since the shacktown sample (as distinct from the truly random non-shacktown sample of 100 cases), was selected to include a quota of unemployed heads of household regardless of sex, disposition to work was not asked of non-working wives of male heads, whereas the 21.2 percent of female heads who are unemployed but willing to work may be an artifact of the sample design (see also note 22.).

An additional 21 percent of female heads declared themselves willing to work in a question asked only of household heads. Thus, according to these data, the women heads sampled seem to have a higher rate of labour force participation than either the wives in the sample *or* the general female population of Venezuela (where, as we mentioned, only

19.5 percent of females 10 and over are in the labour force[23]). The situation is similar in the US where female heads have higher work force rates than their married sisters, especially when groups with children under 6 are compared: 47 percent labour force participation for female heads with preschoolers, versus 29 percent for married women with such young children (Stein, 1970:7). Next we look at employment rates by age of children for the women in the CEVEPOF sample.

Hypotheses 2 and 3: Table 3 shows that for every age of child category, the women heads have higher rates of current employment than the wives (with the exception of a single case of a married woman who proved to be the only female still working when all children were married; she had more than one child and thus shows up on both eldest and youngest child sides of Table 3). The table thus parallels the US data and offers apparent support for Hypothesis 2 – if possible sample bias concerning labour force participation is ignored.[24] The bottom half of the table also offers some apparent support for Hypothesis 3, concerning the curvilinear relationship between women working and age of their oldest child.

Actually, the figures in the left upper half of the table are more interesting. They show a decline in percentage employed for women heads with unmarried eldest child 14 through 19; whereas, conversely, the wives show their highest rate of employment (24.5 percent) when they have a teenaged eldest child. When the eldest child is single, but 20 or over, the female heads' employment rate jumps to 54 percent (tied for first place with the rate for female heads with eldest child 6–13); whereas, the wives' rate is down to 17 percent when their eldest is 20+ and single. The implication may be that the female head benefits from the earnings of any employed children 14 through 19, who would be more likely to remain at home than a child over 20. The latter may be employed, but if he or she is no longer living at home, probably will not be contributing enough to free the mother from labour force participation. This is in line with the results of the recent University of Michigan study of 5,000 US families' economic well-being. This five-year longitudinal study found that 'since all of the economies of scale and most of the help that individuals give to each other are realized through living together rather than through cash transfers *between* households, changes

TABLE 3

(H₂ and H₃): Percent of Mothers Currently Working by Sex of Head of House for (A) Eldest Child; and (B) Youngest Child, where $N > 1$

PART 1 (A) Eldest child

Age of child	Female No.of cases	Female Mother works No.	Female %	Male No.of cases	Male Mother works No.	Male %
< 1 year	0	0	—	13	2	15.4
1 through 5	6	2	33.3	53	6	11.3
6 through 13	13	7	53.8	107	18	16.8
14 through 19	22	10	45.4	53	13	24.5
> 20, single	13	7	53.8	35	6	17.1
At least 1 married child	36	10	27.8	68	7	10.3
All children married	7	0	0	7	1	14.3
(No children)	1	—	—	16	—	—
Totals	98			352		

1 (B) Youngest child ($N > 1$)

Age of Child	Female No.of cases	Female Mother works No.	Female %	Male No.of cases	Male Mother works No.	Male %
< 1 year	2	1	50.0	37	3	8.1
1 through 5	24	10	41.7	137	24	17.5
6 through 13	24	9	37.5	58	11	19.0
14 through 19	15	5	33.3	27	2	7.4
> 20, single	7	2	28.6	17	0	0
Married	6	0	0	7	1	14.3
1 or no children	13			50		
Totals	91			433		

PART 2 Summary of eldest child data for H₄

Age of child	Female % Female working	Male % Female working
< 6	33.4	12.1
6 through 19	48.6	19.4
Single > 20; married	30.4	10.4

in the level and distribution of well-being are mainly caused by changes in household composition' (Morgan et al., 1974:337-38, emphasis in original). Concerning the Venezuelan data, it is plausible that when the child leaves home, he/she contributes less and more female heads are forced to work; wives are apparently not under the same degree of pressure — or may find their families more successful in keeping grown children at home, since the Michigan study also found that the poorest homes (and female-headed ones are, on the average, poorer) are less able to hold their wage-earning offspring. Incidentally, Table 3 also shows that female heads are far less likely to have young children, which leads us to the next topic, stage in family cycle of female-headed families.

Hypotheses 4 through 7: We have predicted that, given the absence of readily available welfare and the economically marginal nature of the activities open to the (poorly educated) mother of young children, female-headed units will tend to form later in the family cycle. Others, including Greenfield (1966) have written of the 'grandmother' family as a frequent form of the female-headed unit. And indeed, the CEVEPOF data indicate (table not shown) that the proportion of three- (or more) generation families is almost double among the female-headed units: 27 percent versus 14 percent among the male-headed households.

Table 4 shows data for two other measures of family cycle: age of children, and age of parents. We see that young children under 6 are by no means absent from the families of female heads — 28.6 percent of women heads have a youngest child under 6. However, the comparable percentage for wives is 52.2 percent. Moreover, there is no mother-headed unit whose eldest child is under one year, and only six women head families where the eldest is under 6 years old; meanwhile close to a fifth of the wives have their eldest child under 6. The reverse side of the coin is equally interesting: the eldest child is 14 or over in over four-fifths of the female-headed families, as compared to just over half of the male-headed ones. The age-of-children data are borne out by the age-of-parents figures, which show the female heads to be five years older, on the average, than the male heads, and at least ten years older than their sisters living in conjugal unions.[25]

This last fact, incidentally, explains an initially anomalous finding: contrary to the situation reported by Stein (1970) for the US, and by

TABLE 4

Hypotheses on Stage in Family Cycle of Female- Versus Male-Headed Households, Part I (H_4 and H_5): Based on (A) Age of Eldest Child and (B) Age of Youngest Child; Part II (H_6 and H_7): Based on Age of Adult Generation

PART I (A) Eldest child

Age of child	Female Head				Male Head
	ΣNo.of Cases	No.	% Total	% Female Head	% Male Head
≤ 1 year	13	0	0	0	3.7
1 through 5	59	6	10.2	6.1	15.1
6 through 13	120	13	10.8	13.3	30.4
14 through 19	75	22	29.3	22.4	15.1
≥ 20 single	48	13	27.1	13.3	9.9
As least 1 married child	104	36	34.6	36.7	19.3
All children married	14	7	50.0	7.1	2.0
No children	17	1	5.9	1.0	4.5
Totals	450	98		99.9	100.0

(B) Youngest child ($N > 1$)

Age of child	Female Head				Male Head
	ΣNo.of Cases	No.	% Total	% Female Head	% Male Head
≤ 1 year	39	2	5.1	2.2	11.1
1 through 5	161	24	14.9	26.4	41.1
6 through 13	82	24	29.3	26.4	17.4
14 through 19	42	15	35.7	16.5	8.1
≥ 20 single	24	7	29.2	7.7	5.1
Married	13	6	49.2	6.6	2.1
1 or less child	63	13	20.6	14.3	15.0
Totals	424	91		100.1	99.9

PART II

Sex of Head	(H_6) Median age of women	(H_7) Median age of head
Female	Between 44 and 45 years old	Between 44 and 45 years old
Male	About 34 years old	Between 39 and 40 years old

Greenfield (1966), Stycos (1963) and Safa (1964) for various parts of the Caribbean or Latin America, the female-headed units in the CEVEPOF sample have *more children* than the conjugal households. This relationship disappears, however, when we control for age of the mother. Then, for virtually every age category, the female heads have fewer offspring than their same-age sisters in conjugal unions.

The low percentage of female-headed families with young children brings to mind a statistic from the US that emphasizes perhaps the main difference affecting family headship between the two countries: in the United States, Stein notes (1970:3), 'by March 1970 about three-fifths of the 3.4 million families with children headed by women were already on welfare and the rolls were still rising'. This absence of welfare in Venezuela may well be a one factor in the rather frequent 'doubling up' encountered in the CEVEPOF sample: one-fifth of male-headed households and one-fourth of female-headed ones contained an additional mother-child or nuclear family. Indeed, it may be the ubiquitousness of urban surplus labour groups and not embedded traditionalism that accounts for the substantial proportions of extended-family households found in studies of numerous Third World cities. An investigation on Cyprus (Balswick and Paschalis, 1973) has revealed a case where more rural than urban households are nonextended nuclear units. Economies of scale of consumption (e.g. housing) not production (e.g. family businesses) seem behind much of this extended family living among marginal, recently urbanized Third World groups.

Finally, the CEVEPOF data in Table 5 show that the women who head their own households have lower education, income, and occupational attainment than their male counterparts. In the US too, female family heads — and females generally — have lower education, income and occupations than males. It would be an equally interesting question in both countries as to whether, within broad social classes, women who head families have lower SES characteristics than women in conjugal unions. Toward this end, in the CEVEPOF sample we are able to compare the currently employed female family heads and their working sisters in male-headed units, and find *no difference* in their job levels.

In short, these Venezuelan data support our simple hypotheses about employment and family cycle stage among female-headed households.

TABLE 5

Education, Income and Occupation by Sex of Head of House

Sex of Head	Education of Head		Income in Bolivares (Bs)+		Occupation		
	% of heads illiterate	% of heads with less than primary education	Median Income per family member per month	Total median monthly family income	A. % of Heads currently working	B. Most common occupations of employed head	C. Most common occupations of employed women**
Male	13.00	52.00	±Bs 210 (200–249)	±Bs 1100 (1000–1249)	80.00	1. Worker (unskilled) 18.1% 2. Driver 15.5	1. Domestic services 32.3% 2. Blue-collar worker 30.6
Female	25.00	72.00	±Bs 149 (100–149)	±Bs 750 (750–999)	39.00	1. Domestic services 29.2 2. Worker (unskilled) 16.7	1. Domestic services 37.0 2. Blue-collar worker 32.6

* Partly because of the sample design, both male and female heads have about 20 percent unemployed. The exact percentages of unemployment are: male heads 19.7 percent; female heads 21.2 percent (see also footnote 22).

+ Bs 4.3 = US $1.00.

** These figures are taken from a different table where there are several additional cases of missing data on female heads (accounting for the 8 percent discrepancy for domestic services for female heads in column B versus column C. Also, column C involves a different method of coding blue-collar occupations, resulting in the figures shown.

Although these results cannot be taken as definitive given the nature of the sample, they are consistent with our theories and seem in harmony with the extant literature.

THE MOTHER–CHILD
RESIDENTIAL UNIT

This section of the paper was sparked by what Murdock and Wilson (1972) call their 'startling and wholly unexpected discovery of a nearly exclusive association between mother-child households and societies that are Negro in race'. Their discovery was made in an analysis of the 186-society Standard Cross-Cultural Sample (Murdock and White, 1969), and as they describe it:

> . . . the most striking regional disparity is the concentration of mother–child households in Africa. This is clearly less a geographic than an ethnic pheno-menon, for the mother–child family does not occur in the non-Negro societies of Africa (the Bushmen, Hottentot, Hadza, and Pygmies), is characteristic of 18 of the 24 Negro societies of that continent in the sample, extends to five Negro tribes in the immediately adjacent Circum-Mediterranean (the Fur, Hausa, Somali, Wodaabe Fulani, and Wolof), and is also reported for the Saramacca Bush Negroes of South America. In short, of the 28 occurrences of such households in our entire sample, 24 are among peoples who are specifically Negro in race (1972:276).

Murdock and Wilson generalize their findings to the 'so-called "matrifocal family" among American Negroes, especially in the Caribbean area', stating:

> Our data confirm the . . . view . . . of Herskovits that the matrifocal family is basically an 'Africanism' imported into the New World with the slave trade. Though doubtless perpetuated there by the conditions of slavery and low economic status, these cannot account for its origin, as various recent authors have maintained. *The ultimate explanation must be sought in the social and*

economic conditions which gave rise to the mother-child household as the predominant indigenous form of family organization *in Africa* (1972:278, emphasis added).

We cannot accept either their apparent assumption that the mother—child dwelling unit is a specific phenomenon of peoples who are 'Negro in race', or their conclusion that the mother-headed family was imported into the New World with the slave trade — any more than we can accept Greenfield's suggestion that in Barbados it was imported with seventeenth-century WASP culture. Instead, for the mother-headed unit, we have argued for a series of conditions linked to the role of the woman in subsistence and the larger political economy of the state. Moreover, our Table 1 shows no difference in the proportions of female-headed households among the poorest urban whites and blacks in the US: for both races, 65 percent of the urban households earning under $2,000 in 1969 were headed by women, and the racial difference was a small 4 percent for urban households earning under $4,000 (59 percent of black, versus 55 percent of white, households in that category were female-headed).

Accordingly, it appears incumbent on us to propose also an alternative explanation than ethnicity for the mother—child dwelling unit. Murdock and Wilson themselves give the clue: 'the ultimate explanation must be sought in the social and economic conditions which gave rise to' the mother—child residential unit in Africa. We agree and shall attempt to delineate and explore these 'social and economic conditions'.

Thus, our proposed explanation of the mother—child residence will be rooted in contemporaneous social structural conditions — as were our suggested Conditions for the emergence and persistence of the mother-headed family. While these two mother—child forms of the household arise among quite different types of societies, they do share two common elements, we suggest. These are: (1) that the woman has the chance for a relatively autonomous subsistence contribution, i.e. that she be able to participate in production and control the allocation of at least a part of the fruits of her labours — or derive an equivalent amount of power from her embodiment of autonomous resources other than her own labour power (for example, she may retain control of part of the bridewealth she costs her husband's kin group, or represent a needed politico-military alliance, or inherit from her own kin group); and (2) that those in control of the larger political economy find it in their interests that she be maintained in a specifically mother—child household unit. The two forms immediately part company in that the mother-headed family is just that; whereas even though the woman in the mother—child dwelling may have a 'home of one's own', to paraphrase Woolf (1929) once again, she is part of a larger polygynous household of which she is not the head.

This brings us to general polygyny, which we consider the key structural commonality uniting instances of mother-child dwelling unit. (Murdock and Wilson themselves suggest that among the social and economic conditions which gave rise to this household form are 'the widespread occurrence of polygyny and slavery, both of which are appreciably more prevalent in Negro Africa than in any other major region of the world'. In this regard, we have found that the mother—child dwelling sometimes occurs — even in Africa — in societies without slavery, but never to our knowledge in the absence of polygyny.)

Specifically, we expect the mother—child residence to be most common: (1) where women are concentrated (especially as producers; see below) by general polygyny; (2) in the home territory of the husband's kin (i.e. marital residence with husband's kin, and/or patrilineal descent); and (3) where women make a substantial contribution to the husband's kin's subsistence resources (either by her own labour, or resources she embodies or controls).

Statistically, these conditions are expected to be more common among societies practising extensive hoe horticulture than among societies involved in other modes of subsistence. Here, the data of the Ethnographic Atlas reveal that women are important contributors to this subsistence economy world-wide (men are the dominant labour force in only 16 percent of the world's extensive hoe cultivation societies). This may be so because the demands of hoe horticulture do not seem to conflict with simultaneous child-care responsibilities (Brown, 1970; Blumberg, 1974b). Moreover, most horticultural societies are at intermediate levels of societal development. They already have begun the route to stratification and societal complexity, we suggest, by attempting to increase production beyond the food and replacement stock needs of the group. In other words, they are attempting to realize the superior production potential of extensive hoe horticulture (versus pre- or incipiently agricultural modes of production) by deliberate efforts to produce and accumulate surplus.

Elsewhere, we have argued that the concentration of producers in a high complexity family and the elaboration of the unilineal descent group are social organizational forms that flourish at intermediate levels of societal complexity — after the beginning of deliberate surplus accumulation, but before the individuation of property and the growing power of the state combine to give youth subsistence opportunities not tied to family-controlled resources while undermining the economic basis of the corporate descent group (Blumberg and Winch, 1972, 1973; Blumberg et al., 1974). So too, we suggest, with mother—child residence.

The entire package we have been discussing — residence with husband's kin (and an associated phenomenon, payment of bridewealth to the wife's kin group for the loss of her services); unilineal corporate descent groups predominantly on the patri- side; the importance of extensive hoe horticulture; a high contribution of women to subsistence production; and their concentration as producers in general polygyny — all tend to go together, at the predicted intermediate levels of societal complexity, in Africa. And Africa, of course, is where most instances of mother—child residence are found. We argue that it is the 'package' and not the 'ethnic location' that influences mother—child residence.

To rephrase, if a woman who has a certain amount of strategic power by virtue of her autonomous contribution to production, bridewealth vested in her, a political or military alliance she cements, or inheritance potential in her kin group is brought to her husband's kin residence and/ or descent group in a situation of general polygyny, there might well be a convergence of interest on the part of the woman and the husband's kin group in giving her the measure of independence represented by 'a home of one's own'. For the husband's kin group, there is the desirability of ensuring that her strategic resources (e.g. labour) remain within the group while keeping her from allying with others in a similar structural situation (e.g. the other co-wives in the household or village) and upsetting the household or kin group control structure.

For the women, it represents a gain in autonomy versus living with other co-wives under the husband's roof and facilitates individual accumulation of property. Missionaries' sermons to the contrary, the status of women under polygyny is not necessarily low, even though they tend to reside with the husband's kin group and have mere usufruct rights to the lands they cultivate. Often, however, they may dispose of surplus production and are in a position to amass wealth by production and/or trade. Sometimes, in addition, co-wives are able to unite and win important powers (as among the Lovedu, where the co-wives are cousins — see Murdock, 1949). Preventing such an occurrence may be behind not only the kin group's approval of separate residences for co-wives but also the two most common organizations of production under African hoe horticulture: the farming of scattered individual plots by individual women (see Kaberry, 1953) or more centralized activity under direct male supervision.

Indeed, we suggest the absence of a 'home of one's own' under conditions of general polygyny may mean that the women are not important producers and/or holders of other strategic resources. Then separate units will be unnecessary, and the husband's discipline, backed by community sanction, should keep co-wives in line.

One other possible reason for the absence of a separate residence for co-wives is *sororal* polygyny. Women raised as sisters presumably are able to cooperate under the same roof, the argument goes (see Stephens, 1963). Also, we might add, sisters are biologically unlikely to be numerous enough to constitute the threat of a producer alliance. It would seem then that there are two basic solutions to the problem of general polygyny: separate residence in the case of non-sisters, and the same dwelling for sister co-wives. Looking at sororal polygyny worldwide (using EA data not shown here) we find 65 instances of sisters sharing a residence (none of these in Africa or the adjacent Circum-Mediterranean region) versus 17 cases of sisters with separate dwellings (all but 3 in Africa). Interestingly enough, our contention that female producers should be more likely to be separately housed is borne out: the subsistence contribution of women in societies where the sisters are housed separately is much higher, on the average, than in the societies where sister co-wives share their husband's roof. The situation is parallel for non-sororal polygyny: separate residence goes with a greater probability that the society in question will have a female-dominated sexual division of labour. Although the figures on sororal versus non-sororal polygyny illustrate that Africa and the Circum-Mediterranean seem to have hit upon the nonsister—separate residence 'solution' to general polygyny while peoples in the other regions with general polygyny have opted for common housing of sisters, the correlation of separate residence with female subsistence production seems more revealing than that with region.

In fact, we predict a positive correlation between female importance in subsistence and mother—child residence, world-wide, and we find it: Table 6 Part A shows a (significant) gamma of 0.45. While this is only moderate compared to the 0.8 or better gammas (not shown) between mother—child residence and (a) marital residence, (b) bridewealth, and (c) descent, we predict that it is not spurious.

To summarize to this point, we have predicted general polygyny and residence with husband's unilineal kin as the common elements in situations of mother—child residence. We have found that general polygyny, due to a coding artifact in the EA, is a prerequisite for mother—child residence, while residence with husband's (unilineal) kin group occurs in 94 percent of the cases of mother—child dwellings. Moreover, 87 percent of the mother—child residence societies fall into the highest category of brideprice, and 61 percent of them are dependent on extensive hoe cultivation as their dominant subsistence activity. Strong as these relationships are, we feel that when they are applied as controls, they will not wash out the basic relationship between a sexual division of labour in which women are important and the provision of separate mother—child dwellings. Nor, we argue, will holding region constant by examining only African cases eliminate the relationship, even though 71 percent of all EA African societies have mother—child residences.

So as our first test of our notion of the conditions under which co-wives are given a 'home of one's own', we predict that the relationship between sexual division of labour and mother—child residence will hold up when we apply successive controls from the rest of the 'package' — including limiting the test to Africa, where the 'package' characterizes the overwhelming majority of societies. First, we control by eliminating

TABLE 6

Testing the Relationship of Sexual Division of Labour with Mother–Child Residence for Spuriousness

PART A. The basic relationship worldwide
Sexual division of labour in the dominant subsistence activity

Household	Labour Force				Female contribution to subsistence
	Male dominant	Intermediate	Female dominant	Total	Averge score*
Mother–child	14.3% (56)	28.5% (65)	39.9% (112)	(233)	40.9% $\gamma=0.45$
Other	85.6 (335)	71.5 (163)	60.1 (169)	(667) $\Sigma=900$	32.4
					$(x^2=51.2,2\mathrm{df},p<0.00001)$

PART B. Sex division of labour – Mother–child residence among societies with (a) general polygyny in (b) Africa

	Male dominant	Intermediate	Female dominant	Total	Average score
Mother–child	75.0% (36)	88.7% (47)	92.7% (102)	87.7% (185)	45.1% $\gamma=0.46$
Other	25.0 (12)	11.3 (6)	7.3 (8)	12.3 (26) $\Sigma=211$	38.5
					$(x^2=9.8,2\mathrm{df},p=0.0075)$

PART C. The relationship among societies with (a) general Polygyny in (b) Africa practising (c) extensive horticulture having (d) marital residence among husbands' kin; and (e) highest brideprice.

	Male dominant	Intermediate	Female dominant	Total	Average score
Mother–child	62.5% (10)	84.0% (21)	92.5% (74)	(105)	48.3% $\gamma=0.59$
Other	37.5 (6)	16.0 (4)	7.5 (6)	(16) $\Sigma=121$	41.9
					$(x^2=8.1,2\mathrm{df},p=0.0177)$

PART D. The relationship among societies with (a) general polygyny in (b) Africa practising (c) extensive horticulture having (d) descent = patrilineal, and (e) highest brideprice

	Male dominant	Intermediate	Female dominant	Total	Average score
Mother–child	61.5% (8)	85.7% (18)	92.3% (60)	(86)	48.1% $\gamma=0.57$
Other	38.5 (5)	14.3 (3)	7.7 (5)	(13) $\Sigma=99$	40.7
					$(x^2=6.5,2\mathrm{df},p=0.0387)$

* This is an index composed of female contribution to five subsistence activities: gathering, hunting, fishing, herding and agriculture. A score of 40.0 would indicate that women did a total of 40 percent of the work in their society's subsistence base (and that the males socre would be 60 percent). Worldwide, for the societies of the EA the median female contribution to subsistence is around 37 percent.

societies lacking general polygyny, since EA coding categories make it impossible for them to be coded as having the mother—child dwelling form. At this point, we also drop non-African societies, predicting that even within African societies with general polygyny, mother—child residence is more likely where women are important subsistence producers. Table 6, Part B shows that the gamma remains the same in absolute value (0.46), and even though we have dropped from 900 to 211 cases by our joint controls, the relationship remains significant.

To summarize the presentation of a whole series of control tables, we shall now (in Table 6, Part C) add three additional controls: residence with husband's kin; highest level bridewealth (either substantial brideprice or exchange of women); and extensive hoe horticulture as the dominant subsistence base. This brings us down to 121 cases, but produces a gamma of 0.59, which remains significant.

Finally, we present Part D of Table 6 just to show what happens when patrilineal descent is substituted for marital residence with husband's kin in the series of controls used in Part C. Since marital residence is with husband's kin even in the situation of matrilineal descent with avunculocal residence (i.e. where the groom goes to live with *his* mother's brother), we end up with fewer cases than in Part C — only 99. But the gamma is still 0.57, and still significant, although at a somewhat reduced level.

In sum, restricting our attention to societies within Africa characterized by the variables we have identified as strongly associated with mother—child residence, we have confirmed our prediction. The relationship between the importance of women's contribution to subsistence production and mother—child dwelling has not washed out.

A second test is possible of our notion of the determinants of a 'home of one's own' for co-wives using Automatic Interaction Detector (AID) analysis (Sonquist et al., 1971). AID is a computer search strategy programme that requires few assumptions about the data. In particular, it does not require additivity or linearity. We shall be predicting to a variable, mother—child residence, which we propose to be curvilinearly related to societal complexity, and will include a number of these societal complexity variables as predictors.[26]

We begin by restricting the AID run to societies with general polygyny.

Of the 1,170 societies of the Ethnographic Atlas, 564 have general polygyny. This then, is our potential maximum N. However, AID in its basic version requires that every case have a value on every variable under analysis. If a case lacks an observation on any variable (and one is unwilling to assign some mean score), the case must be omitted. Following this procedure, and entering the list of predictors to be discussed below, we emerged with an N of 273 societies on which to test our ideas as to the major variables found in the EA which influence the mother–child household.

First, to measure the potential resources which might win a separate house for a co-wife, we include three variables: sexual division of labour in the dominant subsistence activity; bridewealth; and inheritance of moveable property. The EA contains codes on the inheritance of both real property and moveable property. We chose moveable property because of the large (and expected) association of mother–child residence with residence with husband's kin. So if the woman is to inherit something that can be easily convertible to a resource relevant for the husband's kin group, it would seem necessary to be portable (e.g. money, tools, herds, slaves) rather than fixed (e.g. land, coconut palms). Our reasoning was that if co-wives were important in subsistence production, commanded a high brideprice (especially if some of it remained in the women's rather than their parents' control, which unfortunately is not specified in the EA codes), and were persons to or through whom moveable property was inherited, they would be more likely to be housed separately.

Secondly, to measure the fact that mother–child residence is much more likely where the co-wife joins the husband's kin group, we chose two variables: prevalent marital residence, and system of descent.

Thirdly, to tap a variable which is important in determining the sexual division of labour, the level of societal complexity, and in fact many of the other variables in this analysis, we include subsistence economy as our basic measure of the techno-economic base.

Fourthly, we measure various additional indicators of societal complexity, in keeping with our prediction that the mother–child residence phenomenon is most prevalent at intermediate levels of societal complexity, i.e. is curvilinearly related with what we may term 'evolutionary' variables. Those we include are: stratification, political complexity, number of craft-specialized occupations, and permanence of settlement. These four indexes of societal complexity complete our basic list of ten predictors.

But, lurking at the sidelines, is the potentially confounding variable of region (i.e. is it really an ethnically black African phenomenon?). We have argued that 'Africa' seems to stand for a summary or surrogate measure of a whole package of traits (of which the residence, descent, brideprice, and subsistence economy *predictors,* the general polygyny *filter,* and the mother–child *dependent* variable are components) which go together for functional rather than racial or even geographic diffusion reasons. To test this idea, we propose to run AID twice, once without region included among the predictors, and then again with it. If we are right, the total percentage of variance explained should not be significantly less when region is eliminated from the analysis.

The results confirm our expectation. To be sure, the same (rather high) percentage of variance is explained in each of the two AID runs: without region, our predictors of mother–child residence explain 58.13 percent of the variance (where R^2 is calculated by dividing the 'between' sum of squares by the 'total' sum of squares). On the other hand, with region included, the AID explains 57.99 percent of the variance. However, as a comparison of Figures 1 and 2 will reveal, the decision to incorporate or exclude region changes the appearance of the branching 'tree' that is AID's distinctive hallmark. Both AID runs begin with the basic group of 273 cases of general polygynist societies which contain data on each of the predictor variables as well as mother–child residence, the dependent variable. Among these 273 societies, 64.1 percent have separate mother–child residence for co-wives. From this point, the trees generated by AID with and without region diverge. Let us follow each in turn, as the programme attempts to isolate the highest versus lowest branches, i.e. those leading to the group of societies maximally and minimally likely (respectively) to have separate mother–child dwellings.

First we shall consider the AID run from which region was excluded. The first branch is formed by splitting the 273 into two groups on the basis of *subsistence economy.* Those with extensive hoe horticulture, herding, or intensive agriculture with or without irrigation are put into

Figure 1.

Aid Tree for Mother–Child Residence Among Societies with General Polygyny, Region Excluded

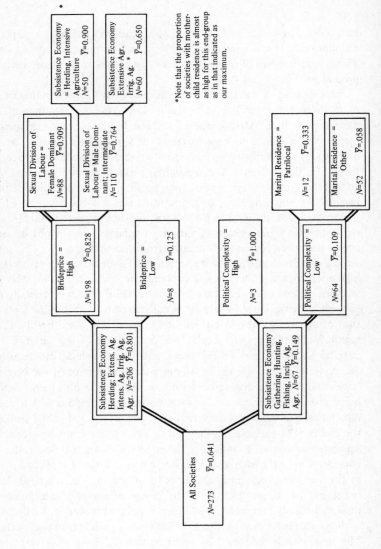

*Note that the proportion of societies with mother-child residence is almost as high for this end-group as in that indicated as our maximum.

All Societies
N=273 $\bar{Y}$=0.641

Subsistence Economy Herding; Extens. Ag. Intens. Ag. Irrig. Ag. N=206 $\bar{Y}$=0.801

Subsistence Economy Gathering, Hunting, Fishing, Incip. Ag. Agr. N=67 $\bar{Y}$=0.149

Brideprice = High
N=198 $\bar{Y}$=0.828

Brideprice = Low
N=8 $\bar{Y}$=0.125

Political Complexity = High
N=3 $\bar{Y}$=1.000

Political Complexity = Low
N=64 $\bar{Y}$=0.109

Sexual Division of Labour = Female Dominant
N=88 $\bar{Y}$=0.909

Sexual Division of Labour = Male Dominant; Intermediate
N=110 $\bar{Y}$=0.764

Marital Residence = Patrilocal
N=12 $\bar{Y}$=0.333

Marital Residence = Other
N=52 $\bar{Y}$=.058

Subsistence Economy = Herding, Intensive Agriculture *
N=50 $\bar{Y}$=0.900

Subsistence Economy Extensive Agr. Irrig. Ag. *
N=60 $\bar{Y}$=0.650

Figure 2.

Aid Tree for Mother–Child Residence among Societies with General Polygyny, Region Included

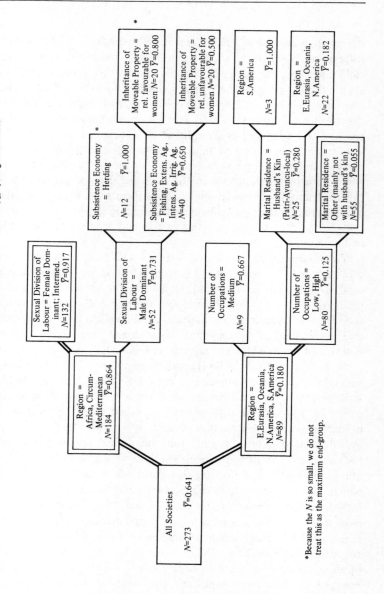

*Because the *N* is so small, we do not treat this as the maximum end-group.

the upper branch (N = 206, 80 percent with mother–child units) which will eventually isolate the societies *most* likely to have separate mother–child dwellings for co-wives. Let us follow this upper branch to its apex – the group having the highest incidence of mother–child residence. The next split is on the *brideprice* variable, with eight societies having the two lowest brideprice categories (token exchange of gifts, or total absence of brideprice) being split away. (These, as we had expected, have a lower incidence of mother–child residence.) The main upper branch next divides on *sexual division of labour,* separating societies where females predominate in the main subsistence activity from all others. These 88 female-labour societies form an 'end group' in that no other meaningful sub-branches are split off from them. And we find that fully 91 percent of the societies in this end group have the mother–child household.[27]

To summarize the results of this first AID tree, from which region was excluded, we explained 58 percent of the variance with ten predictors, with subsistence economy explaining the greater part, and – as predicted – sexual division of labour figuring in the determination of the maximum occurrence of mother–child dwelling units. (Appendix A gives a summary of the explained variance and note 27 gives a further synopsis of the remainder of the tree in Figure 1.)

Now we turn to the AID tree where region was included. Here, the first split is not on subsistence economy, but rather on region. Thus, the sample is split into two groups: an African and Circum-Mediterranean group of 184 societies, 86 percent of which have the mother–child household, comprising an upper branch; and a lower branch of 89 polygynous societies from the other four main world regions (East Eurasia, Insular Pacific, North America, South America, in accordance with Murdock's method of dividing the world; see Murdock, 1967), among which only 15 percent have the mother–child family. Let us once again follow the upper branch to its apex. In fact, that apex is reached in the next step, when the tree branches on sexual division of labour. The 132 societies with either female-dominated or intermediate labour forces constitute our maximum mother–child end group, in which 92 percent of the peoples have mother–child units.[28] Thus, for this tree, region emerged as the factor explaining the majority of the variance (see

Appendix A for a summary of this explained variance, and note 28 for a review of the remaining branches of the tree in Figure 2). However, to reiterate, the fact that analysis without region explained an equal percentage of variance (58 percent, the same as for the run including region) seems to indicate that region is serving as a shorthand symbol for the joint occurrence there of the sorts of variables we have referred to as our 'package'.

Let us review once again what the top-most branch of each of the two AID trees revealed about the maximum occurrence of mother–child residence. First, let us recall that the analysis was confined to groups practising general polygyny – nine-tenths of whom have residence with husband's kin. The maximum branch of the tree in Figure 1 (region excluded) split first on subsistence economy, and then selected societies with relatively higher brideprice, in which women are the primary labour force in the dominant subsistence activity. Incidentally, these turn out to be mainly extensive horticulturalists. In short, the pattern of results seem rather supportive of our paradigm that suggests co-wives are most likely to be housed separately when they make a contribution too important to be ignored – or forgone – to the resources of the group controlling the means of production. The maximum branch of the tree in Figure 2 (region included) split first on region. Then among the African and Circum-Mediterranean groups, it reached its top value among societies in which the sexual division of labour in the dominant subsistence activity was either predominantly female or relatively equal by gender. So here too our predicted sex variable emerges.

As a final point to this section of the paper dealing with the mother–child dwelling unit, it seems we have rendered untenable an interpretation based on race. First, we showed that mother–child residence was correlated with a number of conditions that were indeed more prevalent in Africa. Next, however, we showed that what we viewed as the substantively important correlation between sexual division of labour and mother–child residence held up within Africa, and even when these other factors were held constant (Table 6). Finally, using a different type of analysis (AID) to predict to mother–child residence, we explained the same percentage of variance (58 percent) whether region was included or excluded as a predictor. Moreover, we found that both the region-included and region-excluded AID 'trees' led directly to the importance of women as subsistence producers.

SUMMARY AND CONCLUSIONS

To recapitulate briefly, we have analyzed two very different types of mother—child household — the female-headed family most prevalent among the economically marginal in wage labour societies — and the mother—child residential unit found among societies with general polygyny and residence with the husband's kin or descent group. In both of these cases the literature has identified race (being 'ethnically Negro') as an explanatory factor, with economic variables playing a subsidiary role. Instead, for both of these types of mother—child family, we have managed to eliminate any effect of race, while highlighting the importance of the relationship of the *woman* to her society's mode of production as crucial for the *genesis* of the mother—child family form in question. For its *persistence,* we have speculated, we must look to the degree to which the mother—child household serves the interest of those who control the society's political economy.

NOTES

1. In a less blatant form, the writings about the 'culture of poverty' also blame the victim (see Valentine, 1968, for a devastating critique of the 'culture of poverty' literature). And to Oscar Lewis, who originated the 'culture of poverty' approach, one of its characteristics is matrifocality. Since Lewis was not studying blacks, and claims cross-cultural validity for his approach, this represents an

extension of the *racial* social pathology focus to a world-wide non-racial perspective. Adherents of this approach from the liberal Lewis (see especially 1966) to the ultra-conservative Banfield (1970) may point to structural conditions (e.g. high unemployment rates, low wages) as influences in creating the poor. But what keeps them poor, these authors argue, is their self-perpetuating culture of poverty. Nonetheless, matrifocal families play a less central role in the transmission of poverty in this approach than in that of Moynihan (discussed below).

2. According to Greenfield, 'the sugar industry has developed to the limits of the present level of technology and cannot be expanded by capital investment (pp. 69-70).

3. Although he does not name it, Greenfield has invoked the spectre of 'Galton's problem', which has haunted anthropology since Galton first proposed in 1889 that a relationship may appear in various places by accidental joint diffusion from a common source. Naroll, one of those most concerned with putting Galton to rest, has published various solutions to the problem, but does not claim diffusion distorts basic, 'core' relationships between social and economic structure (see, e.g. Naroll, 1970, 1973; Erickson, 1973). The volume of evidence on covariation of economy and family structure, we argue, is too great to consider that the relationship 'may not be a necessary one' (p. 168) just because both elements came from England.

4. The Blumberg–Winch study utilized an Automatic Interaction Director (AID) computer analysis which explained 40 percent of the variance in a dichotomized measure of family structural complexity.

5. She writes (1970b) of how a social unit possessing a 'culture of poverty' is perpetuated by the role it plays in maintaining the larger political economy, but does not consider how the larger political economy might uphold the matrifocal family of the poor living in the 'culture of poverty'. In the same article, her explication of the 'neoteric society' concept emphasizes that whole nations as well as subgroups within them may be marginal and relatively powerless vis-à-vis a larger system: a world economy in the case of certain Third World societies, and the dominant group and state in the case of marginal subgroups.

6. Gonzalez includes under domestic domain, 'concern with socialization of the young, nutrition, protection and nurturing of group members, health and disease, and so on'. It is less clear what she includes under the jural domain, which apparently includes not just the formal legal system, but also the non-household occupational (and perhaps political) system.

7. She cites Banfield's (1958) description of 'amoral (nuclear) familism' in which no mention is made of female-headed families, but there are indications of low subsistence opportunities for females, and the remnants of an earlier feudal, patrilineal system which may influence inheritance patterns. In other situations where women contribute little to subsistence, but where family resources are concentrated in the uterine line, the male present need not be the husband but perhaps the woman's brother or uncle — or adult son.

8. Elsewhere (Blumberg and Winch, 1973; Blumberg et al. 1974), we have discussed three major components of the mode of production: the subsistence technology, the division of labour, and the social relations of production. The first two are jointly considered the 'forces of production', in distinction to the 'social relations of production' in many Marxian definitions (see, e.g. Edwards, 1972:50).

9. Females might occasionally emerge as heads of three-generation families under some unusual corporate family circumstances (e.g. in mother—daughter matrilineal inheritance systems, which are extremely rare; or in the instances where the widow in a patrilineal inheritance system retains control of her husband's assets — these more frequently pass to the sons (as in India) or husband's brother, without the widow becoming family head).

10. If female-headed units are not viable, they are short-lived. Either they split up or are reabsorbed into some other unit (e.g. the woman's parental home), or they do not survive. Starvation among the underclass has been present, at least periodically, in most agrarian or more complex societies; whereas comprehensive welfare systems have been available in only a few.

11. Boserup (1974:18) notes: 'In most developing countries . . . nearly all of the women employed in urban areas do part time domestic work or are engaged in such activities as crafts, home industries or trade. In these home-based occupations it is possible to continue childbearing and earning wages. In fact, children, from an early age, can contribute to such enterprises'.

12. Folklore has it that rich heiresses and successful Hollywood actresses are the most multiply divorced groups of females in the US. If true, it may in part reflect the low resource gap between these women and their mates. For a more general discussion of relative resources of each spouse and domestic power, see Scanzoni, 1972.

13. These comments concerning surplus labour are more applicable to Asia (and to a certain extent, parts of Latin America), with their plow-agriculture agrarian base, than to Sub-Saharan Africa, where the traditional subsistence base was (and still is for the most part) hoe-horticulture. Surplus labour populations under traditional conditions seem generally confined to the more complex, stratified, and urbanized agrarian systems.

14. It may be that the sorts of exchange networks described for lower income marginal groups, and especially their component mother-headed families (see, e.g. Stack, 1970, 1974 for the US; Peattie, 1968 for Ciudad Guayana, Venezuela) require the input of at least some surplus in order to be viable. Otherwise, with no surplus in the system, and some members falling below zero net available resources, the network might increase the level of general hardship without necessarily saving the worst off members — and collapse. The visible numbers of little shoe-shine/errand boys on the streets of certain Third World cities are sometimes popularly attributed to a two-step process of poverty and abandonment: the father leaving the mother, and she leaving the eldest male child to more or less shift for himself. The family origins and reasons for homelessness of such

children constitute empirical questions, but in the absence of general welfare it can be speculated that the failure or absence of the exchange network might be associated with such outcomes.

15. According to Sackrey (1973:92-93). 'the number of families receiving AFDC funds more than doubled during the 1960s, though it had increased by only 17 percent during the 1950s; and in New York and California, the rise during the 1960s was even greater than the national average, with most of the increase occurring after 1965'. A summary of Sackrey's figures taken from the *Statistical Abstract of the United States*, 1971, p. 271, shows total government expenditures on public aid to the poor at $4.1 billion in 1960; 6.3 in 1965; 8.8 in 1967; and 13.2 in 1969. Urban riots began in 1964, although clearly other factors also influenced the dramatic post-1965 increase in welfare expenditures.

16. Sackrey notes of the Piven and Cloward argument that it 'also explains the relatively low welfare payments in southern states. Since wages in the South are relatively low, it is necessary, in order to regulate the labour force, to keep welfare payments below local wages so that when jobs do appear, welfare recipients can be forced into them at wages higher than their welfare payments' (p. 112). On the other hand, one can argue that low and stringent Southern welfare and unemployment benefits encouraged migration at a time of massive agricultural mechanization and displacement of the rural agricultural population. Piven and Cloward cite a Presidential Commission on Rural Poverty finding that in only 15 years, between 1950-65, US farm output rose by 45 percent while farm employment fell 45 percent. Accompanying this has been a great wave of rural—urban migration. With both wage and welfare rates more attractive in the North, many black farm families (4 million since 1940) joined the tide. Especially in the 1960s when black voting first became a realistic possibility in the South, a welfare policy that encouraged migration must have seemed attractive to local officials (see note 18 below).

17. Despite official rhetoric of equal opportunity, 'schools are financed in such a way that they invest far more in the children of the rich than in the children of the poor . . . tracking and curriculum serve to sort and select children in such a way that the children of blue-collar occupations . . . and the children of the elite will be socialized for positions consonant with their class or origin'. Levin writes (1973:9). To some critics, none the less, these inequalities are the result of 'institutional mindlessness'. Instead, Levin suggests, in a stable social setting the schools' activities 'will correspond to and serve the social, economic, and political relations' of the larger society. We apply Levin's 'principle of correspondence' to the long-established policies of the welfare sector.

18. Welfare is largely funded by Washington, but the states are primarily responsible for the programmes and rates paid; administration is state or local (see Handler, 1972 for a good general discussion). States run the unemployment compensation programmes pretty much as they see fit. With AFDC, 'local government exercised most of the control and paid only about 10 percent of the cost;

the states virtually exercised the rest of the control and paid only about one-third of the cost' (Handler, p. 116). Examples of conflicting interests are many. For instance, the interests of some politicians in a Southern state in keeping welfare rates so low as to encourage out-migration of displaced black agricultural labourers who now have become actual or potential voters may conflict with those of a manufacturing city in the state which may favour a somewhat less penurious standard so as to insure that enough of a surplus labour force remains to take care of fluctuations in local labour needs at low costs to local industry. Conversely, Northern cities and states may want a shrinking gap between Northern and Southern benefit levels so as to stem the tide of migration, and more federal money to help keep welfare and unemployment payments high enough to stave off urban unrest without bankrupting them.

    19. US Department of Labour (1973:8) figures show:

Of the 6,191,000 families headed by women in March 1972, 2,100,000 or 34 percent, had incomes below the poverty line in 1971. The comparable proportion for families with a male head was 7 percent. Among those female-head families where there were related children under age 18, 45 percent were poor. Of those families where the related children numbered five or more, 76 percent were poor. About one-fourth (27 percent) of all white female-head families had incomes below the low-income level in 1971, but more than half (54 percent) of all black female-head families had this little income. Thirty-seven percent of the white female-head families with related children under age 18 were poor in 1971; the comparable proportion for black female-head families was 60 percent.

In this context, it is interesting to note Stein's statistic that three-fifths of female-headed families with children were receiving some welfare assistance. In fact, as Stein's data show, female-headed families are becoming a larger proportion of the below-the-poverty-line population: 'In 1969, 47 of every 100 poor families with children were headed by women. In 1959, the proportion was 28 out of 100'.

    20. The notion of a dual job market has been an important new development in economic theory (see Gordon, 1972, for an excellent discussion and numerous references). Here, we find the ill-paid, often unstable jobs of the secondary labour force; jobs that lead nowhere: 'they are not connected to job ladders of any sort' (Gordon, 1972:45). They often are in small, non-concentrated industries with low and volatile profit margins, high labour intensivity, elastic demand, and intense competition; and even when they are not, women, minority groups, and those with low education are disproportionately found holding them. These findings are supported by the results of the University of Michigan five-year longitudinal study (Morgan et al., 1974) of the factors influencing economic well-being among 5,000 US families. They found that most of the major determinants of well-being were beyond individual control – e.g. sex, race, education and age. However, it turned out that 'family composition change is the

most important of all the variables we included in our analysis of changed well-being'. Partly for this reason, there proved to be a considerable and surprising amount of movement in and out of poverty: 'Only 9 percent of the 5,000 families were in the bottom fifth of the income distribution in each of the five years. On the other hand, 35 percent of the families were in the bottom fifth during at least one of the five years' (Chapman, 1974, reporting on the study). Concerning the relationship between sex of the household head and being consistently in poverty, the study found that: 'A family's chance of being persistently poor is about twice as great if the head is a woman' (Morgan et al.:336).

21.   An Accion en Venezuela study (1969) cites figures that show 32.8 percent of the Caracas 1966 population of 1,720,000 lived in shacktowns. Since then both urban population and proportion living in shacktowns have grown, with informal estimates ranging from a low of 'at least one-third' to figures approaching 40 percent. In contrast, in 1954, the city's population was only 900,000, with only 12.5 percent living in the barrios. Not all barrio residents are poor, but income in them averages well under the city average, and moreover, the dependency ratio is higher than for the total Caracas population: 53.61 percent (in an Accion 1968 sample survey discussed in the study) proved to be below the age of 14. With respect to unemployment, 1968 Accion surveys found 27 percent unemployment in one large complex of shacktowns (Catia) and 20 percent in another (Petare); the report also estimated that at least an equal proportion in each could be classed as underemployed.

22.   The problem of possible sample bias introduced by the quota sampling in the shacktowns (80 percent of our 500 cases) is complex. The original aim was to sample roughly 150 each employed, underemployed and unemployed heads of household in the barrios, and supplement these with 50 cases of heads out of the labour force completely. Attrition resulted in 468 completed interviews, which show the following percentage distribution by sex of head, shacktown–nonshacktown, and labour force status:

| | Sex of Head of House | | | |
| | Female | | Male | |
WORK STATUS	Shacktown(%)	Nonshack(%)	Shacktown(%)	Nonshack(%)
Employed	17	40	42	68
Underemployed	20	4	32	16
Willing to work	25	4	24	9
Not wanting to work	38	52	2	7
Total:	89	25	311	75 (500)

First, let us note that as phrased, the unemployed category is actually a 'willingness to work' category; and second, we observe that shacktown male heads have a negligible rate of being out of the labour force entirely (not willing to work). Was it necessary for the interviewers to look for female heads to reach the goal of roughly 10 percent quota of shacktown interviewees who were out of the labour force? We see that comparing percentages of *currently working* female heads, the nonshacktown women have the higher proportion (44 percent versus 37 percent); but they have very low unemployment rates. So the totals for the potential labour force groups are quite discrepant: 62 percent of shacktown women versus 48 percent of nonshacktown women. Since in the analyses that follow, we use figures only for women currently working, the randomly sampled non-barrio female heads (who turned out to be a very similar proportion of total household heads as the quota-sampled barrio population, we further recall) have a rate not that much higher than their barrio sisters. Incidentally, other figures (not shown) indicate that the barrio female heads are proportionately poorer and less educated than the males of their group, than is the case among nonshacktown female versus male heads. In sum, even though the figures hint that proportion of shacktown females currently working might be understated by the quota sampling, the non-random nature of 80 percent of the sample means that all our findings must be interpreted with extreme caution.

23. Venezuela's population is much younger than that of the United States (half are under 15). And since their female labour force rate is based on females age 10 and up, the figure turns out to be misleadingly low. As it happens, not quite two-thirds of Venezuelan females 10 or over who are not in the labour force are listed as actually being 'in the house', almost all the remaining third are students (Encuesta del Hogar, 1970).

24. Actually, rerunning the tables controlled for shacktown (quota-sampled) versus nonshacktown (randomly sampled) did not change the picture, although the 25 nonshacktown female heads had even fewer young children than their 89 barrio sisters: among both groups, female heads have higher rates of current employment than the wives in virtually every age-of-child category.

25. With respect to age, rerunning the tables controlling for shacktown–nonshacktown shows that shacktown female heads are considerably older than either their male counterparts or their sisters in unions. For the nonshacktown sample, we find that heads of both sexes are older than their counterparts in the barrios, but that the difference between male and female heads almost disappears. However, the nonshacktown female heads are older than the nonshacktown wives, so in general the basic pattern remains supported. Harking back to Greenfield's findings on the prevalence in his Barbados population of the 'grandmother family' of female heads over 60, we find that only one-fifth of the nonshacktown female heads and about one-eighth of the barrio women are 60 or older.

26. Accordingly, at this point we prefer AID to more sophisticated forms of analysis such as path analysis which would require us to make a number of

probably unwarranted assumptions about the EA data. Although AID is a search strategy program, it can be used when one has a good idea of what to look for, i.e. when one has a theoretically-derived list of predictor variables which one proposes will explain a significant proportion of the variance in the dependent variable. As we shall show, that is the case with us. Moreover, when one has a definite paradigm or hypotheses in mind, it is not necessary to randomly dichotomize the sample and run it twice as a check on significant relationships appearing by chance, the procedure used when AID is run as a 'fishing expedition'.

27. There is one other sub-branch which is almost as high on this upper section of the tree. It is formed from the group of societies with male-dominated or intermediate sexual division of labour by another split on the subsistence economy variable. Societies with herding or intensive agriculture as their dominant subsistence base (N = 50) prove to have mother–child residence in 90 percent of these 50 cases. (The final end group on the upper tree is composed of 60 irrigation or extensive horticulture societies, in which 65 percent have mother–child dwellings.)

The lower branch of the tree contains 67 gathering, hunting, fishing or incipient agricultural societies of which only 15 percent have the mother–child unit. After dropping two high-political-complexity societies with mother–child residence, the computer splits the remainder (with low political complexity) on the variable of marital residence. Twelve societies with patrilocal residence are split away from the emergent minimum mother–child sub-branch; three have mother–child dwellings. The remaining 52 societies constitute our 'minimum mother–child family' end group – only 3 cases of the 52 (6 percent) have this household form.

28. Following out the remainder of the upper branch of Figure 2, we start with the sub-branch involving the male-dominated division of labour. It next splits on subsistence economy, where 12 herding societies, all with mother–child residence, are distinguished from the remaining 40 (fishing, extensive horticultural, intensive or irrigated agricultural groups). These 40 split into two end groups of 20 each on the variable of inheritance of moveable property. Where inheritance is matrilineal, or 'other patrilineal heirs' are rewarded (Murdock, 1967, does not further specify, unfortunately) 80 percent of the 20 societies have mother–child residence; in the 20 where inheritance is either classically patrilineal or involves 'daughters receiving less than sons', the proportion with mother–child residence is only 50 percent. The inheritance categories in the former instance might favour women relatively more, thus giving them enough of a resource to justify separate residence, but the coding is not sufficiently explanatory to judge.

Last, we follow the lower branch to the end group of societies with the minimum proportion of mother–child residence. The 89 societies from the remaining four world regions are first split on political complexity to spin off 9 medium complex societies, which furthermore, have 1, 2 or 3 occupations organized as crafts (an intermediate level), and a somewhat higher proportion of mother–child residence. Next, the main lower branch continues with the lowest (no specialized occupations) and highest (four such crafts) complexity societies – in accordance with our suggestion that the mother–child family is maximal at intermediate levels of societal complexity. These high and low-complexity societies are next split on marital residence, where those 25 societies with patrilocal or avunculocal (both *husband's* kin) patterns – and more mother–child residence – are split off. The remainder constitute our *minimum* mother–child household group, where only 5.5 percent of the remaining 55 societies have this form. (The last split separates three South American societies, *all* of which have mother–child residence, from the remaining three world regions, a residual pool of 22 societies of which 18 percent have mother–child domiciles.)

REFERENCES

Acción en Venezuela (1969), 'Basic Population and Income Statistics on the Barrios of Caracas'. Caracas (mimeo).

Adams, Richard N. (1960), 'An Inquiry into the Nature of the Family', in Gertrude E. Dole and Robert L. Carneiro (eds), *Essays in the Science of Culture*. New York: Thomas Y. Crowell Company, pp. 33-49.

Aginsky, B. W. and E. G. Aginsky (1947), 'A Resultant of Intercultural Relations', *Social Forces* 26:84-87.

–– (1949), 'The Process of Change in Family Types: A Case Study', *American Anthropologist* 51:611-14.

Balswick, Jack O. and C. Paschalis (1973), 'The Effect of Urbanization Upon Household Structure in Cyprus'. University of Georgia (mimeo).

Banco Nacional de Ahorro y Prestamo (1971), *MERCAVI 70:Estudio del Mercado real de vivienda en Venezuela. Area Metropolitana de Caracas*.

Banfield, Edward C. (1958), *The Moral Basis of a Backward Society*. New York: The Free Press.

–– (1970), *The Unheavenly City*. Boston: Little, Brown.

Baran, Paul and Paul Sweezy (1966), *Monopoly Capital*. New York: Monthly Review Press.

Bart, Pauline B. (1974), Personal communication concerning unpublished study of divorced men in Cook County, Illinois.

Bascom, W. R. (1941), 'Acculturation Among the Bullah Negroes ', *American Anthropologist* **43**:43-50.

Bell, Norman W. and Ezra F. Vogel (1960), *Modern Introduction to the Family.* Glencoe, III.: The Free Press of Glencoe.

Billingsley, Andrew (1973), 'Black Family Structure: Myths and Realities", *Studies in Public Welfare: Joint Economic Committee.* Paper No. 12, part II.

Blumberg, Rae Lesser (1970), 'Societal Complexity and Familial Complexity: Inter- and Intra-societal Correlates of Family Structure, Functionality, and Influence'. Ph.D. dissertation, Northwestern University.

–– (1973), 'Social Structure, Women and Fertility in Latin America'. Paper presented at Latin American Population Conference (AID auspices), San Jose, Costa Rica.

–.– (1974a), 'The Erosion of Sexual Equality in the Kibbutz: Structural Factors Affecting the Status of Women', in Joan I. Roberts (ed.), *Women: Studies by Women Scholars* (tentative title). Madison: University of Wisconsin Press, forthcoming.

–– (1974b), 'Structural Factors Affecting Women's Status: A Cross-Societal Paredigm'. Paper read at the meetings of the International Sociological Association, Toronto.

Blumberg, Rae Lesser and Robert F. Winch (1973) 'The Rise and Fall of the Complex Family: Some Implications for an Evolutionary Theory of Societal Development'. Paper read at the meetings of the American Sociological Association, New York.

–– (1972), 'Societal Complexity and Familial Complexity: Evidence for the Curvilinear Hypothesis', *American Journal of Sociology* **77**:898-920. See also Vol. 78 (May, 1973):1522.

Blumberg, Rae Lesser, Robert F. Winch and Hazel H. Reinhardt (1974), 'Family Structure as Adaptive Strategy'. Paper read at the meetings of the American Sociological Association, Montreal.

Boserup, Ester (1974), 'Employment and Education: Keys to Smaller Families'. The Victor-Bostrum Fund Report, No.18, Spring.

Boyer, Ruth M. (1964), 'The Matrifocal Family Among the Mescalero: Additional Data', *American Anthropologist* **66**:593-602.

Brown, Judith K. (1970), 'A Note on the Division of Labour by Sex'. *American Anthropologist* **72**:1074-78.

Browning, Harley L. (1967), 'The Demography of the City', in Glenn H. Beyer (ed.), *The Urban Explosion in Latin America.* Ithace, N.Y.: Cornell University Press.

Calley, M. (1956), 'Economic Life of Mixed-Blood Communities in Northern New South Wales', *Oceania* **26**:200-13.

Campbell, A. A. (1943), 'St. Thomas Negroes – A Study of Personality and Culture'. *Psychological Monograph,* no. 55(5).

CEVEPOF and CISOR (1971), 'Survey of Family and Marginality', *Centro*

Venezolano de Poblacion y Familia. Caracas.
— — (1972), *El Status Occupacional de los Jefes de Hogares de Bajos Ingresos en Caracas:* Cordiplan.
Chapman, William (1974), 'Report Challenges War-on-Poverty Assumptions', *Washington Post Special*, p.32 in *Chicago Sun-Times*, 12 May, 1974.
CISOR (1969), 'Barrios Populares de Caracas: Inventario de sus Recursos para su Desarrollo'. Centro Latino Americano de Venezuela (CLAVE), Caracas, mimeo.
Cruickshank, J. Graham (1916), *Black Talk*, Demarara: Argosy Co.
Despres, Leo A. (1970), 'Differential Adaptations and Micro-cultural Evolution in Guyana', in Norman E. Whitten, Jr and John F. Szwed (eds), *Afro-American Anthropology: Contemporary Perspectives.* New York: The Free Press, pp. 263-88.
Edwards, R. C., M. Reich and T. E. Weisskopf (1972), *The Capitalist System.* New Jersey: Prentice-Hall.
Erickson, Edwin F. (1973), 'Beyond Galton's Problem, or Rethinking Blue Butterflies'. Paper read at the meetings of the American Anthropological Association, New Orleans.
Farley, Reynolds (1975), 'Family Types and Family Headship: A Comparison of Trends Among Blacks and Whites'. The University of Michigan Population Studies Centre, Department of Sociology (mimeo). Paper read at the meetings of the American Sociological Association.
Frazier, E. Franklin (1939), *The Negro Family in the United States.* Chicago: University of Chicago Press.
— — (1950, 'Problems and Needs of Negro Children and Youth Resulting from Family Disorganization', *Journal of Negro Education* Summer: 270-77.
Geertz, Hildred (1959), 'The Vocabulary of Emotion', *Journal for the Study of Interpersonal Processes* 22:225.
Gonzalez, Nancy Solien de (1959), 'The Consanguineal Household Among the Black Carib of Central America'. Ph.D. dissertation, University of Michigan.
— — (1969), *Black Carib Household Structure.* Seattle and London: University of Washington Press.
— — (1970a), 'Toward a definition of matrifocality', in Norman E. Whitten Jr and John F. Szwed (eds), *Afro-American Anthropology: Contemporary Perspectives.* New York: The Free Press, pp. 231-43.
— — (1970b), 'The Neoteric Society', *Comparative Studies in Society and History* 12:1-13.
Goode, William J. (1963), *World Revolution and Family Patterns.* New York: The Free Press.
Gordon, David M. (1972), *Theories of Poverty and Underemployment.* Lexington, Mass.: Heath.
Gough, Kathleen (1952), 'A Comparison of Incest Prohibitions and the Rules of Exogamy in Three Matrilineal Groups of the Malabar Coast'. *International Archives of Ethnography* 46:82-105.

Greenfield, Sidney M. (1966), *English Rustics in Black Skin.* New Haven, Connecticut: College and University Press.

Handler, Joel F. (1972), *Reforming the Poor.* New York: Basic Books.

Handwerker, W. Penn (1973), 'Technology and Household Configuration in Urban Africa: the Bassa of Monrovia', *American Sociological Review* 38:182-97.

Harvey, Edward (1968), 'Technology and Structure of Organization', *American Sociological Review* 33:247-58.

Hauser, Philip M. (1963), 'The Social, Economic and Technological Problems of Rapid Urbanization', in Bert Hoselitz and Wilbert Moore (eds), *Industrialization and Society.* Paris: UNESCO, p. 203.

Henriques, Fernando (1953), *Family and Colour in Jamaica.* London: Eyre & Spottiswoode.

Herskovits, Melville J. (1937), *Life in a Haitian valley.* New York: A. A. Knopf.
—— (1941), *The Myth of the Negro Past.* New York: Harper & Brothers.
—— (1943), 'The Negro in Bahia, Brazil: A Problem in Method'. *American Sociological Review* 8:394-404.

Herskovits, Melville J. and F. Francis (1947), *Trinidad Village,* New York, A. A. Knopf.

Hill, Robert B. (1971), *The Strengths of Black Families.* New York: Emerson Hall, Inc.

Kaberry, Phyllis (1953), *Women of the Grassfields.* London: HMSO.

Kay, Paul (1963), 'Aspects of Social Structure in a Tahitian Urban Neighbourhood', *Journal of Polynesian Society* 72:325-71.

King, C. E. (1945), 'The Negro Maternal Family: A Product of an Economic and a Culture System', *Social Forces* 24:100-104.

Knudsen, Dean D. (1969), 'The Declining Status of Women: Popular Myth and the Failure of Functionalist Thought', *Social Forces* 48:183-93.

Lee, Richard B. (1968), 'What Hunters do for a Living, or, How to Make Out on Scarce Resources', in Richard B. Lee and Irven DeVore (eds), *Man the Hunter.* Chicago: Aldine Publishing Company, pp. 30-48.
—— (1969), '!Kung Bushman Subsistence: An Input–Output Analysis', in Andrew P. Vayda (ed.), *Environment and Cultural Behaviour.* Garden City, New York: The Natural History Press, pp. 47-76.

Lenski, Gerhard E. (1966), *Power and Privilege: A Theory of Social Stratification.* New York: McGraw-Hill.

Levin, Henry M. (1973), 'Educational Reform: Its Meaning?' Occasional papers in the Economics and Politics of Education. School of Education, Stanford University.

Lewis, Oscar (1966), *La Vida: A Puerto Rican Family in the Culture of Poverty.* New York: Random House.

Lombardi, John R. (1973), 'Exchange and Survival'. Paper read at the meetings of the American Anthropological Association, New Orleans.

Lopreato, J. (1965), 'How Would You Like to be Peasant?' *Human Organization* 24:298.

Mamdani, Mahmood (1972), *The Myth of Population Control: Family, Caste, and Class in an Indian Village*. New York: Monthly Review Press.

Ministerio de Fomento (1970), 'Encuesta del Holgar', Caracas, Venezuela (April).

Morgan, James N. et al., (1974), *Five-Thousand American Families – Patterns of Economic Porgress*. Ann Arbor: Institute for Social Research, University of Michigan.

Moynihan, Daniel Patrick (1965), *The Negro Family: the Case for National Action* (The Moynihan Report). Office of Policy Planning and Research of the Department of Labour.

Murdock, George P. (1949), *Social Structure*. New York: The Macmillan Company.

–– (1967), Ethnographic Atlas: A Summary', *Ethnology* 7:109-236.

–– (1968), 'World Sampling Provinces', *Ethnology* 7:305-26.

Murdock, George P. and Caterina Provost (1973), 'Factors in the Division of Labour by Sex: A Cross-Cultural Analysis', *Ethnology* 12:203-25.

Murdock, George P. and Douglas R. White (1969), 'Standard Cross-Cultural Sample', *Ethnology* 8:329-69.

Murdock, George P. and Suzanne F. Wilson (1972), 'Settlement Patterns and Community Organization: Cross-Cultural Codes 3', *Ethnology* 11:254-95.

Myrdal, Gunnar (1944), *An American Dilemma*. New York: Harper & Brothers, 2 vols.

Naroll, Raoul (1970), 'What Have We Learned from Cross-Cultural Surveys?' *American Anthropologist* 72:1227-88.

–– (1973), 'Galton's Problem' in Raoul Naroll and Ronald Cohen (eds), *A Handbook of Methods in Cultural Anthropology*. New York: Columbia University Press, pp. 974-89.

Nimkoff, M. F. and Russell Middleton (1960), 'Types of Family and Types of Economy', *American Journal of Sociology* 66:215-25.

Opler, Marvin K. (1943), 'Woman's Social Status and the Forms of Marriage', *American Journal of Sociology* 49:125-48.

Oppenheimer, Valerie Kincaid (1973), 'Demographic Influence on Female Employment and the Status of Women', *American Journal of Sociology* 78:946-61.

Parsons, Talcott (1955), 'The American Family: Its Relations to Personality and to the Social Structure', in Talcott Parsons and Robert F. Bales (eds), *Family Socialization and Interaction Process*. Glencoe: The Free Press, pp. 3-33.

Parsons, Talcott and Robert F. Bales (1955), *Family, Socialization and Interaction Process*. Glencoe: The Free Press.

Peattie, Lisa R. (1968), *The View from the Barrio*. Ann Arbor, Michigan: University of Michigan Press.

Perrow, Charles (1967), 'A Framework for the Comparative Analysis of Organizations', *American Sociological Review* 32 :194-208.

Piven, Frances Fox and Richard A. Cloward (1971), *Regulating the Poor: the Functions of Public Welfare.* New York: Random House.

Polgar, Steven (1972), 'Population History and Population Policies from an Anthropological Perspective', *Current Anthropology* 13:203-11.

Powdermaker, Hortense (1939), *After Freedom: A Cultural Study in the Deep South.* New York: Viking Press.

Sackrey, Charles (1973), *The Political Economy of Urban Poverty.* New York: W. W. Norton and Company.

Safa, Helen L. (1964), 'From Shantytown to Public Housing: A Comparison of Family Structure in Two Urban Neighbourhoods in Puerto Rico', *Caribbean Studies* 4:3-12.

Sahlins, Marshall D. (1965), 'On the Sociology of Primitive Exchange', in Michael Banton (ed.), *The Relevance of Models for Social Anthropology.* A.S.A. Monograph I. London: Tavistock Publications; New York: Praeger.

Scanzoni, John (1972), *Sexual Bargaining: Power Politics in the American Marriage.* New Jersey: Prentice-Hall.

Schnaiberg, Allan and David Reed (1974), 'Risk, Uncertainty and Family Formation: the Social Context of Poverty Groups', *Population Studies* 28:513-533.

Simey, Thomas (1946), *Welfare Planning in the West Indies.* Oxford. Clarendon Press.

Smith, Raymond T. (1956), *The Negro Family in British Guiana.* London: Routledge & Kegan Paul.

Sonquist, John A., Elizabeth Lauh Baker and James N. Morgan (1971), *Searching for Structure.* Ann Arbor, Michigan: Institute for Social Research, University of Michigan.

Stack, Carol D. (1970), 'The Kindred of Viola Jackson: Residence and Family Organization of an Urban Black American Family', in Norman E. Whitten, Jr and John F. Szwed (eds), *Afro-American Anthropology: Contemporary Perspectives.* New York: The Free Press, pp. 303-12.

— (1974), *All Our Kin: Strategies for Survival in a Black Community.* New York: Harper & Row.

Staples, Robert (1972), 'The Matricentric Family System: A Cross-Cultural Examination', *Journal of Marriage and the Family* 34:156-65.

Stein, Robert L. (1970), 'The Economic Status of Families Headed by Women', Reprint 2703 from the December *Monthly Labour Review* 93:1-8.

Stephens, William M. (1963), *The Family in Cross-Cultural Perspective.* New York: Holt, Rinehart & Winston.

Stycos, Mayone J. (1968), *Fecundidad en America Latina.* Bogota: Tercer Mundo S.A.

US Bureau of the Census (1970), *United States Summary,* PC(1) D1, 1970, Detailed Characteristics. Computed from Table 258, 1-959-61.

US Department of Labour, Employment Standards Administration, Women's

Bureau (1973), *Facts About Women Heads of Households and Heads of Families*. Washington, D.C.

Valentine, Charles A. (1968), *Culture and Poverty: Critique and Counterproposals*. Chicago: University of Chicago Press.

—— 'Blackston: Progress Report on a Community Study in Urban Afro-America'. Mimeographed. St Louis: Washington University.

IX Venezuelan Census (1961), Ministerio de Fomento, Oficina Central del Censo, Republic of Venezuela, Caracas.

Winch, Robert F. and Rae Lesser Blumberg (1968), 'Societal Complexity and Familial Organization', in Robert F. Winch and Louis Wolf Goodman (eds), *Selected Studies in Marriage and the Family*. New York: Holt, Rinehart and Winston, 3rd edn, pp. 70-92.

Wolf, Eric R. (1966) *Peasants*. New Jersey: Prentice-Hall.

Woofter, T. J. (1930), *Black Yeomanry*. New York.

Woolf, Virginia (1929), *A Room of One's Own*. New York: Harcourt.

Young, M. and P. Willmott (1957), *Family and Kinship in East London*. London: Routledge & Kegan Paul.

APPENDIX A

'Explained' Variance of Mother–Child Residences

I. Region excluded split number	Variable name	Proportion of variance 'explained'
1	Subsistence economy	0.3417
2	Brideprice	0.0605
3	Sexual division of labour	0.0165
4	Subsistence economy	0.0271
5	Social class	0.0168
6	Descent	0.0161
7	Political complexity	0.0362
8	Descent	0.0133
9	Marital residence	0.0118
10	No. of specialized occupations	0.0442

$0.5842 = \Sigma \text{BSS/TSS}$

II. Region included split number	Variable name	Proportion of variance 'explained'
1	Region	0.4472
2	Sexual division of labour	0.0205
3	No. of specialized occupations	0.0378
4	Subsistence economy	0.0180
5	Inheritance of moveable property	0.0143
6	Marital residence	0.0139
7	Region	0.0281

$0.5798 = \Sigma \text{BSS/TSS}$ *

*Differences in rounding make the total slightly discrepant (in the third or fourth decimal) from the figures given for R^2 above.

6

CULTURE, CRISIS, AND CREATIVITY OF FAMILIES IN BOMBAY, SAN JUAN AND MINNEAPOLIS

Dennis C. Foss and Murray A. Straus
University of New Hampshire, U.S.A.

As is the case in most areas of research, the assumptions underlying the study of creativity tend to guide the theoretical reasoning as well as the empirical research. While most assumptions remain assumed because they are incapable of test, some assumptions are indeed capable of either direct test or indirect test in terms of their correlates. It is, of course, highly beneficial to test assumptions whenever possible, in that the acceptance or rejection of basic assumptions has wide ranging impact on the theorizing and research in an area.

This paper presents an examination of four of these assumptions regarding creative production. Furthermore, the paper reports the findings of a research designed to test three of them. These assumptions entail large issues to which the present research cannot provide a definitive answer, partly because the data are based on the relatively small samples of families which it was possible to study by means of laboratory experimental methods. But these same experimental methods also have obvious advantages, especially in respect to causal inference and to control of extraneous variables.[1]

Assumption 1. Creative ability and therefore creative production is a relatively stable personal trait

Creative ability can be conceived as a special type of cognitive ability which allows one to arrive at objects, ideas, actions, etc. that are considered by others to be creative (Guilford, 1967; Cattell and Butcher, 1967). Thus, creative ability is analogous to other abilities such as the ability to do well in athletics, the ability to make friends readily, and the ability to grasp difficult concepts. Similarly, creative production can be viewed as the fruits of creative ability. Creative products are viewed broadly and would include behaviours,[2] and verbalized ideas as well as objects. Creative ability and production are easily distinguished conceptually (although interrelated) and are as distinct as one's ability to bake pies, and the quantity and quality of the pies one actually bakes.

Since one's ability to perform in a given area, and the actual performance seem obviously tied to one another, the variance in creative production among individuals has largely been sought in the varying degrees of creativity that individuals possess. Consequently, inquiry into the nature and genesis of creative production has taken the actor as its focal point, and the individual has been the major recipient of empirical and theoretical time and energy. Creative production has been studied in terms of the modes of thought of individual producers (i.e. 'ideational fluency', 'flexibility', etc., Guilford, 1967:138), from the vantage point of personality correlates of creative production (i.e. Barron, 1963; Feldheusen et al., 1965; Eisenman and Cherry, 1968), and differences in the way creative persons perceive situations, and a wide variety of other personal characteristics (i.e. Getzels and Jackson, 1962; Henle, 1962; Roe, 1960; Bruner, 1962:11-17).

While we do not deny the importance of individual differences in creative ability, the dominance of this assumption may be one reason why the situation, as reported by a committee on creativity research a decade ago, remains essentially unchanged: 'Our committee's first and foremost important recommendation is a plea.' Research on these general environmental conditions — cultural, professional, and institutional — conducive to [creativity] ... needs encouragement (Taylor, 1964:144; see also the similar statement by Stein, 1968:963).

To some extent this plea has been met by two types of studies.

First, is the 'socialization perspective'. The question here is what types of family educational, societal, cultural and economic environments tend to enhance creative ability (Getzels and Jackson, 1962; Nichols, 1964; Straus, 1971; Straus and Straus, 1968; Dye, 1964; Oden, 1968; Torrance, 1962). Secondly, the relationship between the environment and the actor has been examined from what might be called the 'labelling perspective'. The primary issue in this perspective is which individuals, objects, behaviours, and ideas will come to be labelled by others as creative (for example, Stein, 1953). Interest focuses on the factors that operate in the decision-making process by which some products and individuals come to be viewed as creative while others come to be viewed as deviant or ordinary.

Important as are the socialization studies and the examination of creativity in terms of the labelling of creative products, neither of these focus on the social structural and environmental circumstances which can *directly* influence creative performance. On the other hand, the brainstorming studies and the research of Torrance and Arsan (1963) and Yamamoto (1964) are examples of the type of research which is needed to clarify the many important issues concerning the social conditions for creative performance.

Assumption 2. Creative ability and creative production and relatively stable characteristics of social groups

Some research on creativity has focused on the group level (for review of this area see Zagona et al., (1966). Thus, some families, corporations, universities, nations, cultures, etc. have come to be viewed as more creative than others. While there has been a shift from the individual to the group, the explanation of creative production is still sought in characteristics of the actor, and the only change is that the actor is shifted from the individual to a group such as the family. Again creative production is assumed to be a relatively stable characteristic which ensues from the *group's* creative ability, and the key to understanding the occurrence in production is assumed to be located in differential characteristics of the group actor rather than the individual actor (for example, Gibb, 1951; Thomas and Fink, 1963; Hoffman and Maier, 1961; Smith and Kight, 1959).

Assumption 3. Creative performance is a function of the immediate environment in which the behaviour takes place

While the dominant assumption made in the literature is that creative performance — whether the groups or individuals — tends to be relatively constant as the result of a relatively stable ability, we suggest a counter assumption that might prove useful. Stated in an extreme form, creative performance may be assumed to be function of the immediate physical or social environment in which the behaviour takes place. In short, at any particular point in time the differences between the creative performance of various individuals and groups is primarily a function of the differing situations in which they act (including their status and roles in the situation) rather than differences in some quality that inheres within them.

This counter assumption suggests a need for research on whether creative behaviours are the result of the extent to which the situation or environments in which the individual or group finds itself demands creativity, as well as the extent to which the larger social structure of which they are a part permits and encourages creative performance. Such studies have been urged by some, as indicated by our quotation from Taylor, but the actual prevalence of research on situational and structural factors that directly influence creative behaviour seems to be minimal (but see Bruce, 1974). Instead, as we pointed out, both individual and group creative *production* have been viewed largely as the result of differential levels of creative *ability* and, like creative ability, production has been viewed as relatively stable and seemingly unaffected to an important degree by the immediate environment in which the production occurs. The environment is considered, not as to its direct impact on creative behaviour, but rather in its relation to creative ability and to the process by which others come to view the product as creative.

*Assumption 4. Creative production, being a basic
trait of the human condition, is universal in its nature,
negesis, and make-up*

Creativity often has conferred upon it the status of being a basic characteristic of the human condition. Men and women in all cultures and in all times have been found to create. Since creative production is both universally present and viewed as basic, it has been assumed that its nature and origin must also be universal. While it is admitted that there are differences between cultures — for example, some cultures abound in poetry and verbal expression and others in musical or technological innovation — it is seemingly assumed that at bottom creativity is everywhere the same. With rare exceptions such as the work of Torrance (1973) the lack of cross-cultural research on creativity seems to point to an assumptive lack of need for this type of research. One quite simply does not run across the pleas for cross-cultural research that one finds in many other areas of sociological research. The vast literature in the area indicates an implicit assumption that to study creative functioning of a sample of Americans is to study creativity per se. It is a difficult task to find a journal article on creativity which contains a disclaimer that the findings are representative of a single culture rather than universally applying to all men.

METHOD

The data for this paper are from a larger experimental study of family interaction in three societies — Minneapolis, San Juan and Bombay — using the SIMFAM technique (Straus and Tallman, 1971). This is a laboratory procedure which involves families in an interesting and absorbing task. The task is a puzzle in the form of a game played with balls and pushers. This game is played on a court, about 9 by 12 feet, marked on the floor. There are two wood target boards at the front on the court (see Figure 1). Also, at the front of the room are a blackboard and three pairs of red and green lights mounted on a single board. One pair of these lights is for the husband, one pair for the wife, and one

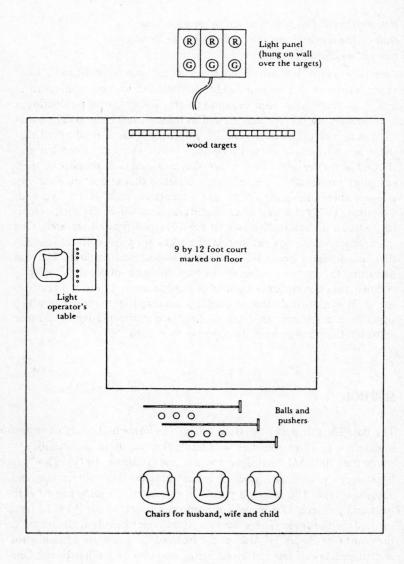

Figure 1.

pair for the child. The family plays this game for eight 3-minute trials.

After the family is seated, a white band is tied to the husband's wrist, a yellow band to the wife's wrist, and a blue band to the child's. The family is then told: 'The puzzle to be solved is to figure out how to play this game. If what you do is correct, a green light will be flashed. If what you do is wrong, a red light will be flashed. By noting which colour light flashed, you can figure out the rules of the game and use this information to get as high a score as possible.'

In addition to the lights, a family could judge how well it was doing from fictitious scores which were written on the blackboard after each 3-minute trial. There are actually only three rules that a family needed to learn: (1) the colour of the pusher and ball must match the colour of the arm band, (2) the ball must hit one of the wooden target boards at the end of the court, and (3) the ball must not roll out of the court after it hits the target.

The Sample

A questionnaire was given to children in schools selected on the basis of their location in middle-class or lower-class parts of Minneapolis, San Juan and Bombay. This questionnaire permitted selection of families to meet certain requirements of the larger study. The resulting samples consisted of 63 families in Minneapolis, 45 in San Juan, and 64 in Bombay (see Straus, 1971 for the sampling design). In Minneapolis 64 percent of the eligible families who were originally asked to participate did so, in San Juan 88 percent, and in Bombay the figure was 93 percent.

The experiment was divided into two 'periods' or 'blocks' of 3-minute trials. In the first block of four trials all families were treated alike. For the second block of trials (5 through 8) a random half of the families were assigned to a control condition and the other half experienced what can be called a 'simulated crisis'. This was achieved by simply giving all red lights, irrespective of what the family did. However, two random green lights were also flashed to add realism (see Straus and Tallman, 1971:398).

Measurement of creative behaviour

For each member of the family a verbatim record was kept of the ideas put forward concerning how to play the game or each new mode of play which was tried. This is the 'creativity' protocol. Actual use of practicality of the idea is ignored in recording the creativity protocol and in scoring.

The resulting protocols were scored for two variables. They are patterned after the scoring systems developed by Wilson et al., (1953). One score is comparable to their 'fluency' factor score. It is the number of different ways of playing the game originated by each person, for example, 'shoot from the left corner'. The second score is comparable to Guilford's 'flexibility' factor and is the number of different principles or approaches used in responding to the task. For example, 'shoot from the left corner' and 'shoot from the centre' would contribute two points to a family's fluency score, but only one point to their flexibility score, since the same principle (angle of shot) is involved in both. But it someone suggests, 'bounce the ball', this would fall into another of the 12 categories used to score flexibility and hence would be scored for flexibility as well as fluency. The creativity score used in this paper is the sum of the fluency and the flexibility scores. Details on the conceptual basis, scoring categories, and scoring critieria for these measures are given in Straus and Tallman (1971).[3]

Measure of problem-solving success

As previously noted, green lights were used to indicate a correct action and red lights indicates violation of a rule of the game. Electric counters connected to each signal light recorded the number of successes and errors. The data reported here on success in problem solving is the proportion that green lights are of all lights flashed during the course of each trial.

CONSISTENCY OF CREATIVE PRODUCTION: THE CONTROL GROUP

If the assumption that creative production among families is a relatively stable characteristic is valid, we should expect that the level of creative production in an earlier period of time will be highly correlated with the level of production at a later point (if the span of time is not too great). More specifically, among the *control group* families, those who were high in creative production in the first period (trials 1–4) should remain at a high level in the second period (trials 5–8). Those with lower levels of creativity should tend to remain low.

The results of the experiment were mixed. In Bombay the San Juan correlations approaching zero were found (0.02 and 0.07, respectively). In other words, for both the Indian and Puerto Rican samples, there was little or no relationship found between earlier creativity and later creativity. In short, little support for the stable characteristic assumption was found.

In Minneapolis, on the other hand, a high correlation was found between earlier and later creativity (0.46).[4] The Minneapolis finding would seem to offer support for the notion that creative production is a stable trait of groups, and that over time there tends to be relatively creative and relatively non-creative families. Further analysis in order to better interpret the significance of these results will be offered later in the paper.

Prior success

Again, the assumption that creative production in groups is a fairly stable characteristic suggests the corollary that immediate situational factors will have little effect on that production. The first situational factor to be explored is the previous success experienced in that situation by the family.

To the subjects in an experiment, the laboratory is often unfamiliar and sometimes even threatening. It seems reasonable to expect that those families associating the laboratory environment with a high degree of success will tend to feel more secure in that environment and, at a later time, be more willing to attempt more creative, yet more risky, behaviours. It is argued that a situation or environment in which one has success will be one in which an individual will feel more secure and in turn be more willing to take the risk of being creative.

In this experiment, the families were able to judge their success at the problem-solving task by the number of green and red lights they received. Thus, the most successful families were those who received the greatest number of green lights and the fewest number of red lights. If there were little or no relationship between early success in the situation and later creativity, this suggests that the environment may be relatively unimportant and that creativity is relatively stable.

Again, the results are mixed. In India and Puerto Rico, positive correlations between success and later creativity were found (0.22 and 0.28, respectively). In Minneapolis, however, a low negative correlation of -0.12 was found. As in the previous test, the Minneapolis data seem to support the stable characteristic assumption, as well as offer little support for the importance of the immediate creative situation. But the Indian and the Puerto Rican data support the situational rather than the stable trait assumption.

THE EFFECT OF CRISIS

The second situational factor to be examined for its effect on creativity is the simulated crisis which was experienced by a random half of the families. For these families, a rather major alteration in the immediate situation occurred in trials 5–8. The rules of the game were changed so that the previously successful problem solutions were not incorrect. In fact, no matter what their behaviour, the treatment families received all red lights with the exception of two random green lights. This experimentally produced situational crisis should have an effect on the families' creative production if situational counter assumption is correct, and little effect if the 'stable family trait' assumption is followed.

At the same time, situational factors can also be reflected in the performance of the control group families. For those experiencing the control situation, if the nature of the situation plays an important role in creative production, creative production should start high in the first trial in response to situational demands and begin to decrease through trial 8 as the situational demands are met. Therefore, to the extent that situational factors are important:

(1) The *control group* families, after having high creative production in the first period in order to find the problem solution demanded by the situation, should decrease their creative production in the second period because the situational demands for creativity had been met.

(2) The *crisis treatment group,* like the control should start high in creative production, but rather than decreasing in the second period trials, they should increase or stabalize their creative production due to the further demands placed upon them by the crisis situation.

Contrary to this line of reasoning, in all three societies both the control and the treatment families decreased their output of creative production in the second period. Such findings – that the treatment also decreased their creative production in the crisis situation – seem to refute the situational assumption. However, that data must be interpreted in the light of possible ceiling effects and of our findings on the trends from trial to trial.

Ceiling effects

The measure of creative production behaviour allowed any given type behaviour to be labelled as creative only once. Thus, if a subject decided to stand on a chair while attempting to guide the ball toward the target, this act would become part of his creative production score. If in later trials he also stood on a chair, these acts would not be considered as part of his creative production. The reason for not considering the act as creative more than once is quite straightforward: creative acts are usually considered to be novel; when they are repeated they are no longer novel or innovative and would more likely be a function of memory than creativity.

The significance of the single inclusion of creative behaviour for the creative production score is that each additional creative behaviour becomes incrementally more difficult. Consider for example one of the standard creativity test items: 'how many uses for a paper clip can you think of?' At first, possible uses such as holding papers together, cleaning fingernails, using it as a book mark, etc. come to mind, but the larger number of uses one has already suggested, the more difficult it becomes to arrive at further suggestions. Thus, the decrease in creative production for both control and treatment groups may, at least in part, be due to the increasing difficulty of arriving at the behaviours not already tried.

Within-period trends

Since the decrease in creative production scores between periods 1 and 2 may have been the result of the ceiling effects of single measurement of creative behaviour, rather than a lack of impact of the crisis condition, further analysis of the effect of the crisis environment is necessary. Specifically, we may examine the scores trial by trial to determine if the change in the experimental situation experienced by the treatment group brought about any changes in the trial to trial *trend* of creative production in the last four trials.

For this purpose we plotted the mean scores for each trial. A visual inspection of the resulting graphs revealed that for the control group families in all three societies, the mean creative production declined in an almost perfect linear pattern from trial 1 through trial 8. The first column of Table 1 shows the same thing expressed as standardized regression coefficients. In addition to showing the ceiling effects, this

TABLE 1

Regression of Creative Production Score on Trial Number

| | Standardized regression coefficients | | |
	All Trials (control families)	Crisis trials (5–8) Control families	Treatment families
Bombay	–0.98	–0.94	–0.61
San Juan	–0.67	–0.93	–0.88
Minneapolis	–0.95	–0.99	–0.98

mode of analysis can also be used to examine the effects of crisis. The data under the heading 'Crisis trials' indicates that, in Bombay, the decline in creative production was much less for the families who experienced the crisis than for the control group families in these same trials (-0.61 compared to -0.94). Among San Juan families the crisis produced only a small arresting of the typical drop in creativity (-0.93); and in Minneapolis, there is essentially no difference. Thus, we again have some indication that families in Bombay are the ones most influenced by situational factors (in this case, the simulated crisis), families in Minneapolis least affected by such factors, and families in San Juan fall in between, but in this case closer to the Minneapolis pattern.

It is possible that these differences grow out of differences in the nature of Indian, Puerto Rican and North American social organization. India is the least urbanized and industralized of these three countries, Puerto Rico is intermediate, and the United States is the most urban and industrial of the three. In addition, we assume that as agricultural societies become urbanized and industrialized, the individual and the nuclear family become less subject to control by the larger kin group (a major type of situational influence) and that the values of the society come to emphasize individual autonomy and self-direction of performance (i,e. more subject to influence by the characteristics of the individual person or individual nuclear family). Thus, if this reasoning is correct, properly socialized members of a kinship oriented agricultural society learn that the standards for appropriate behaviour are best determined by cues from the social situation to a great extent, whereas properly socialized members of an individualistic, nuclear family oriented society learn that it is best to guide behaviour on the basis of the individual interests and abilities.

It seems plausible that these principles apply to the behaviour we have labelled creativity. Hence, families in the most kinship oriented agricultural society (India) are responsive to situational influences and there is little consistency of creative performance across situations. At the other extreme, in the most urbanized and industrialized of the three societies (US) the creative performance of the families we studied is relatively little influenced by the situational factors (crisis and prior success) and reveal considerable consistency of creative behaviour across situations. The society which is intermediate in its level of urbanization and industrialization (Puerto Rico) is also intermediate in response to situational factors and in consistency of creative performance across situations.

The results presented up to this point are consistent with such an interpretation. Specifically, the data in the section on the control group families showed that the creative production of Minnesota families in the second period was strongly related to their earlier creativity and thus their creative production seems to be a relatively stable characteristic of the families themselves. In less urbanized and industrialized India and Puerto Rico no such consistency of creative production was found. In India and Puerto Rico creative production in the second period was found to be correlated with how much success the families had earlier experienced in the experimental situation. However, this dependence relationship between creative production and success in the situation did not hold for Minneapolis. Finally, in the present section, the crisis environment had least effect on the trend of decreasing creative production in Minneapolis families, the most on families in Bombay, and an intermediate impact on those families in San Juan.

These findings suggest that there may be no universal or general importance of either situational factors or stable group traits for creative production. Rather, the importance of each may vary culturally. In particular, it is suggested that there may exist an inverse relationship between urbanization—industrialization and the influence of situational factors on creative production. That is, the greater of urbanization—industrialization the weaker the impact of situational factors on creative production and conversely the more creative production seems to be a stable trait of family members.

JOINT EFFECTS OF SUCCESS, CREATIVITY AND CRISIS

Given that the simulated crisis situation does seem to have an impact on creative production (although an impact that varies by culture) a closer examination of the creative production of the crisis treatment families in the three cultures should give us a better idea of some of the factors that are important for understanding creative production. In accordance with the theory and data presented earlier in this paper at least four possible 'hypotheses' could be made.[5]

Hypothesis 1: Stable Group Characteristic Hypothesis

To the extent that there are typically creative and non-creative families, it is expected that in virtually any situation or environment some families will have greater creative production than others. Thus, those who showed themselves to be the most creative in period one are expected to be the most creative in period two. This will occur irrespective of whether they had been highly successful in this environment or not.

Hypothesis 2: Situational Hypothesis

In contradiction to Hypothesis 1, an extreme situational environmental argument may be offered. It is here suggested that traits or characteristics of the actors, be they individuals or families, are really of secondary importance since the traits themselves are functions of general environments and immediate situations, and behaviour can best be explained in terms of differences in the situations in which the behaviour takes place. Therefore if a family had a high degree of success within the environment they will be more likely to be creative than a family who found less success within the environment and thus found it less rewarding and secure. Those families who have had greatest success within the environment will have higher creative production in the crisis period, regardless of their previous level of creative production.

Hypothesis 3: Linear Additive Hypothesis

An obvious line of reasoning is that both of the previous hypotheses are partially right. Thus, a linear additive effect is hypothesized. That is, those families who were highest on both earlier success and earlier creativity dimensions will be highest in creative production in the second period, those who were lowest on both will be lowest on creative production, and those with mixed earlier success and earlier creativity will be in the middle.

Hypothesis 4: Cultural-Specificity Hypothesis

Although each of the above hypotheses suggests a different impact of personal trait and situational factors on creative production, each assumes that the hypothesized impact is universal rather than culture bound. A rival assumption and hypothesis is suggested here. Rather than situational and/or family characteristics having some universal relationship to creative production, it hypothesized that the influence on creative production is dependent on the larger socio-cultural environment in which the creative production takes place.

To test these hypotheses the samples of families were divided at the median for each society to produce a low and high success group based on their problem solving success score for performance in period 1, and also a low and high creativity group based on their creativity score in period 1. The cross-classification of these two variables produced the four groups of families shown in each of the tables to follow.[6]

Part A of Table 2 shows the behaviour of the treatment group families in Minneapolis corresponds to that predicted by the 'stable group characteristic' hypothesis (Hypothesis 1). Those Minneapolis families who had high creative production scores in the first period also had the highest scores in the second period (19.8 and 19.4). Similarly, those Minneapolis families who in the earlier period had the lowest creative production scores also had the lowest scores in the later creative production (16.8 and 16.9). In Minneapolis, creative production appears to be a stable group characteristic. Regardless of whether the families earlier had a low or high degree of success in the experimental environment, their behaviour during the crisis period was consistent with the creative behaviour they had earlier exhibited. Thus, earlier creative production rather than the situational factor was the better predictor of creative behaviour in the second period in Minneapolis.

In Bombay, as seen in part B of Table 2, the situational factor or

TABLE 2

**Creative Production in Trials 5-8, by Success
and Creativity in Trials 1-4 (Crisis Group Families only)**

Creative production in Trials 1-4	Success in Trials 1-4		
	Low	High	Total
A. *Minneapolis*			
High	19.8	19.4	19.5
Low	16.8	16.9	16.8
Total	17.9	18.4	
B. *Bombay*			
High	12.8	15.0	14.4
Low	13.0	14.3	13.8
Total	12.9	14.8	
C. *San Juan*			
High	8.9	14.6	11.3
Low	2.8	8.0	6.1
Total	6.3	10.4	

earlier success within the environment is the better predictor of creative production. Those families which had had the highest degree of success in period 1 were the most likely to be creative in the crisis period (with mean scores of 15.0 and 14.3), while those who had the least earlier success had the lowest mean creative production scores (12.8 and 13.0). Earlier creative production on the other hand, seems to have little value in predicting which families would later have the highest creative production. Thus, in Bombay, the 'situational hypotheses' (no. 2) was supported in that earlier success in the environment had the greatest impact on creative production.

In San Juan, the data supports the 'linear additive hypothesis' (no. 3), in that a combination of earlier creative production, and earlier success was necessary for the most accurate prediction of creative production scores during the crisis period. Table 2, part C shows that those families who both have experienced a high degree of success within the environment and had earlier exhibited a high degree of creative production had the highest mean creative production score in the later period (14.6). Similarly, those who had been low on both were the lowest in their creative production in the second period (2.80). Those who had mixed earlier success and creativity (either high-low or low-high) had creative production scores which were in the middle (8.9 and 8.0). Thus while neither creativity as a stable trait or the situational factor is alone sufficient to account for the variance in the second period creative production scores for San Juan families, both together do account for the variance in an additive way.

The first three hypotheses suggested earlier in the section have each found support in one of the three cultures studied but little support in the other two. Thus no hypothesis was found to have general or universal support, which in turn suggests the 'cultural-specificity' theory of the fourth hypothesis. Rather than family characteristics and/or situational factors having some universal relationship to creative production, their influence on creative production seems dependent on the larger social-cultural environment in which the creative functioning occurs.[7]

SUMMARY AND CONCLUSIONS

If it is assumed that the urban–industrial setting poses a recurrent series of unfamiliar problems for families, and that the creativity of the family group is an important aspect of the ability of families to adapt to such an urban–industrial setting (Straus, 1968), then a great deal needs to be known about the factors influencing creativity in family groups. The present study was undertaken to examine four of the possible influencing factors, two of which were simply assumed in the previous analysis. These are: (a) the extent to which creativity in families is a stable characteristic of individual family groups; (b) the effects of prior success within a situation on creativity; (c) the effects on creativity of a problem so intransigent that it can be labelled as a 'crisis', and (d) the effects of the socio-cultural setting on these relationships.

To examine these issues, 172 three-person family groups were studied (64 in Bombay, 45 in San Juan and 63 in Minneapolis) by use of a laboratory problem solving task (SIMFAM). This task, and the associated scoring procedures, enabled us to observe the creativity displayed by families in attempting to solve the laboratory problem under normal non-frustrating conditions and under frustrating conditions which we have labelled as a simulated crisis.

The results show that all four factors are operating, but in ways that differ from society to society. The society to society differences in the factors affecting creativity under normal conditions and in the face of the simulated crisis are related to the degree to which the city of residence is located in a society which is urbanized and industralized, ranging from Bombay at one end of the continuum, to San Juan at an intermediate level, to Minneapolis at the other end. Specifically, our findings indicate that the greater the urbanization—industrialization the weaker the impact of situational factors on creative production and conversely, the more creative production seems to be a stable trait of family members. In Minneapolis, where the social organization is most urban and industrial, with concurrent accent on individuality and individual autonomy, creativity seemed to be by and large a stable characteristic of the families themselves with the situational factors having little impact. In Bombay, which is the least urbanized and industrialized of the societies studied, earlier levels of creative functioning had little predictive value for later creative production in the crisis situation. Rather, the more important factor in determining later creative production was the degree of success that the families had had in the experimental situation. In San Juan, which is intermediate and industrialization—urbanization, the creative production of families was found to be dependent on both prior creativity and prior success.

In conclusion, bearing in mind the qualifications imposed by the small samples studied in each society, the results of this study suggest that the influence on creativity of (a) the individual characteristics of family groups, (b) the experience of prior success, and (c) the experience of high goal blockage or 'crisis', rests on culturally specific conditions. To the extent that these findings are correct, it would seem that: (1) the implicit universal applicability which tends to characterize the reporting of findings in American research on creativity is unwarranted, and (2) the validity of the assumptions underlying the study of creative behaviour may not be general but rather culturally specific. In particular, the 'creative ability perspective' which assumes that creative acts reflect intra-individual or intra-group characteristics is most applicable to societies which are highly urbanized and industrialized, perhaps because of the emphasis in such societies on individualism and individual autonomy. Conversely, the 'situational perspective' which assumes that creativity is a function of the social situation, may be most applicable in kinship oriented agrarian societies, perhaps because of the emphasis in such societies on the importance of conforming to the standards of kin and community.

NOTES

This research was supported by NIMH grant number MH-15521. Earlier phases of the study were supported by grants from the National Science Foundation and the University of Minnesota Graduate School, and by a Fulbright grant for research in India. Some of the many people who have contributed to this long and com-plicated research have been acknowledged in a previous paper (Straus, 1968). In relation to the present paper, we would like to express our appreciation to Joyce Foss and Martha Huggins for valuable comments and criticisms of an earlier draft.

    1. It is not contended that all investigators in the area of creativity make these assumptions, or that those who do usually either make them explicit or hold them in the extreme form in which they are cast in this paper for the purpose of exposition. However, these assumptions, while often implicit, are widely held.

    2. Behaviour is often considered to be merely a means of arriving at creative products, rather than as a potential product itself. Behaviours such as acting and dancing which while not issuing into a tangible object, yet which are considered themselves to be creative suggest the inclusion of such behaviours in the concept of creative production.

    3. The validity of this measure of creativity is not well established. However,

some suggestion of validity may be inferred from the fact that (1) the behaviours scored are congruent with the main conceptualizations of creativity outline earlier in this paper, (2) the measure has proved fruitful in the analysis of two other issues (Straus, 1968; Straus and Straus, 1968) and may therefore be judged to have at least a minimum level of 'construct validity', (3) the creativity scores of the Minneapolis children in this study are about as highly correlated with Torrance's Minnesota Test sample and 0.33 for the working class) as any of the correlations between different measures of creativity to be found in the literature.

    4. Since we are using the product–moment correlation these statements should all have the qualifier 'relatively' low or 'relatively' high.

    5. The use of the phrase 'hypotheses *could* be made . . .' is not just a cumbersome stylistic peculiarity because, in fact, there were no formal a priori hypotheses. Rather, we started this analysis only with the idea that the four factors under investigation (i.e. the individual family group trait factor, the effect of prior success, the effect of goal blockage or crisis, and cultural differences) were worth exploring. Subsequently, on the basis of inspecting the initial two-variable correlations and cross-tabulations, we decided to look into the combinations of factors indicated in these 'hypotheses'. The lack of a priori hypotheses is also the reason why statistical tests of hypotheses are not reported.

    6. The reader is advised against tempting but hazardous generalizations based on inter-societal comparisons of raw mean scores. Use of mean scores in this way is hazardous in that slight differences existed in the way the experiment was adminstered in each society (to insure that the game be both challenging. and yet capable of being solved by all subjects in all three socieites before the introduction of the crisis treatment). In addition, people of different cultures are likely to manifest differing amounts of behaviour of all types, act with differing amounts of reserve in the experimental situation, etc. Thus, for example, it would be questionable to conclude on the basis of their higher socres that families in Minneapolis are the most creative. On the other hand previous papers have suggested that it is quite legitimate to make intersocial comparisons of either trends or correlations of measures which are 'conceptually equivalent' even though not 'phenominally identical' (Straus, 1969; 1970:572-573).

    7. From a sociology of knowledge perspective it is interesting that the individual trait assumption which is predominant in the American creativity literature is supported by the behaviour of the Minneapolis rather than the Bombay families. Thus, the conceptualization of the research community parallels the characteristics of the society in which the research in conducted.

REFERENCES

Barron, F. (1963). 'The Disposition Toward Originality' in C. W. Taylor and F. Barron (eds), *Creativity: Its Recognition and Development.* New York: Wiley, pp. 139-52.

Bruce, P. (1974), 'Reactions of Preadolescent Girls to Science Tasks', *Journal of Psychology* 86:303-308.

Bruner, J. S. (1962), 'The conditions of creativity', in Gruber, Terrell and Wertheimer (eds), *Contemporary Approaches to Creative Thinking.* New York: Atherton Press, pp. 1-28.

Cattell, R. B. and H. J. Butcher (1967), *The Prediction of Achievement and Creativity.* New York: Bobbs-Merrill.

Dye, M. E. (Sister) (1964), 'An Inquiry into Creativity and its Nurturing Climate: An Exploratory Study', *Dissertation Abstracts* 25 1:320.

Eisenman, R. and H. O. Cherry (1968), 'Creativity and authoritariansim', Paper presented at the April meeting of the Southeastern Psychological Association, Roanoke, Va.

Feldheusen, J. W., T. Denny and R. F. Condon (1965), 'Anxiety, Divergent Thinking and Achievement', *Journal of Educational Psychology* 56 (1);40-45.

Getzels, J. W. and P. W. Jackson (1960), 'Occupational Choice and Cognitive Functioning: Career Aspirations of Highly Intelligent and Highly Creative Adolescents', *Journal of Abnormal and Social Psychology* 61:119-23.

–– (1962), *Creativity and Intelligence.* New York; Wiley.

Gibb, J. R. (1951), 'Effects of Group Size and Threat Reduction Upon Creativity in a Problem-Solving Situation', *American Psychology* 6:324.

Guilford, J. P. (1967), *The Nature of Human Intelligence.* New York: McGraw-Hill.

Henle, M. (1962), 'The Birth and Death of Ideas', in Gruber, Terrell and Wertheimer (eds), *Contemporary Approaches to Creative Thinking.* New York: Atherton Press, pp. 31-60.

Hoffman, L. R. and H. R. Maier (1961), 'Quality and Acceptance of Problem Solutions by Members of Homogeneous and Heterogeneous Groups' *Journal of Abnormal and Social Psychology*,62:401-7.

McCandless, B. R. (1967), *Children: Behaviour and Development.* New York: Holt, Rinehart & Winston, pp. 330-33.

Nichols, R. C. (1964), 'Parental Attitudes of Mothers of Intelligent Adolescents and Creativity of their Mothers', *Child Development* 35:1041-50.

Oden, M. H. (1968), 'The Fulfillment of Promise: 40-year Follow Up of the Terman Gifted Group'. *Genetic Psychology Monograph* 77:1-29.

Roe, A. (1960), 'Crucial Life Experiences in the Development of Scientists' in E. P. Torrance (ed.) *Talent and Education.* Minneapolis: University of

Minnesota Press, pp. 66-77.

Smith, E. E. and S. S. Kight (1959), 'Effects of Feedback on Insight and Problem-Solving Efficiency in Training Groups', *Journal of Applied Psychology* 43:209-11.

Stein, M. I. (1953), 'Creativity and Culture', *Journal of Psychology* 36:311-22.

−− (1968) 'Creativity', in Edgar F. Borgatta and William W. Lambert (eds), *Handbook of Personality Theory and Research*. Chicago; Rand McNally & Company, pp. 900-42.

Straus, M. A. (1968) 'Communication, Creativity, and Problem-Solving Ability of Middle- and Working-Class Families in Three Societies', *American Journal of Sociology* 73 (January) :418-30.

−− (1969). 'Phenomenal Identity and Conceptual Equivalence of Measurement in Cross-National Comparative Research', *Journal of Marriage and the Family* 31 (May) :233-39.

−− (1970) 'Methodology of a Laboratory Experimental Study of Families in Three Societies' in Reuben Hill and Rene Konig (eds), *Families in East and West*. Paris: Mouton, pp. 552-77.

−− (1971), 'Social Class and Sex Differences in Socialization for Problem Solving in Bombay, San Juan, and Minneapolis', in Joan Aldous et al. (eds), *Family Problem Solving*. Hinsdale, Illinois: Dryden Press, pp. 282-301.

Straus, J. H. and M. A. Straus (1968), 'Family Roles, and Sex Difference in Creativity of Children in Bombay and Minneapolis', *Journal of Marriage and the Family* 30 (February) :46-53.

Straus, M. A. and I. Tallman (1971), 'Simfam: Technique for Observational Measurement and Experimental Study of Families', in Joan Aldous et al. (eds), *Family Problem Solving*. Illinois: Dryden Press, pp. 380-438.

Taylor, C. W. (1964), *Creativity: Progress and Potential*. New York: McGraw-Hill.

Thomas E. O. and C. F. Fink (1963), 'Effects of Group Size', *Psychological Bulletin* 60:371-84.

Torrance, E. (1962), *Guiding Creative Talent*. Englewood Cliffs, N.J.: Prentice-Hall.

Torrance, E. (1973), 'Cross-Cultural Studies of Creative Development in Seven Selected Societies', *Educational Trends* 8:29-39.

Torrance, E. P. and K. Arson (1963), 'Experimental Studies of Homogeneous and Heterogeneous Groups for Creative Scientific Tasks', in W. W. Charters, Jr and N. L. Gage (eds), *Readings in the Social Psychology of Education*. Boston: Allyn and Bacon, pp. 133-40.

Wilson, R. D., J. P. Guilford and P. R. Christensen (1953), 'The Measurement of Individual Differences in Creativity', *Psychological Bulletin* 50:362-70.

Yamamoto, K. (1964), 'Creativity and Sociometric Choice Among Adolescents', *Journal of Social Psychology* 64:249-61.

Zagona, S. V., J. E. Willis and W. J. MacKinnon (1966), 'Group Effectiveness in Creative Problem-Solving Tasks: An Examination of Relevant Variables', *Journal of Psychology* 62:111-37.

7

MARRIED AND UNMARRIED COHABITATION
The Case of Sweden, With Some Comparisons

Jan Trost
Uppsala University, Sweden

DEFINITIONS OF THE TERMS 'UNMARRIED COHABITATION' AND 'MARRIAGE'

There is often some uncertainty as regards the meaning of the term 'unmarried cohabitation' and similar terms. The married situation is much more simple to define since it is based upon what the law says. In modern societies all laws are written and with marriage is meant a ceremony and some kind of registration. In older laws, however, as well as in some 'pre-literate' societies the degree of clarity is based upon a law remembered and used by means of oral repetition of the unwritten rules. Even in those societies, however, the marital status of an individual as well as a recognition of the marriage group and the family is obvious for all persons being involved in any way.

As an example from ancient times we can use the rules of the Swedish society from around AD 1,000. At that pre-Christian time the three most important parts of the wedding ceremonies were:

(1) the betrothment (fästningen) or the engagement to be married;

(2) the marriage (giftermalet), i.e. when the bride was given to the bridegroom by the guardian; and

(3) the bedguidance (sängledningen), i.e. when the bride and the bridegroom went to bed together in front of witnesses (Carlsson, 1972, p.3).

At this time it was evident that the marriage was based upon an economical contract between the lineages, so the man and the woman could not act upon their own will. Today marriage is probably viewed by most persons as a personal informal contract the aim of which is an emotional connection between the two spouses/partners. From the viewpoint of modern civil law, e.g. the new Swedish law (cf. SOU 1972:41), marriage is a way for two partners in a cohabiting situation to adopt a set of rules indicating division of household properties during marriage, indicating how to dissolve the marital group, indicating how to divide the properties in case of a dissolution through death or divorce. The religious as well as the emotional aspects cannot reasonably be dealt with by civil law. These rules are valid not only for the two partners/spouses, their children and society as a legal system but for third parts too — a understanding not entirely valid for personal contracts.

The implications of the term unmarried cohabitation (and similar) seem to be *legio*. A few examples might be reasonable to mention. Löcsei (1970) has suggested a term for both married and unmarried cohabitation; *syndyasmos*, which he defines as 'legalized and not legalized varieties of *lasting* living community between men and women'. He does not clarify if the term is reserved for dyads only or if it is applicable to larger groups also — it seems however as if he intends to mean dyads only. The term is new and might seem to some colleagues and especially some laymen somewhat odd — according to our view the term is valuable in our jargon, thus simplifying our communication. Although Löcsei seems to have some ideas about the unreasonability of differentiating between married and unmarried cohabitation, he has implicitly delivered a definition of unmarried cohabitation: i.e. legalized varieties of lasting living community between a man and a woman.

Näsholm (1972a : 356-57) defines nominally unmarried cohabitation as 'two adult persons of different sex living together under marriage-like conditions in the same household without having officially confirmed their relation through marriage' (our translation from Swedish). This definition is evidently similar to the one of Löcsei. In one of her studies, however, Näsholm had to use an operational definition with an unknown degree of validity: the respondent decided at the time of answering a mailed questionnaire if she/he was to be regarded as cohabiting. According to our experience most respondents probably had in their minds something very similar to the nominal definition of Näsholm.

Claesson et al. (1973) define unmarried cohabitation as when 'man and woman live together, with or without children, and fulfilling family functions without formally marrying' (our translation from the Swedish) — again a definition similar to Löcsei's and Näsholm's.

There are, however, other types of definitions. One of them being 'two non-related members of the opposite sex sharing common habitate, duties and responsibilities of housekeeping with or without sexual relationships and without any marriage ceremony' (Hickrod, 1972). The earlier definitions implicitly or explicitly presume a sexual relationship between the two 'spouses' (no good non-pejorative term available), the last definition does not. The earlier definitions stem from Hungary and Sweden where pre-marital sex has never been so tabooed as probably has been the case in US from which the later definition comes. This might explain the difference between the two types of definitions.

Macklin (1972) presents another variant when trying to include as many types of unmarried cohabitation as possible in the nominal definition: 'to share a bedroom for at least four nights per week for at least three consecutive months with someone of the opposite sex'.

There are some differences between the American and the Swedish ways of looking upon the concept and thus upon the term unmarried cohabitation — at least these differences are obvious for the author, being a Swede, when reading for example the Cohabitation Newsletter. In Sweden we know that unmarried cohabitation is nothing unusual. We have for a long time known that pre-marital sex occurs and has occurred among almost all couples. One of the many indicators is the high rate of children born out of wedlock, another the high rate of pregnant brides.

SOME EXAMPLES OF LEGAL
DIFFERENCES BETWEEN MARRIED
AND UNMARRIED COHABITATION

As mentioned, the family laws can be perceived as aimed at helping the couple during the marriage and when a dissolution is actual or has happened – in technical–economical matters. Thus there are almost no rules helping the unmarried cohabiting couple. Most dramatically this is actualized at the dissolution through separation or the death of one of the partners. In the case of divorce/separation most of the partners dislike or hate each other (often the reason for the dissolution and at the same time caused by the problems arising during the dissolution process). As Simmel (1922) says, the intensity of the hatred is equivalent to the intensity of the love once existing. In case of married partners the Swedish law states that if no marriage settlement says otherwise, the property should in principle be put in one pile and then divided in two equal parts – one for the man and one for the woman. But in the unmarried case what the person owns is her/his own property – this often means that the woman owns nothing. She might have been a housewife engaged in bringing up the children and doing the field service in the old-fashioned way, or since in traditional society (which still exists around us) the contracts on the TV, the piano, the car, the washing machine, the sofa, etc. are written in the name of the man, he is the formal owner. During the calm and loving cohabitation the partners do not normally bother about this type of reality but at time for dissolution many of us want to hurt the one earlier loved.

In case of death, however, these reasons are not actual but instead of the partner (the memory of which often is kept with love) the dead partner's/relatives often claim their inheritance rights, despite the fact that the surviving partner in the cohabiting unit reasonably (from her/his own point of view and in correspondance with the laws relevant for the married couple) claims ownership over most of the property.

In cases when the dissolution is caused by separation as well as by death the situation is in many ways more complicated when the partners have children (cf, Claesson et al., 1973).

What we have here called the 'family law' is not however the only set of rules influencing the dyads in different ways for the married and for the unmarried. The social welfare system contains many laws and rules as well as applications in their effects differing between the two types of cohabitation — some of them favouring one and some the other; some of them favourable in the short run and unfavourable in the long run.

There is a shortage in crèches and day-homes for pre-school children in most places in Sweden so poorer parents are favoured as are unmarried mothers as well as other one-parent families. This rule evidently favours the unmarried cohabiting couple if they do not inform the officials that they are cohabitating — it is almost impossible to control if the unwed mother is single or cohabiting. The fee for the day-care system is dependent upon the economy of the family and in most cases the unwed mother with her low income will gain economically from not informing the officials that the father of the child is living with her and the child. A widower with a pension might lose the pension when remarrying, and a divorced person with an alimony from the ex-spouse will lose the alimony at remarriage.

The taxation system still favours the one-parent family; some of the welfare subsidies do too. University and college students can borrow money with state-guarantee and if they borrow some money they receive a sum which they do not have to pay back. The size of the loan is dependent upon the spouse's economic situation as well as upon the applicant's; in the short run this favours the unmarried but in the long run it is unfavourable since the money borrowed must be paid back. The exemplification could be extended for several pages but we prefer to present this small sample.

The law and the social welfare rules, etc. are of greatest importance in many senses but the behaviour of the individuals and the couples are based upon their perception of reality and not reality per se.

Of the two reasons it is impossible to say which is the best for a specific couple — to marry or to cohabit unmarried. One reason is that no one person knows all the relevant laws and rules. The other reason is that even if we could build a robot and program it with all the rules possible to indicate what would be the best for a specific couple in a specific situation at a specific time, the robot still would not know anything about the laws and rules coming and could not foresee the couple's future situation. It is obvious, however, that marriage has the advantage of all the important rules concerning a dissolution of marriage — all marriages end with divorce or the death of one of the spouses.

HOW COMMON IS UNMARRIED COHABITATION?

The question and the answer depend upon what we mean by unmarried cohabitation. Since we perceive unmarried cohabitations as equivalent to married cohabitation a definition should differentiate between the two concepts only in one aspect: the formal marital status of the dyad. Thus we agree with the view of Löcsei (1970) and Näsholm (1972a).

There were no reliable data available for Sweden or any other country (as far as we know) until very recently. Näsholm (1972a and 1972b) gave us the first data for Sweden from 1969 and 1970. She estimated that about 6.5 percent of all syndyasmos were unmarried and 93.5 percent married couples. (It should be noted that the two partners in an unmarried cohabitation can be married but not to each other. When talking about married couples, however, we mean that the two partners are married to each other.) The most recent figures available are the result of a nation-wide data collection during the spring of 1974 which show that 12 percent of the syndyasmos were unmarried (Trost, 1975).

According to Hayner (1966:113) 20 percent of the syndyasmos in Mexico in 1950 were unmarried — a figure that might have decreased through the 'Wedding Days' promoted by the Mexican Government and especially by the wife of the President of Mexico some ten years ago. Some 240 000 couples have legalized their cohabitation through these 'Wedding Days' (according to a letter to the author from Pablo Pindas, 21 June 1973).

For the US some figures exist but the problem is that they deal with students in colleges and thus cannot be assumed to be representative;

sometimes the definitions are so wide that it seems as if the interest lies not in cohabitation but in having a sexual affair of the 'one-night stand' type — a kind of definition not relevant for our interest (this does not mean that we find the students' figures of no interest at all, on the contrary they might be seen as indicators of what is going on in society and thus be grounds for predictions). These data are the only ones we know of in spite of having searched through literature and having had correspondance with colleagues in many parts of the world. It seems as if the same tendency can be found in many countries but no clear evidence is available.

Another type of indicator is the changes in the nuptiality rate. If we assume that the frequency of syndyasmos is constant in a given culture in a fairly short time period (say ten years) then if the marriage rate decreases or increases during that time period the rate of unmarried cohabitation will increase or decrease, respectively. When the marriage rate decreases some say that the marital dyad has grown less popular, but according to our point of view that statement is reasonable only if we lay heavy stress upon the work 'marital' and less upon the concept of social group or syndyasmos.

In 1966 we had 61,101 marriages in Sweden. This number decreased steadily during the following years and was, in 1973, only 37,500; a decrease of 40 percent during seven years. The loss of marriages during this seven-year period was about 120,000 i.e. the number who would have married if the marriage rate had been constant. However, 12 percent of all the syndyasmos is equivalent to something like 200,000 cases. The difference between these two figures might be smaller when calculated more carefully than here, but still there is an important difference. This is as far as we can see mainly due to two causes. The first is a decrease in the average age at first syndyasnis) during the last decades until 1966 the average age at first marriage decreased for both men and women by 0.1 year per year. This tendency would probably have been going on if the marriage rate had been unchanged. Thus, we assume that the average age at first formation of the dyad has continued to decrease.

The second cause for the difference is probably connected with an increase in the total number of syndyasmos, not as a result of the lower age of formation of the dyads. A more permissive attitude can be found today than one or two decades ago; permissive in the sense that earlier those engaged couples were 'allowed' to live together over the weekends and over the vacations, but were in most social environments not allowed to steadily live together; but now anyone is 'allowed' to live together. Those married couples wanting a divorce in order to remarry do not today have to wait for a divorce before openly living together — this tendency is indicated by the fact that during the last years the relative number of divorces based upon the paragraph of adultery (GB 11:8) has decreased. In fact this paragraph has to a very large extent been used as a way of getting a quick divorce wanted not by the plaintiff but by the defendant in order to remarry.

Another explanation for the difference is that even before 1966 we had some unmarried cohabiting couples — an estimate is 1 percent.

The nuptiality rate calculated in a more reasonable way than with raw figures — the number of marriages in relation to the number of unmarried men and women age-specifically — shows a more remarkable decrease, partly dependent upon the fertility boom in the 1940s (cf, Holmbeck, 1974). So the increase in the number of unmarried cohabiting couples corresponds to the decrease in nuptiality.

Let us check the marriage rate for some countries, the data for which happen to be available. Table 1 shows first marriage rates by age and sex. In Denmark the marriage rate has decreased remarkably for both men and women, so according to our assumption the rate of unmarried cohabitation has increased considerably, also — but not as much as in Sweden (it should however be noticed that the time period differs between the countries in table 1). In Finland there are no changes to be found from this table — comments from colleagues in Finland say that there is a trend toward an increase in unmarried cohabitation which might be visible in the vital statistics in some years.

The data for Norway are somewhat confusing; in the lower age range there is an increase but in the higher a decrease — the period of comparison is long and fairly old.

The crude marriage rate in Sweden has decreased from 7.83 in 1966 to 4.76 in 1972. In Denmark from 8.63 in 1966 to 6.61 in 1971, in Finland from 8.35 in 1966 to 7.69 in 1972 (a very small decrease

TABLE 1

First Marriage Rates, by Sex and Age

	Sex	Persons married first time per 1,000 unmarried by age										Average age at first marriage
		-19	20-24	25-29	30-34	35-39	40-44	45-49	50-54	55-59	60-	
Denmark 1961/65	Males	20.3	145.3	211.5	105.2	50.4	24.9	12.7	6.9	4.2	1.3	25.3
	Females	50.2	259.8	187.1	71.7	32.7	16.4	8.7	4.7	2.8	0.6	22.5
1971	Males	8.7	103.8	136.9	65.2	31.2	18.6	9.1	5.0	3.5	1.7	25.2
	Females	28.0	187.6	137.0	59.9	28.5	15.9	8.9	5.3	3.2	0.6	23.0
Finland 1966/70	Males	13.2	133.3	156.9	76.6	36.6	21.5	11.6	7.1	3.7	1.5	24.7
	Females	47.9	184.1	133.0	63.0	31.1	16.2	8.9	4.5	2.1	0.5	22.0
1970	Males	11.9	133.0	151.6	74.4	33.9	19.8	10.6	8.0	3.0	1.7	24.0
	Females	45.3	189.1	133.0	65.6	31.4	16.1	8.9	5.0	1.9	0.7	23.0
Iceland 1966/70	Males	11.6	158.5	145.4	79.3	42.2	22.9	14.3	10.4	6.4	2.8	25.0
	Females	49.0	207.3	165.5	77.9	46.0	22.8	12.9	9.3	4.8	1.0	22.9
Norway 1959/62	Males	7.3	101.3	168.2	107.0	58.1	32.8	17.3	9.6	5.7	1.8	
	Females	38.8	217.0	203.0	99.7	49.5	24.8	13.1	7.3	3.3	0.8	—
1969/70	Males	10.1	132.4	170.3	84.2	40.0	21.6	11.5	7.0	4.0	0.9	24.6
	Females	47.5	226.3	157.6	74.2	32.3	19.2	9.9	6.5	2.8	0.6	22.2
Sweden 1966/70	Males	3.6	90.0	140.7	78.2	35.9	17.5	10.3	5.5	3.4	0.9	26.0
	Females	27.8	158.6	144.1	67.6	32.2	17.7	10.7	6.0	3.0	0.6	23.6
1972	Males	1.3	51.0	88.2	51.8	24.8	12.0	6.5	4.1	2.2	0.8	26.6
	Females	12.2	96.4	102.5	52.8	24.4	13.0	8.5	4.3	2.4	0.4	24.4

Source: Nordic Yearbook of Statistics, vol. 12 (Stockholm, 1973).

visible only the last year), in Norway the rate has been constant: 7.37 in 1966 and 7.27 in 1972, Iceland has had a steady rate of around 8.

We have consulted the statistics edited through UN and it seems as if Sweden and Denmark are the only two countries showing a remarkable and significant (in non-statistical meaning) change in the nuptiality rate during the last decade. We have checked the crude rates for the following countries, some showing a steady rate, some showing changes not seemingly consistent or trend-like (in spite of the crude rate not being the best measurement we have to use it in the absence of better and when comparing the same country over a short time span the biasing effects are not so serious): Scotland, Romania, USSR, Hungary, GDR, Switzerland, Spain, GFR, Austria, Yugoslavia, Belgium, Greece, The Netherlands, Italy, Australia, Canada and Japan.

Another way of looking at the nuptiality is to calculate the number of unmarried persons in different ages at different times. Table 2 give data for Sweden and the US. From these data we find a similar increase in these two countries in spite of the fact that they start on different

TABLE 2

Proportion of unmarried women at different ages in Sweden and US

Age (yrs)	1960		1970	
	Sweden	US	Sweden	US
20	78.0	45.8	84.8	56.7
25	27.6	13.1	32.0	16.2
30	13.5	7.9	14.1	8.6

Sources: Bernhardt and Holmbeck (1974) and data presented by Michael Gordon at a lecture in Uppsala, 17 May, 1974.

base lines (the fact that the US has fewer unmarried women has to do with the lower average age at marriage in the US than in Sweden − the fairly high age in Sweden might have to do with the high degree of permissiveness toward pre-marital sex).

The increase in the number of unmarried women in Sweden is still more pronounced later than table 2 shows. Thus in 1972 the three figures are 20 years = 89.2 percent, 25 years = 38.2 percent, and 30 years = 15.7 percent.

Thus, according to the presented data there probably is a decrease in the nuptiality in the US too, but it is not yet visible from the crude rate. Since we do not believe in a decrease in the popularity of the syndyasmos we presume that the decrease in the marriage rate is compensated by an increase in the unmarried cohabitation rate, and many of the cases of unmarried cohabitation at colleges in the US for example, should not be seen as substitutes for marriage but as an increase in the number of syndyasmos.

From the data in this section we can conclude that at present Sweden has around 12 percent unmarried couples of all syndyasmos, that Denmark and US probably has a fairly high rate, and that we have found no evidence that other countries have the same tendency. Personally, however, we assume that the same tendency is going on in many parts of the world, the mentioned countries might be early in the change-sequence, and since Sweden is such a small country and with good official statistics we have found the tendencies most remarkable.

UNMARRIED COHABITATION – A DEVIANT BEHAVIOUR?

It is evident that many scholars all over the world look upon unmarried cohabitation as something odd or even something deviant. Eleanor Macklin is kind enough to serve those involved in research in this field with the spreading and editing of a *Newsletter*. Many of the notes in the *Newsletter* contain views in this mentioned direction – according to an agreement no quotations are to be made from the *Newsletter* so we cannot be more precise. On the American scene unmarried cohabitation has not been unusual in some strata – evidently it has been fairly common among poor people. This also seems to be the case in Mexico (cf. above).

If unmarried cohabitation is usual only in some parts of the society it can be said to be deviant — at least in the meaning deviating from the normal or deviating from the cultural standard. This is probably the case in some states in the US where, according to our informants, unmarried cohabitation had for a long time been prevalent among the poor but only the last few years unmarried cohabitation has become not unusual among college and university students. This type of deviance — i.e. among the so-called intellectuals — is often rightly or wrongly assumed to be an innovating deviation. If that assumption is right the deviance will soon go over into conformity.

We do not know how the case has been with Sweden — has the unmarried cohabitation gone through the stage of intellectualists deviance? A couple of years ago, before Näsholm (1972a and 1972b) published her data, most Swedes believed that the unmarried cohabitation was a youth and intellectualism phenomenon. Näsholm showed that there is an over-representation among student/similar but no high over-representation and an over-representation among workers (which absolutely is not equivalent to poor people — no really poor people exist in Sweden today; there are a few poor individuals but none that can really be termed 'poor'). Näsholm shows that there are no differences between the married and the unmarried cohabiting couples as regards annual income. Some differences exist, all of them however evidently having to do with the age difference, which is almost a necessity since most of the syndyasmos are formed by young persons. Such differences are the number of persons in the household, for example, and the duration of the dyad.

Trost (1974) shows that out of persons younger than 25 years living in a syndyasmos 53 percent are cohabiting unmarried and 47 percent married; in the age category 25–34 one-fifth are unmarried and among those older than 55 years only 3 percent are unmarried and 97 percent married. As in Näsholm's material from the end of the 1960s Trost's data collected 1974 show no differences between the two types of syndyasmos and income. In a sequence of yearly studies at a Swedish Coastartillery unit, Trost (1970–1974) shows that the relative number of married privates has decreased. The material consists of data collected in 1969–1973 among the about 20-year-old privates, a new set of boys each year. In 1969–1971 4–5 percent of the boys were married, in

1972 2 percent, in 1973 only two boys, less than 1 percent. On the other hand the number of unmarried cohabiting boys has increased steadily, thus in 1969 10 percent were cohabiting unmarried, while in 1973 more than 20 percent were so.

In a study made by Hartmann and Jenner (1972) it is possible to find comparisons between the unmarried and the married cohabiting couples. Their study dealt with the attitudes and opinions of university students toward a Swedish military defence system. In their study half of the respondents cohabiting did so unmarried and half married. These two categories differed in many respects as number of children, how they finance their studies, how long they had been students, etc. – all differences referrable to differences in age.

From the examples above we can conclude that unmarried cohabitation in Sweden can neither be perceived as a deviant phenomenon nor as a conformity since there are no norms existing that one should cohabit unmarried. It is evident from the indicators we have that the unmarried cohabitating couples are as heterogeneous as are the married couples – the difference being the legal marriage.

As is shown by Trost (1974) there is among a nation-wide sample of Swedes a tendency to perceive unmarried cohabiting couples as less economically integrated than married couples. Three situations were presented to the respondent:

(1) Think about a couple having been married for 30 years. The wife has been at home taking care of the children. They are now going to divorce. Except for the common household goods, the man owns 35,000 kronor and the woman owns 5,000 kronor. In your opinion, how should this money be divided?

(2) Think about a couple in their thirties, having been married for five years. They are now going to divorce. They agree upon the wife to take care of the children. Except for the common household goods, the man owns 35,000 . . . (as the first question).

(3) Think about a couple in their thirties who have been living together unmarried for five years. They are now going to separate . . . (as the last question).

According to the ordinary rules of the law the couples in the first two cases should divide equally so that they get 20,000 each but in the unmarried case they keep what they own. The answers show the opinions as follows: the number of cases saying an equal share to be most reasonable is in the first case (the long-lasting couple) 83 percent, in the second case (the young married couple) 72 percent, and in the unmarried case 57 percent. There is a possibility that some persons know the law and therefore we find a part of the tendency. Since the figures show a declining trend, Trost (1974) assumes that one explanation is that many of the respondents perceive a decrease in the economical integration in the three situations presented. Thus, the common man is assumed to perceive the unmarried cohabitation as less integrated which could be seen as an indicator of a perception of the unmarried as less stable than the married cohabitation.

We have no knowledge of why some people marry and some do not. We do not know if those now cohabiting unmarried will one day marry each other. We do not know how the unmarried perceive their situation and the law and other rules, etc. During the autumn 1974 we collected data through personal interviews with both partners separately in about 100 cases of unmarried cohabiting couples and about 100 newly married couples. This material has not yet been analyzed; we have, however, the impression that all (or almost all) of the couples marrying have been cohabiting unmarried for some time and we know that in many parts of the country during the last century couples were cohabiting unmarried without being viewed as deviant (see, for example, Sundt. 1967). Their reason for not marrying can in some (probably very few) cases have been that they wanted to be sure that the woman could give birth to a child, alternatively a son. In many more cases probably, the reason was that it had not happened that they had married.

The dissolution rate of the unmarried cohabiting couples is much higher than among the married couples (Näsholm 1972a). This statement should, however, not be seen as an indicator of the unmarried cohabiting casses as being dyads with less commitment or less feeling. Many do probably cohabit unmarried in order to find out if they can go along for a long time — thus, this is some kind of test- or trial-marriage. the aim of which is to be dissoluted in case the partners realize that they do not fit together. It does not seem unrealistic that unmarried cohabitation will in some years become a social institution with the most important aim or function to be a test- or trial-marriage. If this assumption is correct the marriage rate will increase again and in some years reach a level slightly lower than the level in the mid-1960s. Since there will be many cases of unsuitable partners not marrying, those marriages being formed will be 'happier' and thus the divorce rate, ceteris paribus, will be lower.

REFERENCES

Bernhardt, Eva M. and Britta Holmbeck (1974), 'Fertility Trends in Sweden, in *Scandinavian Population Studies,* 3, Third Scandinavian Demographic Symposium, Helsinki.

Carlsson, Lizzie (1972), *Jag giver Dig min dotter,* II (*I Give You my Daughter,* II). Lund.

Claesson, Agneta, Ragna Lindgren and Goren Lindh (1973), 'Samvetsaktenskapet och juridiken' (The Conscience marriage and the Law), Uppsala, mimeo.

Hartmann, Jurgen and Birgit Jenner (1973), 'Studenter och försvar' ('Students and Defence'). Stockholm, mimeo.

Hayner, Norman, S. (1966), *New Patterns in Old Mexico.* New Haven

Hickrod, Lucy Jen Huang (1972), 'Religious Background of College Students and Attitudes Toward Living Together before Marriage', mimeo.

Holmbeck, Britta (1974) 'Giftermalens och skilsmässornas utveckling efter 1950', *Information i prognosfragor,* 4:1-59.

Locsei, Pal (1970), 'Syndyasmos in Contemporary Budapest', Budapest, mimeo.

Macklin, Eleanor D. (1972), 'Heterosexual Cohabitation among Unmarried College Students, *Family Coordinator,* pp 463–72.

Näsholm, Astrid (1972a), 'Sammanboende gifta och sammanboende ogifta' ('Married Cohabitation and Unmarried Cohabitation'), in SOU 1972:41;

Näsholm, Astrid (1972b), 'Riksförsäkringsverkets föräldraundersökning' ('The Parents study by the State Insurance Company') in SOU 1972:41.

Simmel, Georg (1922), *Soziologie,* Munchen.

SOU 1972:41: *Familj och aktenskap,* 1 (*Family and Marriage,* 1), Stockholm.

Sundt, Eilert (1967), *Om Giftermaal i Norge (On Marriage in Norway)*. Oslo.
Trost, Jan (1970-1974), *En undersökning av värnpliktiga vid KA 5, argangarna 10-14. (A Study of Privates at KA 5, years 10-14)*, MPI-reports nos 8, 12, 14, 17 and 20, Stockholm.
Trost, Jan (1975), *En undersökning av allmänhetens inställning i nagra familjeekonomiska fragor* [A study of the public's opinion to some family economical questions], in SOU 1975:24: Tre sociologiska rapporter, Stockholm, 7-32.

8

RELATIONSHIP BETWEEN DIFFERENTIATION AND EQUALITY IN THE SEX ROLE STRUCTURE
Conceptual Models and Suggested Research

Harold T. Christensen
Purdue University

It can be taken as a given, I believe, that throughout history man has tended to dominate woman in both private relationships and public affairs. This is a historical fact, whether one likes it or not. But increasingly today many women, and some men, simply do not like it and are agitating for change.

Man's physical strength, plus his freedom from the childbearing function, have permitted him to define and direct the social structure pretty much to his own advantage. And in this 'man's world' women have been stereotyped as being both different and inferior; then treated accordingly. It has been convenient for men to overlook the individual potentials of women and to view them as a class and as having a common purpose or destiny — that of mothering, homemaking, serving; certainly not governing in the larger sense or even much 'bothering themselves' with intellectual concerns. Because of this, there is some justification in the claims of many neo-feminists that men are inclined to be 'chauvinistic' and 'sexist'. Still, it is probably carrying things a bit too far to imply (as some seem to) that all men are that way and that this perversity is intrinsic to man's nature.

Few would question the major thrust of today's Women's Liberation Movement — that the sex role structure needs to be re-examined and reworked to give greater expression to all human potential, female as well as male. Surely women are right in reacting to male-imposed stereotypes which put them at a disadvantage. Yet, when in doing so they assume an emotionally biased, anti-male stance, this impresses me as over-reacting. For example, in my own teaching and writing on sex roles I occasionally have had females respond with the inference that my analysis needed to be discounted simply because I am male and so can be assumed to be biased. While this has not been a frequent occurrence, it has happened; and I have heard other men relate similar experiences. When this happens we have sexism in reverse, for women then may be charged with the same thing some have been accusing men of doing with reference to them; applying a derogatory stereotype.

There appear to be extremists on both sides of the debate, whose emotionalism only beclouds the issue. Arguments, whatever the source, should be allowed to stand or fall on their own merits. Assuming objectivity, it is simply irrelevant whether the proponent of any idea be male or female.

In the sex role issue, as with many other controversies, there has been too much polemical debate and too little objective research. One sex role controversy of this nature is the dispute over whether being different (in roles as well as in biology) inevitably leads to being unequal. The remainder of this discussion is to focus upon that specific problem. It will not report the results of any research, for that is yet to be carried out, but will deal with conceptual models — yet pointing toward needed research.

NATURE OF THE CONTROVERSY

The Contemporary Women's Liberation Movement has not only challenged the inequality of traditional concepts and structures that distinguish men and women but has even brought into question the validity or propriety of maintaining *any* distinctions based upon gender (see, for example, Millett, 1970). Many of today's neofeminists are saying that only elementary biological differences need to be recognized, and that even these should be de-emphasized by erasing the sex role structure imposed by the culture and by establishing a more or less uniform socialization process for the early years whereby males and females would be reared in essentially the same manner] It is common-place in feminist literature to see arguments to the effect that 'separate but equal' cannot really mean *equal.*

In making this kind of case, writers frequently have used the Jim Crow analogy. For example, Simone De Beauvoir (1952:xiii-xxix), who is regarded by some as the high priestess of neo-feminism, put it this way:

> In proving woman's inferiority, the antifeminists then began to draw not only upon religion, philosophy, and theology, as before, but also science – biology, experimental psychology, etc. At most they were willing to grant 'equality in difference' to the *other* sex. That profitable formula is most significant; it is precisely like the 'equal but separate' formula of the Jim Crow laws aimed at the North American Negroes. As is well known, this so-called equalitarian segregation has resulted only in the most extreme discrimination.

She then proceeded to spell out deep seated similarities between the situation women find themselves in and that of the American Black. In both cases, one segment of the population is relegated to an inferior status and kept there by devious and sundry means; this condition she thought to be, not inborn, but created by the dominant class.

While I feel that Simone De Beavoir is essentially correct in her overall assessment of woman's condition, two qualifications in the argument as she presented it seem necessary. In the first place, I would find her case more convincing if she had left room for an impartial variety of *non*feminists – without using the label '*anti*feminists' and without implying that everyone who does not agree fully with the feminist position is engaging in '*proving* woman's inferiority' (italic added). There are both partial and impartial nonfeminists. Surely it cannot be claimed that *all* scientists lack objectivity on this matter. In the second place, the Negro analogy – while extremely helpful in understanding woman's condition – must be interpreted with some caution. Like most analogies, there are points at which the fit is less than perfect. Men and women are biologically interdependent by nature, whereas Blacks and Whites are not. Furthermore, the 'separate but equal' doctrine back of the Jim Crow laws (which the United States

Supreme Court struck down in 1954, subsequent to Simone De Beauvoir's writing) is not the same thing as the 'different but equal' possibility that is being examined here for sex role interrelatedness. Separate and different are not synonymous concepts. The first is defined by the dictionary as 'to keep apart, as by an intervening barrier or space' whereas the second is defined as 'differing in character or quality, not alike, dissimilar'. It should be possible, therefore, for sex roles to be differentiated without the sexes being physically separated, or vice versa; and it follows from this that the arguments which support the linkage of discrimination with segregation do not necessarily hold when applied to the question of sex role differentiation.

Nevertheless, sex role differentiation frequently gets blamed for society's discrimination against women, as if the two were inseparably connected. Those who argue for the complete elimination of the sex role structure for the avowed purpose of doing away with sex discrimination, do so either because they loosely confuse the distinct meanings of the terms, or else because they believe that role differentiation almost invariably results in inequality between the sexes. Two noteworthy writers who seemingly hold to this latter view are Alice S. Rossi and Harriet Holter. Both of these important scholars, while clearly distinguishing the two concepts, go on to describe them in a manner that seems to imply an intrinsic linkage.

According to Rossi (1969:548), 'a group may be said to suffer from inequality if its members are restricted in access to legitimate valued positions or rewards in a society for which their ascribed status is not a relevant consideration'. She points out that this inequality may exist either in the form of explicit legal statutes or as informal social pressures, and that the latter type is the more difficult to remove. She refers to woman's ease in empathizing with minority groups, saying (p. 549):

> Women know from personal experience what it is like to be 'put down by men, and can therefore understand what it is like to be 'put down' as a black by whites. But there are also fundamental differences between sex as a category of social inequality and the categories of race, religion, or ethnicity.

The three most important differences which set sex discrimination apart are, according to her: that women do not constitute a true minority in terms of population size, nor are they segregated from men with the population; that for sex roles, socialization generally comes earlier and is more pervasive and tenacious than is true with the other categories; and that the special kind of intimate relationship which exists between men and women — not present between categories in the ethnic, religious, or racial spheres — puts a brake on any development of solidarity among women as women.⌋

⌊ Rossi then outlines three potential equality models for structuring relationships between the sexes (and among ethnic, religious, and racial groups as well), only the last of which she finds fully acceptable. They are the *Pluralist Model*, which recognizes innate differences and which values diversity, but in doing this is apt to disguise and perpetuate inequalities; the *Assimilation Model*, which, although not based upon innate differences, nevertheless accepts the traditional system of male ascendancy and asks women to move into already-established male areas and thus to give up their own role distinctiveness; and the *Hybrid Model*, which seeks fundamental reorganization in the social system itself and requires corresponding role changes on the part of men and women alike⌋. She illustrated these as follows (pp. 556-57):

> . . . the pluralist model says the woman's nurturance finds its best expression in maternity; the assimilation model says women must be motivated to seek professional careers in medicine similar to those pursued now by men; the hybrid model says, rather, that the structure of medicine can be changed so that more women will be attracted to medical careers, the male physicians will be able to live more balanced, less difficult and status-dominated lives.

Of the pluralist model she says:

> It is dubious whether any society has ever been truly pluralist in the sense that all groups which comprise it are on an equal footing of status, power, or rewards. Pluralism often disguises a social system in which one group dominates . . . (p. 552).

> The odds are heavily stacked against the pluralist model of society as a goal in terms of which racial, ethnic, or sex equality can be achieved (p. 554).

And she appears to be almost as rejecting as this, of the assimilation, model, implying that it is demeaning to women and pointing out that it involves an implicit fallacy (p. 555):

> No amount of entreaty will yield an equitable distribution of women and men in the top strata of business and professional occupations, for the simple reason that the life men have led in these strata has been possible only because their own wives were leading traditional lives as homemakers, doing double parent and household duty, and carrying the major burden of civic responsibilities. If it were not for their wives in the background, successful men in American society would have to be single or childless. This is why so many professional women complain privately that what they need most in life is a 'wife'.

This, of course, leaves only the hybrid model. Rossi favours that model — which calls for an across-the-board reworking of the social structure and whose ideology 'invisages a future in which family, community, and play are valued on a par with politics and work for both sexes' (p. 557) — because she believes its alternatives either are not viable or are productive of inequality.

Holter (1970, 1971) takes a very similar view but expresses it somewhat differently. She distinguishes between sex differentiation and sex stratification, but believes that the first quite naturally leads into the second:

> The more differentiated the roles of men and women in a society or a group, the larger is the difference in power and prestige according the two genders (1970:42).

> . . . it is maintained that sex differentiation, like other functional differentiations, entails a rank ordering of the positions of men and women (1970:53).

> Gender differentiation is here used primarily to include a division of tasks between men and women which is accompanied by a consistently different personality formation of the two genders. Such differentiation usually also discriminates against women, and it is the contention of the present author that discrimination of women necessarily follows from most known gender differentiations (1971:5).

Since Holter quite understandably does not want sex discrimination (believing that such discrimination is an outgrowth of differentiation) she argues for the diminution and perhaps elimination of sex differentiation. There are two types of equality that may be arrived at in that manner:

> One may roughly distinguish at least between equality within the framework
> of the present Western societies on the one hand, and equality in a radically
> changed society on the other. The first may be termed equality on masculine
> premises, or briefly 'masculine equality'; the other — or others — is equality in
> a qualitatively different society, that is, a society which is not dominated by
> masculine values as we know them (1971:10).

Again understandably, given her premises, she opts for the second of
these alternatives: equality brought about by far-reaching changes in
the social structure — in the educational, the political, and particularly
the economic spheres. She believes that this will require a virtual social
revolution, that the battles which can take place within the four walls
of a home simply are not enough.

Parallels between this analysis and the one by Rossi will be readily
apparent to the reader. Holter's stratified society based upon sex
differentiation is essentially the same as Rossi's pluralist model; her
'masculine equality' type, the same as Rossi's assimilation model; and
her type that requires societal restructuring, the same as Rossi's hybrid
model. Both writers see sex role inequality as being linked to sex role
differentiation and both propose to eliminate the former by reducing
the latter; not by any halfway measures but rather through fundamental
changes in the social structure.

What is not entirely clear to me in reading these authors is whether
they are proposing that society move the *full distance* in eliminating sex
differentiation, or if they would accept the retention of at least a minimum role structure that might be suggested by biological differences
and perhaps by society's needs for greater efficiency found in division-
of-labour arrangements. They seem in places to be contending against
the very relevancy of biology. But how can this be so? Although
undoubtedly social psychological factors must take precedence in
explaining role structure and role behaviour, men and women do have
biological natures and I fail to see how this fact can be ignored.

At any rate, I have long held — and still do — to the desirability of
some kind of *differentiated equality*. This position accepts parts of
Rossi's pluralist and hybrid models: the former in that it would retain
some sex role structure, and the latter in that it favours social change
to further reduce the prescriptions and proscriptions imposed upon

both sexes; and it thus leaves more to personal choice. I first coined the phrase, 'differentiated equality', and declared myself in favour of what position, about a quater of a century ago (Christensen, 1950:111; quotation from 1958:146).

Equality does not require similarity. People can be dissimilar and still be on the same level. Nature made men and women different as classes but did not make them unequal. Society then established divergent roles for the two sexes, corresponding roughly with the biological differentiations already established. But the social alignment between men and women somehow or other got tipped at the axis; it tends to become vertical in arrangement, with men having most of the advantage. Sex assumed status.

Recent developments have been away from stratification within marriage, and in the direction of partnerships. The older patriarchal family is yielding to an emerging democratic or equalitarian type. The newer assumption is that of a love relationship based upon a horizontal division of labour; it is the application of democracy to marriage.

Sex equality, therefore, shall mean that neither men nor women will be discriminated against because of their sex. They will have somewhat different roles to play, both biological and cultural, but roles of equal dignity and opportunity. There will be individual differences in ability and achievement, but these will not be drawn along sex lines. It will be a *differentiated equality* where opportunity is the same for all but where men and women are given certain divided functions. The sexes will be equal, each within its own sphere.

The heart of the controversy is not whether the social structure (including sex roles) is in need of reworking to permit greater self determination and greater equality. Most thinkers agree that this should take place. But the really difficult questions have to do with the extent to which sex role differentiation and sex role inequality might be inter-related; and, following this, whether it is possible or even desirable to realistically think in terms of a differentiated equality. Definitive answers to such questions will require, first, better conceptualization of the relevant variables; and second, more and better research using empirical data.

A TYPOLOGY OF EQUALITY –
DIFFERENTIATION INTERRELATEDNESS

If we can agree that equality and differentiation are separate concepts, it next will be helpful to try to distinguish various ways in which they might interrelate. Figure 1 has been designed with that in mind. It presents models of the equality–inequality structure and of the differentiated–undifferentiated structure, superimposed upon each other. Since the notion of equality implies the total absence of superordination and subordination, a horizontal bar is used to picture it; and since inequality means the opposite, a vertical bar is used for that. With reference to the other factor, a lined bar is used to designate the differentiated male role; a white bar, the differentiated female role; and a shaded or black bar to picture roles that are undifferentiated by sex (or what might be called role overlap, or role blurring, or role homogenization).

It first should be notes that model E, the centre cell, is the only one that permits varying the equality factor and the differentiation factor both at the same time. Since it may be presumed that very few real life situations reach their ultimate extremes – extremes of 'all or none' – it is this model that comes closest to empirical reality and is therefore the most useful when dealing with actual cases. I shall illustrate with one such case, that of sex role change, a little later on. But before that, it will be well to describe further both the nature and the limitations of the typology employed.

As can be observed, the top row of Figure 1 (A, B, C) pictures the differentiation factor as varying with the assumption of complete equality; and the bottom row (G, H, I) does the same except on the assumption of complete inequality. Similarly, the left-hand column (A, D, G) pictures the equality factor as varying, with the assumption of complete differentiation; while the right-hand column (C, F, I) does the same except on the assumption of complete nondifferentiation. Thus, in every model shown – except E of course – one factor is varied while the other is held constant.

The four corner cells (A, C, G, I) will be recognised as being farthest from reality, since each pictures hypothetical combinations of the most

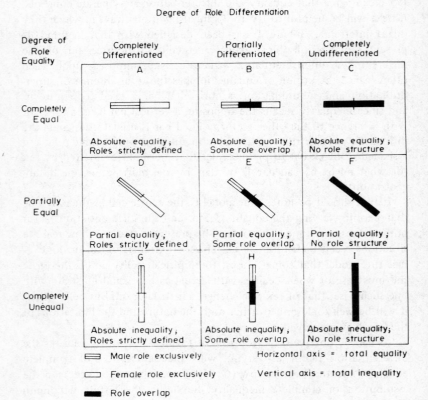

Figure 1. Models of sex role structure, showing interrelationships between equality and differentiation.

extreme positions on the equality—differentiation continua. They are what Max Weber would speak of as 'ideal types' — not ideal in the sense of being better, but only in the sense of being abstractions or logical constructs which describe ultimate extremes, used for orientation purposes in conceptualization and measurement. While it is not expected that many, if any, actual cases will fall at these extremes, the mental formulation of them can help give meaning and interpretation of the concrete situations one may wish to study. These latter will fall in the remaining cells of the graph, especially in E.

Each of the four middle-border cells combines one extreme with one 'partial' position: total equality with partial differentiation (B); total differentiation with partial equality (D); total nondifferentiation with partial equality (F); and total inequality with partial differentiation (H). It seems probable that very few empirical cases would fall precisely at any of these points, since each model assumes some kind of absolute position. I would expect intersex relationships to come close to one or another of these rarified models on occasion, but seldom if ever to constitute a perfect fit. For this reason, they also might be thought of as 'ideal types', although somewhat more reachable than the corner models. They picture logical possibilities but are not presumed to describe many actual cases. Perhaps model B represents the most attainable of these four possibilities and I shall have more to say about that one later on.

There is one small exception to the above characterizations. In the strictest sense, F and I should be eliminated since they represent a contradition of terms. They picture a superordinated—subordinated sex role structure along with the assumption that no sex role structure exists, and this cannot be. Still, providing their purely fictional nature is kept in mind, leaving them in place can do no harm and they do service to preserve the symmetry of the schema.

Cell C, however, does not represent a contradiction of terms, since equality cannot be considered as precluding a nondifferentiated structure nor vice versa. As was pointed out earlier, there are those today who claim that equality of the sexes and freedom from any kind of sex role structure are one and the same, or that the former *requires* the latter. Without too much anticipating a point to be discussed later on, let me simply say here that, if my typology is correct, it should be possible to attain equality following any one of models A, B or C; but that, since B is the least extreme of the three, it may well be the most attainable of these absolute equality models.

In interpreting Figure 1, the reader also should keep in mind certain things that it does not show. Like most models, this one is nothing more than a schematic design set up to add conceptual clarity and thereby facilitate the ordering and testing of data. Hence, because of its schematic nature as well as its brevity, there are inevitable omissions. One such as that it pictures only the male role in superordinated positions, not the female — cells D, E, G and H. This is not a reflection of any value judgement on my part, but is only because of a need to economize, plus the fact that role domination patterns most generally have favoured the male.

A second limitation lies in the fact that the middle categories for both factors — cells B, D, E, F and H, which are labelled 'partially' — do not picture the full range of variability that is possible. This also is because of the need to economize. For these in-between areas, the reader is asked to visualize both the axis tipping and the role overlapping as varying from nearly complete equality and/or differentiation on the one hand to nearly complete inequality and/or nondifferentiation on the other. Figure 2 is an elaboration of model E and it illustrates the point just made. Nevertheless, even this elaboration is schematic in nature; it does not, and cannot, picture every possible combination.

Finally, the graphical devices used here (Figures 1, 2 and 3) do not suggest anything about the *quality* of the sex norms pictured — 'quality' in terms of such considerations as norm flexibility and the severity of the sanctions imposed. A more detailed or complete portrayal might have shown the 'overlap' segments of the appropriate bars with different degrees of shading, to signify qualitative differences. Cultures vary greatly in their sex role structures, not only as to *how much* differentiation and/or equality they promote, but as to *which role tasks* are involved and the *degree of permissiveness* regarding roles that is tolerated. To capture some of these qualitative dimensions, I could, for example, have shown the bars in the partially differentiated cells as broken down into five segments rather than three: exclusively male, favoured for the

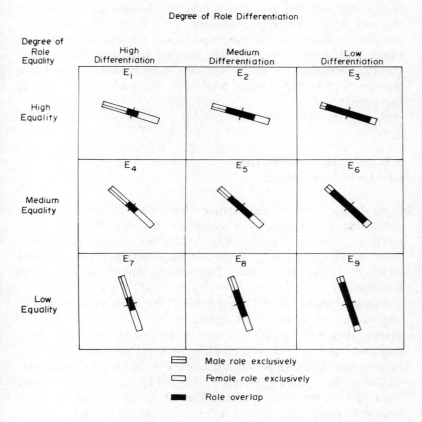

Figure 2. Models of partial equality combined with partial differentiation (an elaboration of E from Figure 1).

male but permitted for both, permitted equally for males and females alike, favoured for the female but permitted for both, and exclusively female. But even this would have failed to take into account some of the finer points on quality. Furthermore, this might have complicated the picture drawn for present purposes so I chose to leave that for future exploration. In the meantime, however, one should keep in mind that the lines separating the bar segments of the partially differentiated cells are not intended to imply breaks that are as arbitrary or sharp as they appear here.

A SCHEMATIC PORTRAYAL
OF SEX ROLE CHANGE

From the many possible combinations of sex role equality with sex role differentiation that it would be possible to derive from Figures 1 and 2, I shall select here just a single series to illustrate change. This will have to do with long-range time trends that are presumed to have occurred within the United States — and also, perhaps, throughout most of the Western world. .

Figure 3 borrows from Figures 1 and 2, but carries the analysis one step farther by applying the schema to the phenomenon of social change. Models G (vertical axis with differentiation complete) and C (horizontal axis coupled with no differentiation) are carried over from Figure 1 and used to represent the logical extremes between which our society has been moving. Models E_3, E_5 and E_7 are carried over from Figure 2 (and two additional bars inserted for showing an even finer breakdown) to picture the trends that are presumed to have occurred.

I estimate that the sex role structure of colonial America would fall at about E_7, and of contemporary America perhaps midway between E_5 and E_3. Some persons might contend that we are no farther than E_5 today while others would see E_3 coming closer to describing the present situation. But my concern now is not with determining the exact distances travelled; only with trying to establish directions of travel.

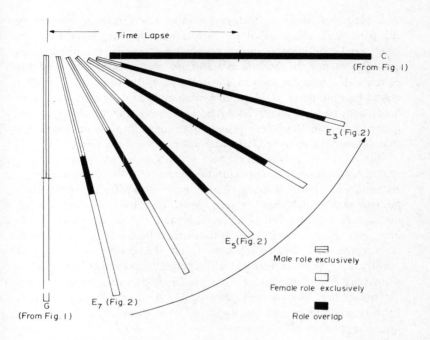

Figure 3. Model of changes in the sex role structure of the United States, showing trends toward equality and overlap.

If this schema is at all correct, two trends in the sex role structure of our society become evident, and a third is suggested. The first is a tipping of the axis in the vertical-to-horizontal direction, which means movement toward greater equality. The second is an expansions of role overlap, which signifies a breakdown of differentiation and means that the separate worlds of men and women are tending to merge. The third — which some might choose to classify as just a sub-category of the second — is the decline of cultural ascription to make room for greater individual choice. Along with movements toward greater equality and more role overlap, society is becoming less prescriptive and proscriptive concerning relationships between the sexes, which means that self-determination is becoming the accepted norm.

Students of American history are in general agreement concerning the patriarchal character of the early family system, which gave the male head considerable power over other members (although his control was not as absolute or arbitrary as has been described for certain other societies such as, for example, early Rome). Woman's lot was to bear numerous children, to work hard in looking after the household, and perhaps above all to be submissive and obedient to her husband. And in all of this she had little choice, for the role structuring that dictated it was embedded within the culture of the time.

But times have changed. Technological advancements, plus legislative enactments, plus newer opportunities opening up in the educational, economic, and political spheres have combined to lift many of woman's burdens and to make her life vastly more attractive. Although she has not as yet achieved full equality with man, the distance travelled is impressive. Families are significantly smaller; homes generally are more comfortable and housework easier; and the doors to non-familial pursuits have been at least partially opened to her. Most importantly, woman has been given greater freedom to choose, to more completely determine her own destiny. But again, these movements towards equality, and homoginization, and freedom of choice are merely trends; none has gone the full distance.

SOME SUGGESTIONS FOR RESEARCH

My own position favouring a differentiated equality was outlined earlier in this paper. In terms of the typology developed here, it is best pictured by model B of Figure 1: absolute equality coupled with some sex role differentiation, but with the amount and the task content of this latter yet to be determined. As for the equality dimension, I recognize equal opportunity as being intrinsic to both democratic and Christian principles as well as being a part of my perosnal value system; and I view sex role equality as being just as important as any other kind of equality. Furthermore, I see no logical or sociological reason why this goal cannot in time be reached — or at least nearly reached (after allowing for human imperfections). In my way of thinking, there are ethical imperatives that require us to move as far in that direction as proves possible. As for differentiation, I hold no brief for the approximately equal thirds into which the bar of the model is divided. But then that part is left flexible and is negotiable. One can expect that in time it will be further defined by the kind of experimenting now going on and by research. I expect the optional or 'overlap' portion of the bar to end up in a position of great preponderance, which will mean that the biological and social prescriptions will remain only at their essential minimums. Yet, I also expect that there are and will remain some such minimums worth preserving.

Nevertheless, this position — along with the various alternatives to it — is just that: a position; a hypothesis in need of testing.

The models presented in Figures 1, 2 and 3 represent an exercise in conceptual exploration. My attempt has been to clarify certain issues in the sex role controversy as background for needed research. Although some of these issues have been, or are now being studied, to a limited extent we still seem to be a long way from empirically-based, definitive answers. I shall end by briefly listing important next-steps as I see them, first those derived from the models themselves and then some which reach out into related areas of concern.

Suggestions from the Models

Explore both historical and contemporary data to determine empirically how sex role differentiation and sex role equality interrelate.

(1) Does the overall frequency distribution for Figure 1 support the several assumptions I have made: that the four corner cells (which assume absolute positions for both factor) will almost never be reached; that the four adjoining border cells (which assume absolute positions for only one factor at a time) will seldom be reached; and therefore that the middle cell E (which assumes both differentiation and inequality) will capture the vast majority of all actual occurrances?

(2) Assuming that at least some cases will fall outside of middle cell E, does a preponderance of this residue fall in cell B (absolute equality with some role overlap)? If so, this will lend support to my assumptions

that cell B is the most attainable of the completely equalitarian models, and that role equality does not require the complete elimination of the sex role structure.

(3) What is the frequency distribution when cell E is broken down into the schema of Figure 2? Also, how close to complete differentiation—nondifferentiation and to complete equality—nonequality will the actual cases fall? Answers here should throw important additional light on the attainability of each of the respective models. The two factors could be analyzed one at a time while the other is held constant. Furthermore, the placement of various cultures on this schema could be determined and then compared.

(4) Does the schema of Figure 3 hold up when tested against a wide range of American data? Also, approximately where on this graph (or an expansion of it showing finer breakdowns) can different time periods and different subcultures be placed?

(5) To what extent are females found in superior or dominant positions within the sex role structure; and what are the frequency distributions of such cases according to models that could be set up similar to those in Figures 1, 2 and 3?

Related Areas of Concern

Develop additional models to conceptualize still other aspects of the sex role phenomenon, and then validate and utilize these by means of empirical research.

(1) How can 'sex role strain' — seen as arrangements within the sex role structure which prove to be dysfunctional to the individual, to interpersonal relationships (such as marriage), and/or to society at large — be measured? How do strains at these three levels interrelate? And, most importantly, what are the many effects of these strains at each level?

(2) What are the various factors or conditions that produce these strains in the individual, in his relationships with others, and in the society that surrounds him? Pursuing this broad but highly important concern (important because it can provide a basis for judging the relative desirability of the several role patterns) must of necessity

involve finding answers to a number of more specific questions, such as the following:

(a) How do the typologies pictured in Figures 1, 2 and 3 relate to the phenomenon of sex role strain? Which model, in other words, is found to be associated with the most strain? Which with the least?

(b) Is strain in any way dependent upon the content of the sanctions used? Or upon their prescriptive—proscriptive quality? Or upon the severity with which they are enforced?

(c) Is sex role strain any greater when males and females perform certain prescribed tasks than when other tasks are performed? Is there, in other words, any kind of 'natural' division-of-labour pattern as measured by low strain probability? Are there certain irreducible minimums, at least, that each sex had best keep to itself; or, are all tasks interchangeable from this standpoint?

(d) Is there any kind of optimum balance between social prescription, on the one hand, and self-determination on the other — in terms of absence from strain? For example, does a socially-promoted division of labour result in less confusion and greater efficiency; and, if so, when does this reach a point of diminishing returns? Or conversely, is it possible to enjoy too much personal choice (because of both the ambiguity and the possible lost motion involved)? When does self-determination cease to be functional?

(e) How do incongruities between the personality structure and social norms, or within interactional patterns, affect sex role strain as defined and measured? Some examples might be: when either the self-concept or personal values are out of line with social norms; when behaviour is out of line with either the self-concept or social norms; and when a person is in role conflict with one or more significant others.

(f) How do either strain, or role changes to escape it, affect significant others and/or the role patterns of the opposite sex? Roles, by definition, are reciprocal; yet writers and researchers frequently limit themselves to just one side of the issue. Male role problems, for example, have been notoriously neglected.

This list of suggested research is not intended to be exhaustive and the several points made are not spelled out in any detail. Nevertheless, it hopefully should provide leads. Whatever future study there can be, which can pin down answers to these and related questions, will most certainly prove useful, both in personal decision making and in the formulation of social policy affecting the sex role structure.

REFERENCES

Christensen, Harold T. (1950), *Marriage Analysis.* New York: Ronald Press.
—— (1958), *Marriage Analysis,* 2nd edn. New York: Ronald Press.
De Beauvoir, Simone (1952), *The Second Sex.* New York: Knofp. Translated by H. M. Parshley.
Holter, Harriet (1970), 'Sex Roles and Social Differentiation', in Harriet Holter, *Sex Roles and Social Structure.* Oslo, Norway: Universitetsforlaget, ch.1.
—— (1971), 'Sex Roles and Social Change', *Acta Sociologica,* **14**:(1-2).
Millett, Kate (1970), *Sexual Politics.* New York: Doubleday and Company.
Rossi, Alice S. (1969), 'Sex equality: the beginnings of ideology', in Ira L. Reiss (ed), *Readings on the Family System.* New York: Holt, Rinehart and Winston, 1972, ch. 36, pp. 547-57. (Originally published in *The Humanist,* Sept./Oct., 1969).

NOTES ON CONTRIBUTORS

Rae Lesser Blumberg is Acting Associate Professor in the Department of Sociology at the University of California, San Diego. She received her doctorate in sociology from Northwestern University (1970), and has taught previously at the University of Wisconsin at Madison. She has conducted research in Australia, Israel, and South America, where she lived for some years in Bolivia and Venezuela. In Venezuela, she has taught at Andres Bello University and has served as resident sociological research adviser to the Ministries of Education (1970-72) and of Health and Social Welfare (1973). In 1973-74 she held a Ford Foundation Faculty Fellowship on the Role of Women in Society. She has published numerous articles dealing with cross-cultural paradigms of sexual stratification, the inter-relationship of economic factors, female status and fertility, societal complexity and familial complexity, ethnicity and extended families, and has written on education, family, urban ecology and political economy in developing countries. She has in press (1976) a book, *Stratification: Socio-economic and Sexual Inequality,* and is working on a book detailing her theory-testing research (utiliz-ing a 61-society pilot sample) on women's relative economic power as a primary determinant of their status and life options vis à vis men.

Harold T. Christensen is Professor Emeritus of Sociology, Purdue University, Indiana and is currently Visiting Professor at San Diego State University. He received in 1967 the Burgess Research Award (for continuous and meritorious contributions to theory and research in the family field) and has published six books, including the editorship of *Handbook of Marriage and the Family* (Rand McNally, 1964), and some sixty articles in professional journals.

Dennis C. Foss is Assistant Professor of Sociology at Sangamon State University, Springfield, Illinois. He has written articles dealing with systems theory and its application to sociology, theory construction, and philosophy of social science, and is the co-author of *The American View of Death: Acceptance or Denial?*

Maria Pilar Garcia is a doctoral candidate at the University of Chicago. She has extensively participated in field work in Venezuela where she is currently directing a major research project about urban development and planning in Ciudad Guayana. Areas of interest and research include demography, urban development and planning in Latin America. Her main publications include the two volumes, *Planificación urbana y realidad social en Ciudad Guayana* (Corporación Venezolana de Guayana. Caracas, 1976) and with Rae L. Blumberg, 'The Unplanned Ecology of a Planned Industrial City: The Case of Ciudad Guayana, Venezuela' in the book, *Urbanization in the Americas, From the Beginnings to the Present.* (Vol. III, The Hague, Mouton Press. 1976)

A. A. Khatri is Professor of Sociology at the University of Alabama, Birmingham, Alabama. He is the author of *A Manual of Scale T Measure Jointness of Families in India;* and the co-editor of *Perspectives on Marriage and the Family,* and of *Developmental Psychology: An Anthology.*

Luis Lenero-Otero is President of the Instituto Mexicano de Estudios Sociales, A.C. He has published *Investigacion de la Familia en Mexico* (IMES, Mexico, 1978), *Desarrollo Social* in collaboration with José Trueba (IMES, Mexico, 1972) and was editor and main author of *Poblacion Iglesia y Cultura* (IMES-FERES, 1970).

William T. Liu is Professor of Sociology and Director of the Centre for the Study of Man in Contemporary Society at the University of Notre Dame, Notre Dame, Indiana. He has done extensive research in a number of southeast Asian countries on the family and on teenagers.

Murray A. Straus is Professor of Sociology at the University of New Hampshire. He holds his PhD in Sociology from the University of Wisconsin (1956), and has taught and done research in Sri Lanka, India, and Puerto Rico, as well as the USA. He is a past-President of the National Council on Family Relations (USA).

Jan Trost is a family sociologist at Uppsala University, Sweden. He has published textbooks in family sociology, and articles in international journals dealing with social psychology and family sociology.

Jan Turowski is Professor of Sociology at the Catholic University of Lublin, Poland, and Head of the Department of Sociology.

Tsuneo Yamane is a graduate of Tokyo University, and is Professor of Sociology in the Department of the Science of Living at Osaka City University, Japan. He is the author of the article 'Isolation of the Nuclear Family and Kinship Organization in Japan' in the *Journal of Marriage and the Family* (1967).